MW01630154

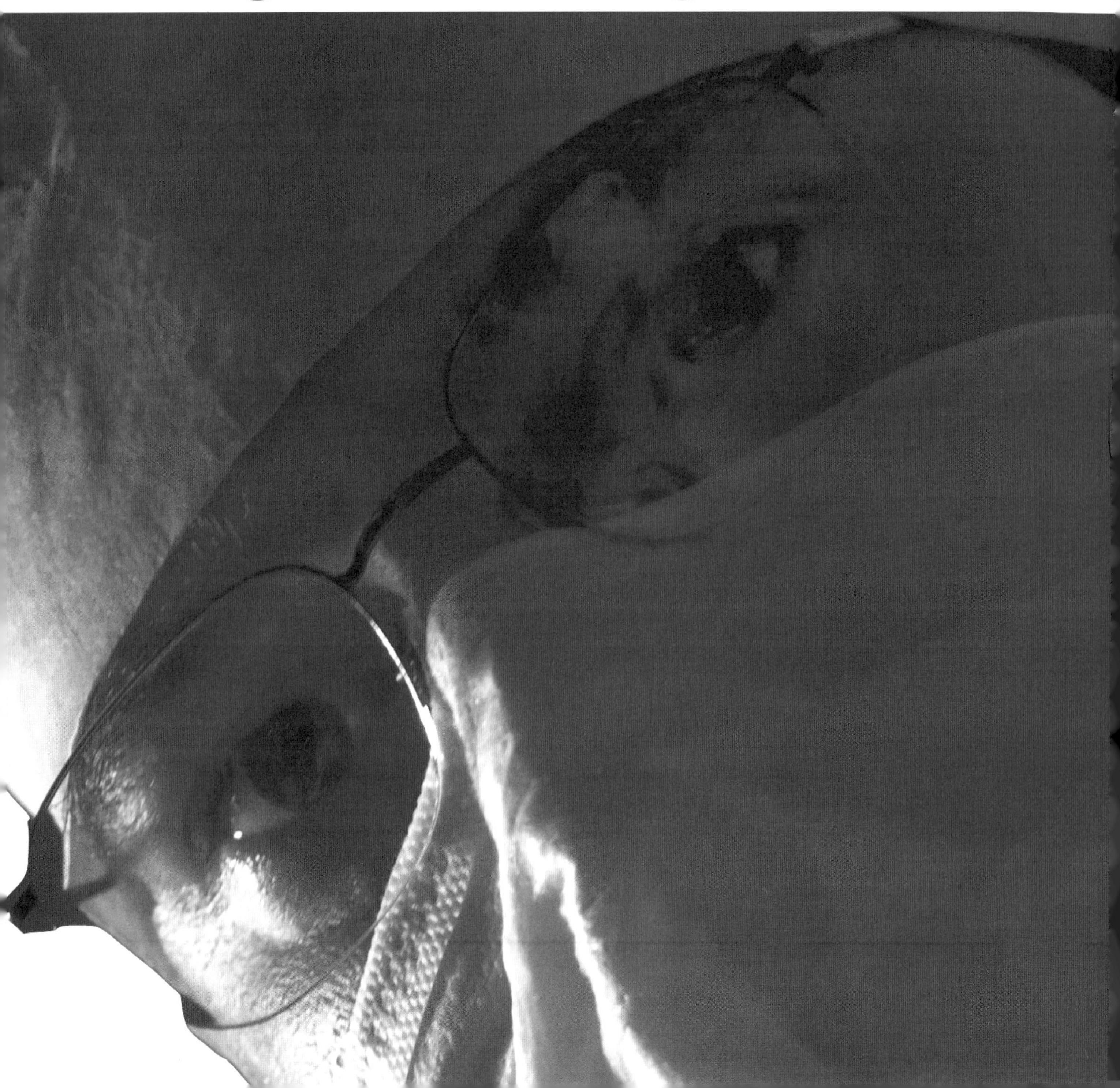

Your Jewish Guide Through Life's Tough Decisions

Medicine and MORALS

Course Author
Rabbi Yehuda Pink MSc

Dr. Chana Silberstein, editor-in chief
Rabbi Mordechai Dinerman, associate editor

Rabbinic Advisory Board
Rabbi Yosef Feigelstock
Rabbi Feitel Levin
Rabbi Shlomo Yaffe

Editorial Board
Rabbi Yisrael Rice, chairman
Rabbi Sholom Adler
Rabbi Levi Kaplan
Rabbi Yosef Loschak
Rabbi Levi Mendelow
Rabbi Dr. Shlomo Pereira
Rabbi Avraham Steinmetz

The **Rohr Jewish Learning Institute**
gratefully acknowledges
the pioneering support of

George and Pamela Rohr

SINCE ITS INCEPTION
the **Rohr JLI** has been
a beneficiary of the vision, generosity,
care and concern
of the **Rohr family**

In the merit of
the tens of thousands of hours of Torah study
by **JLI** students worldwide,
may they be blessed with health,
Yiddishe Nachas from all their loved ones,
and extraordinary success
in all their endeavors ❧

כִּי יְדַעְתִּיו לְמַעַן אֲשֶׁר יְצַוֶּה אֶת בָּנָיו וְאֶת בֵּיתוֹ אַחֲרָיו
וְשָׁמְרוּ דֶּרֶךְ ה' לַעֲשׂוֹת צְדָקָה וּמִשְׁפָּט
(בראשית יח,יט)

Dedicated with eternal gratitude by

George and Pamela Rohr

to his parents

Mrs. Charlotte Rohr

מרת **שרה** ע״ה

בת ר׳ יקותיאל יהודה קסטנר הי״ד

and

יבדל לחיים טובים וארוכים

Mr. Sami Rohr

ר׳ **שמואל** שיחי׳

לאורך ימים ושנים טובות

whose towering example is a constant source of inspiration,

and with boundless love to their children
Rivkah Malca, Daniella Esther, Meir, and Rayzel.

May G-d grant you peace, health, and happiness.
May you know the fullness of a life enriched by the study of Torah
and the practice of *chesed*.

May you be a source of *nachas* to our family, and of light and strength to *klal Yisrael*.

Endorsements for
Medicine and Morals

"**O**ver the past two years I have examined much of the material prepared for courses offered at the Rohr Jewish Learning Institute. This material has uniformly been of high caliber and of meaningful intellectual weight. Additionally, the course books are aesthetically attractive. I recommend without reservation their use, particularly by persons who are in the major professions and in business."

Marvin Schick, PhD
Founder, National Jewish Commission on Law and Public Affairs (COLPA),
Liaison to the Jewish Community under NYC Mayor John V. Lindsay
New York, NY

"**I** am most impressed with the course on Jewish medical ethics, Medicine and Morals. As the title suggests these two topics should and must go hand in hand, not only to treat our patients but to understand them too. The topics are right in line with modern day realities, but put an important time and Torah honored perspective that will help the health care provider see these issues in a different, helpful and more appropriate light."

Robert Kliegman, MD
Professor and Chair, Department of Pediatrics, Medical College of Wisconsin,
Executive Vice President, The Children's Hospital of Wisconsin
Milwaukee, WI

"**T**he content is truly unique, yet obviously relevant to the issues facing physicians daily."

John Jane, Sr., MD
Chair, Department of Neurological Surgery
University of Virginia Health System
Charlottesville, VA

"**T**he Medicine and Morals course provides an important grounding in the halachic approach to a variety of thorny issues confronting medicine today. For those looking for an overview of traditional rabbinical thinking in these issues, the course seems ideal."

Paul Root Wolpe, PhD
Director, Center for Ethics
Emory University
Atlanta, GA

"**T**he course gives a thoroughly researched and well-explained tutorial on Jewish law and organ donation. It is an excellent review of the issues and enormously intellectually stimulating."

Sally Satel, MD
U.S. Senate Committee on Health, Education, Labor and Pensions,
Recipient of a gratuitous organ donation
Washington, DC

"**A**s a practicing critical care physician, I draw on my Jewish ethical training cross culturally and have found it helpful in my discussions with my non-Jewish patients as well."

Dr. Joel B. Zivot, MD, FRCPC
Medical Director, Cardio-thoracic Intensive Care Unit,
Winnipeg Regional Health Authority
Winnipeg, Canada

"These materials place some of the most urgent contemporary problems of medical ethics into the context of one of the world's oldest and most sophisticated ethical systems. Not only practicing Jews will find value in studying the issues presented in this program. Anyone who needs to grapple with the practical and policy dimensions of modern medical practice and delivery will profit from the work of the Rohr Jewish Learning Institute."

Daniel D. Polsby, JD
Dean and Professor of Law,
George Mason University School of Law
Arlington, VA

"Jewish philosophy and ethics has from its origin, and will continue in the future to engage with and influence medical thought and practice. The opportunity to showcase this intimate relationship through the JLI course Medicine and Morals is a source of great pride."

Natan Bar-Chama, MD
Director Male Reproductive Medicine and Surgery,
The Mount Sinai School of Medicine
New York, NY

"I came to Rabbi Pink's lecture to learn about the Jewish perspective and learnt about medical issues as well."

Graham Lipkin
Clinical Director of Renal Medicine
University Hospital of Birmingham Foundation
NHS Trust
Birmingham, England

"Medicine and Morals-Your Jewish Guide Through Life's Tough Decisions is the premier initial offering of the Touro College Continuing Professional Development Institute and JLI. JLI aspires to be the preeminent provider of adult Jewish learning, and continues to set new standards in the field. Its numerous offerings are superior.

"This new curriculum on Jewish medical ethics will enable health care professionals to be informed by the insights of our sages. Physicians will be better prepared to confront the tough issues facing modern medicine. I enthusiastically endorse this new academic partnership."

Dr. Steven Huberman
Dean, Graduate School of Social Work,
Touro College and University
New York, NY

"I am very impressed with the topics covered in the course Medicine and Morals. The class covers some of the most critical issues in law, medicine and religion, and I applaud your efforts to expand learning in this area. Thank you for your fine contributions."

Robert Steinbuch
Professor of Law, University of Arkansas,
Commissioner on the Arkansas Commission for
Newborn Umbilical Cord Blood Bank Initiative
Little Rock, AR

"The course in Jewish Medical Ethics offered by the Rohr Jewish Learning Institute is a fascinating and engaging tour of the subject. Dealing with a variety of the most compelling questions including: refusing medical treatment, organ donation, and assisted reproduction, the course juxtaposes the current trends in secular law as embodied in recent cases with traditional Jewish views on the same questions. The questions and materials used to illustrate and educate are well chosen."

Lloyd R. Cohen, PhD, JD
Professor of Law, George Mason University
School of Law
Author of "Transplant Organs,"
The Encyclopedia of Law and Society
Arlington, VA

"The course clearly incorporates all the key themes of modern medicine and the ethical challenges that we face. The course will enable a greater understanding of how Jewish medical ethics can make a distinctive contribution to modern medicine. The course comes at a time where scientific advancements are producing increasing numbers of ethical dilemmas. There is a great need for people to think through these issues and be equipped to make choices. I am delighted that such a course has been developed and wish it every success."

June Jones, PhD, MSc
Senior Lecturer in Biomedical Ethics
University of Birmingham
Birmingham, England

"I support these excellent seminars in Jewish Medical Ethics developed by Rabbi Pink. They are of great value both clinically and academically."

Anthony D. Hockley (OBM), FRCS, LLM
Neurosurgeon,
Queen Elizabeth Hospital and Birmingham
Children's Hospital
Birmingham, England

"An interesting course and an important area for dissemination of information."

Jeffery Klein, MD
Reproductive Endocrinology
and Infertility Specialist
Reproductive Medicine Associates of New York
White Plains, NY

"Science and technology advance at such a rapid pace that we often don't stop to understand the implications of medical breakthroughs. Through the lens of Jewish law and perspective, Medicine and Morals brings a framework of understanding to some of the most difficult medical ethics questions we face."

Bradley W. Kesser, MD
Department of Otolaryngology-Head and Neck Surgery,
University of Virginia Health System
Charlottesville, VA

"With the advent of new technology and treatment modalities, the physician and communities of today need guidance from several sources with regard to the ethical and moral issues of caring for our patients. The Rohr Jewish Learning Institute has gathered many professionals from the clergy and the non-clergy to shed light on these complicated issues. Our Acharonim and Rishonim have debated these issues in the Talmud and through compilation of laws in Shulchan Aruch, have guided us in these difficult matters.

"I congratulate the Rohr Jewish Learning Institute for undertaking this immense task to illuminate light on these complex issues. The Institute has my good wishes and full support for this most worthwhile project."

Avi Pandey, MD, FACS, PC
Associate Director, Department of Ophthalmology,
Queens Hospital Center
Queens, NY

"**R**ecent advances in clinical knowledge and technology enable solutions that, until not long ago, remained in the imaginary realm. However, do we have the Halachic answers to questions arising from these cutting-edge, never-before available, clinical solutions? Maimonides would be very proud of this promising JLI Medicine and Morals course."

Gill Heart, PhD
Former Commanding Officer, Special Forces
Israel Defense Force
Director, Mind in Control
Atlanta, GA

"**I** am a pulmonary and critical care physician who deals with the type of ethical areas that you highlight. I am impressed with your simple but insightful approach. The subjects that you bring forward reflect significant problems that we encounter commonly. The discussion is a 'must read' for all in medicine."

Mark J. Rumbak, MD
Pulmonary Critical Care Physician
Tampa, FL

"**A**s a pediatrician, the necessity of education in the field of medical ethics is all too real for me. It is clear that a thorough and multi-faceted approach to these questions is vital. I applaud the Rohr Jewish Learning Institute on their new course, Medicine and Morals."

Rachel D. Rosenbaum, MD
Doctor of Pediatrics
Bristol-Myers Squibb Children's Hospital at
Robert Wood Johnson University Hospital
New Brunswick, NJ

"**A**s a physician I find myself in the trenches of medical ethics. I frequently turn to my friends, colleagues, and senior faculty for insight as well as shoulders to lean on. I appreciate a course that recognizes that Jewish and secular medical ethics often, but not universally concur. It is an asset to me that there exists education which balances the medical and Jewish perspectives on these difficult questions of ethics."

Rachel Kassel, MD, PhD
Doctor of Pediatrics
St. Louis Children's Hospital, Washington
University School of Medicine
St. Louis, MO

"**A**s we face new issues in the field of medical ethics, it is important to remember that the human element is present in all of these questions. The Rohr Jewish Learning Institute's new course Medicine and Morals explores medical ethics from not only a legal and medical perspective, but also the 3000-year-old Jewish tradition. By examining these contemporary questions through the lens of an ethical framework that has guided people for centuries, we can strive to treat our fellow human beings with the utmost standard of morality."

Stephen Rozenberg, OD
Doctor of Optometry and Homeopathic
Medicine
Queens, NY

The course

Medicine and Morals

has been approved
in these states
for fulfillment of
the requirements for
continuing legal education

Alabama
California
Colorado
Delaware
Florida
Georgia
Idaho
Illinois
Louisiana
Minnesota
Missouri
Montana
Nevada
New York
North Carolina
Ohio
Oregon
Pennsylvania
Rhode Island
South Carolina
Utah
Vermont
Virginia
Washington
Wisconsin

This course is approved by:

**Rohr JLI/Touro Division
of Continuing Professional Development**

TOURO COLLEGE

Orde van Vlaamse Balies
Order of Flemish Bar Associations
Belgium

Accreditation & Credit Designation Statement

The State University of New York (SUNY) Downstate Medical Center is accredited by the Accreditation Council for Continuing Medical Education to provide continuing medical education for physicians.

The SUNY Downstate Medical Center designates this educational activity for a maximum of 30 *AMA PRA Category 1 Credits™*. Physicians should only claim credit commensurate with the extent of their participation in the activity.

Table of Contents

Lesson **1**

Choosing Life:
The Obligation to Seek Healing

Introduction

While a central pillar of medical ethics is the principle of patient autonomy, this is no guarantee that people will not make decisions that are capricious or unwise.

If to be human is to have the right to choose, to be ethical is to make the right choice.

Judaism has this to say to those grappling with how best to exercise their freedoms:

"I have set before you life and death, the blessing and the curse. You shall choose life" (Deuteronomy 30:19).

In a free society, it is up to you to decide whether to engage in medical care. Will you choose life?

Case **Study**

At an age when most teenage girls are thinking about having fun, Hannah Jones is hoping only to be allowed to die with dignity. Hannah, who is thirteen and terminally ill, has persuaded a hospital to withdraw a High Court action that would have forced her to have a risky heart transplant against her will. Instead, Hannah said she would prefer to spend her remaining days in the care of her family, rather than take the chance of dying in the hospital. Her mother, Kirsty, an intensive care nurse, and her father, Andrew, an auditor, say they respect their daughter's wishes.

Hannah has been in and out of the hospital since having leukemia diagnosed at the age of five. The chemotherapy left her with a hole in her heart and, as her body has grown, her heart has been unable to keep pace. It has only ten percent of normal function and she quickly gets short of breath. Doctors have warned Hannah that a transplant is her only hope of long-term survival. However, doctors have also warned her that a heart transplant is risky, especially due to her weakened condition.

"I know there's a big waiting list for heart transplants and I'm happy to save someone else's life," she said. "I just decided that there were too many risks, and even if I took it, there might be a bad outcome afterwards.

"I've been in hospital too much and I've associated hospital with bad memories, so that's why I didn't want the transplant. There is a chance that I may be OK, and there is a chance that I may not be as well as I could be, but I'm taking that chance."

Adapted from *The Times of London,* November 11–12, 2008

Learning **Activity 1**

Turn to your neighbor and discuss the following question:

Every day, many people refuse medical care and their autonomy is respected. What aspect of this story made it newsworthy enough to gain international coverage? In two minutes, you will be asked to share your responses with the class.

The Obligation to Seek Healing
The Case for Doctors

Rabbi Moshe ben Maimon (1135–1204). Better known as Maimonides or by the acronym Rambam; born in Córdoba, Spain. After the conquest of Córdoba by the Almohads, he fled Spain and eventually settled in Cairo, Egypt. There, he became the leader of the Jewish community and served as court physician to the vizier of Egypt. His rulings on Jewish law are considered integral to the formation of halachic consensus. He is most noted for authoring the *Mishneh Torah*, an encyclopedic arrangement of Jewish law, and for his philosophical work, *Guide for the Perplexed*.

Text 1

וכן כל מכשול שיש בו סכנת נפשות מצות עשה להסירו ולהשמר ממנו ולהזהר בדבר יפה יפה שנאמר (דברים ד,ט) השמר לך ושמור נפשך.

רמב״ם, הלכות רוצח ושמירת הנפש יא,ד

Similarly, it is a positive mitzvah to remove any obstacle that could pose a danger to life, and to be very careful regarding these matters, as it states (Deuteronomy 4:9), "Be cautious and guard your life."

Maimonides, *Mishneh Torah*, Laws of the Murderer and Guarding Life 11:4

Text 2a

אֲנִי ה' רֹפְאֶךָ.

שמות טו,כו

I am the Lord your healer.

Exodus 15:26

Text 2b

רְאוּ עַתָּה כִּי אֲנִי אֲנִי הוּא וְאֵין אֱלֹהִים עִמָּדִי
אֲנִי אָמִית וַאֲחַיֶּה מָחַצְתִּי וַאֲנִי אֶרְפָּא וְאֵין מִיָּדִי מַצִּיל.
דברים לב,לט

See now that it is I! I am the One, and there is no god like Me. I cause death and grant life. I strike and I heal, and no one can rescue from My Hand.

Deuteronomy 32:39

Text 2c

וַיֶּחֱלֶא אָסָא בִּשְׁנַת שְׁלוֹשִׁים וָתֵשַׁע לְמַלְכוּתוֹ בְּרַגְלָיו עַד לְמַעְלָה חָלְיוֹ
וְגַם בְּחָלְיוֹ לֹא דָרַשׁ אֶת ה' כִּי בָּרֹפְאִים.
דברי הימים ב, טז,יב

And Asa suffered from a foot ailment in the thirty-ninth year of his reign until his ailment spread upward; and even in his illness, he did not seek the Lord, but the physicians.

II Chronicles 16:12

Text 3a

וְכִי יְרִיבֻן אֲנָשִׁים וְהִכָּה אִישׁ אֶת רֵעֵהוּ בְּאֶבֶן אוֹ בְאֶגְרֹף וְלֹא יָמוּת וְנָפַל לְמִשְׁכָּב.
אִם יָקוּם וְהִתְהַלֵּךְ בַּחוּץ עַל מִשְׁעַנְתּוֹ וְנִקָּה הַמַּכֶּה רַק שִׁבְתּוֹ יִתֵּן וְרַפֹּא יְרַפֵּא.
שמות כא,יח–יט

nd if men quarrel, and one strikes the other with a stone or with a fist, and the victim does not die but is confined to bed, if he gets up and walks about outside on his staff, the assailant shall be cleared; he shall only pay for the victim's idleness, and he shall provide for his cure.

Exodus 21:18–19

Text 3b

דבי רבי ישמעאל אומר: ורפא ירפא, מכאן שניתן רשות לרופא לרפאות.
תלמוד בבלי, בבא קמא פה,א

he school of Rabbi Yishmael taught, "He shall provide for his cure"—from this [verse we learn] that permission is granted to physicians to heal.

Talmud, Bava Kama 85a

Rabbi Shlomoh Yitschaki (1040–1105). Better known by the acronym Rashi. Rabbi and famed author of comprehensive commentaries on the Talmud and Bible. Born in Troyes, France, Rashi studied in the famed *yeshivot* of Mainz and Worms. His commentaries, which focus on the simple understanding of the text, are considered fundamental to Torah study. Since their initial printings, the commentaries have appeared in virtually every edition of the Talmud and Bible. Many of the famed authors of the *Tosafot* are among Rashi's descendants.

Text **3c**

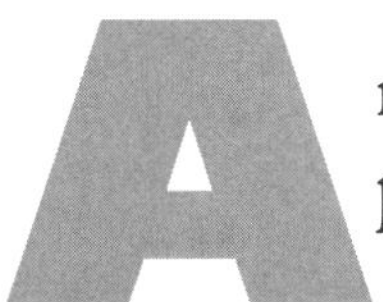

ולא אמרינן רחמנא מחי ואיהו מסי.

רש"י, שם

And we do not say, "G-d has struck; will the physician then go and heal!"

Rashi, ibid.

Question for Discussion

Do readings 3a–3c make a strong case for permitting healing in the case of G-d-inflicted illness? Explain the reasoning behind your conclusion.

Text **3d**

והא מרפא לחודיה שמעינן ליה. ויש לומר דהוה אמינא הני מילי מכה בידי אדם אבל חולי הבא בידי שמים כשמרפא נראה כסותר גזירת המלך קא משמע לן דשרי.

תוספות, שם

Tosafot. A collection of French and German talmudic commentaries in the form of critical explanations; written during the 12th and 13th centuries. Among the most famous authors of *Tosafot* are Rabbi Ya'akov Tam, Rabbi Shimshon ben Avraham of Sens, and Rabbi Yitschak "the Ri." Printed in almost all editions of the Talmud, these commentaries are fundamental to basic talmudic study.

From the word *verapo* alone we can derive [that there is permission to heal. What then is the purpose of the double expression *verapo yerapei*]?

Without it, one might think that only wounds inflicted by humans [may be healed], whereas healing an illness that is divinely inflicted could be construed as defying the edict of G-d. [Therefore, the word is repeated,] to teach us that it is permitted [to heal *all* illnesses].

Tosafot, ibid.

The Theology of Medical Treatment

Text 4a

מעשה ברבי ישמעאל ורבי עקיבא שהיו מהלכין בחוצות ירושלם, והיה עמהם אדם אחד. פגע בהם אדם חולה, אמר להם רבותי אמרו לי במה אתרפא, אמרו לו עשה כך וכך עד שתתרפא. אמר להם ומי הכה אותי. אמרו לו הקב״ה. אמר להם: ואתם הכנסתם עצמכם בדבר שאינו שלכם, הוא הכה ואתם מרפאים, אינכם עוברים על רצונו. אמרו לו מה מלאכתך, אמר להם עובד אדמה אני הרי המגל בידי. אמרו לו מי ברא את הכרם, אמר להם הקב״ה. אמרו לו ואתה מכניס עצמך בדבר שאינו שלך, הוא ברא אותו ואתה קוצץ פירותיו ממנו. אמר להם אין אתם רואים המגל בידי, אילולי אני יוצא וחורשו ומכסחו ומזבלו ומנכשו לא תעלה מאומה. אמרו לו שוטה שבעולם, מימיך לא שמעת מה שכתוב אנוש כחציר ימיו (תהלים קג,טו), כשם שהעץ אם אינו מנכש ומזבל ונחרש אינו עולה, ואם עלה ולא שתה מים ולא נזבל אינו חי והוא מת, כך הגוף הזבל הוא הסם ומיני רפואה ואיש אדמה הוא הרופא.

מדרש תמורה, אוצר המדרשים ב 580–581

Rabbi Yishmael and Rabbi Akiva were once walking through the streets of Jerusalem accompanied by another person. They encountered a sick man.

He said to them, "Rabbis, tell me how I can be cured."

They replied to him, "Do such and such until you are cured."

He asked them, "Who afflicted me?"

They replied, "G-d."

The sick man responded, "You have interfered in an area that is not your domain. G-d afflicted me and you advised me how to be cured. Are you not defying G-d's will?"

The rabbis asked him, "What is your occupation?"

He replied, "I am a farmer; this is my scythe in my hand."

They asked him, "Who created the vineyard?"

He answered, "G-d."

They said to him, "You interfere in an area not under your domain. G-d created it and you are cutting its fruits!"

He responded, "Do you not see the scythe in my hand? If I did not plow, trim, fertilize, and weed, nothing would grow."

The rabbis said to him, "Foolish man, have you never heard of the verse (Psalms 103:15), 'As for man, his days are like grass'? Just as a tree without weeding, fertilizing, and plowing will not sprout, and after sprouting, without water and fertilizer it will not live but will die, so too with the human body: the drugs and medication are [like] fertilizer and the doctor is [like] the farmer.

Midrash Temurah, Otsar Hamidrashim, vol. 2, pp. 580–581

Learning Activity 2

Turn to your neighbor and discuss the following questions:

According to the Midrash, what is the problem in seeking medical care?

How does the Midrash respond to this problem?

Text 4b

אם רעב אדם ופנה אל הלחם ואכלו שמתרפא מאותו הצער הגדול בלי ספק, האם
נאמר שהסיר בטחונו מה׳, והוי שוטים יאמר להם, כי כמו שאני מודה לה׳ בעת האוכל
שהמציא לי דבר להסיר רעבוני ולהחיותני ולקיימני, כך נודה לו על שהמציא רפואה
המרפאה את מחלתי כשאשתמש בה.

פירוש המשנה להרמב״ם, פסחים ד,י

If a person is hungry and eats food in order to relieve himself from that great discomfort, will we say that he disregarded his trust in G-d? Only fools would say such a thing! Just as I thank G-d when I eat for giving me something to remove my hunger and giving me life and sustenance, likewise it is proper to thank Him for creating the treatment which I can use to heal my illness.

Maimonides, commentary to the Mishnah, Pesachim 4:10

Question for Discussion

In light of readings 4a and 4b, why was King Asa condemned for seeking the counsel of doctors?

Text **5a**

רְפָאֵנוּ ה׳ וְנֵרָפֵא, הוֹשִׁיעֵנוּ וְנִוָּשֵׁעָה . . .
וְהַעֲלֵה אֲרוּכָה וּרְפוּאָה שְׁלֵמָה לְכָל מַכּוֹתֵינוּ, כִּי אֵ-ל מֶלֶךְ רוֹפֵא נֶאֱמָן וְרַחֲמָן אָתָּה.
בָּרוּךְ אַתָּה ה׳, רוֹפֵא חוֹלֵי עַמּוֹ יִשְׂרָאֵל.
תפלת העמידה, סדור תהלת ה׳

Heal us, O Lord, and we will be healed; help us and we will be saved . . . Grant complete cure and healing to all our wounds, for You, Almighty King, are a faithful and merciful healer. Blessed are You, Lord, who heals the sick of His people Israel.

Amidah Prayer, Sidur Tehilat Hashem

Text **5b**

מי שברך אבותינו אברהם יצחק ויעקב משה ואהרן דוד ושלמה הוא ירפא את (. . .)
בעבור שנדר לצדקה בעבורו (בעבורה).
בשכר זה הקדוש ברוך הוא ימלא רחמים עליו להחלימו ולרפאותו ולהחזיקו ולהחיותו
(עליה להחלימה ולרפאותה ולהחזיקה ולהחיותה). וישלח לו (לה) מהרה רפואה
שלמה מן השמים . . . רפואת הנפש ורפואת הגוף ונאמר אמן.
מי שבירך, סידור תהלת ה׳

May the One who blessed our patriarchs, Abraham, Isaac, Jacob, Moses, Aaron, David and Solomon, heal (. . .) in the merit of the charity being given for his/her sake.

In this merit, may G-d grant compassion to him/her, to restore him/her, to heal him/her, to strengthen him/her, to enliven him/her, and He shall send speedily from heaven a complete healing for him/her . . . a healing of the spirit and healing of the body, and let us all say: Amen!

Prayer for the Sick, *Sidur Tehilat Hashem*

The Role of Spiritual Healing

Text 6a

חש בראשו יעסוק בתורה . . . חש בגרונו יעסוק בתורה . . . חש במעיו יעסוק בתורה . . .
חש בעצמותיו יעסוק בתורה . . . חש בכל גופו יעסוק בתורה.
תלמוד בבלי, עירובין נד,א

One who feels pain in the head should engage in the study of the Torah . . . One who feels pain in the throat should engage in the study of the Torah . . . One who feels pain in the bowels should engage in the study of the Torah . . . One who feels pain in the bones should engage in the study of the Torah . . . One who feels pain in all of the body should engage in the study of the Torah.

Talmud, Eiruvin 54a

Text **6b**

היה הקדוש ברוך הוא מביט בתורה, ובורא את העולם.
בראשית רבה א,א

G-d was looking into the Torah as He was creating the world.

Midrash, Bereishit Rabah 1:1

Text **6c**

רצונו לומר שהתורה בעצמה היא סדר הכל, ולכך כאשר רצה השם יתברך לברא את
עולמו ולסדר אותו, היה מביט בתורה שהיא סדר הכל ובורא את עולמו . . .
אם יש לאדם חולה בגופו שכל אשר הוא חולה יוצא מן הסדר
יעסוק בתורה שהיא סדר העולם, ואז האדם אשר היה מקבל חולי שהוא שנוי
יחזור אל הסדר שהוא בריאתו.
נתיבות עולם, נתיב התורה א

Meaning, that the Torah itself is the regulator of everything. Thus, when G-d wanted to create and order His universe, He peered into the Torah—the regulator of everything—and created His universe. . . . Therefore, if one has an illness of the body—meaning that he departed from the normal order—he should study Torah, which is the regulator of the universe. Then, the person who received this illness, which is a change [from the normal], will be able to return to the normal order.

Rabbi Yehudah Loew of Prague, Netivot Olam, Netiv HaTorah 1

Jewish vs. Secular Perspective
Right of Refusal of Treatment

Questions for Discussion

1. What are the most common reasons given for the refusal of treatment?

2. Based on Text 7, what is the primary cause for Hannah's refusal of the treatment?

Text 7

Liz Hayes: What is it about the heart transplant you don't like?

Hannah Jones: Not coming around from the anesthetics if something goes wrong in the theater and they can't do it.

Liz Hayes: So it's the operation?

Hannah Jones: The operation, yeah. If they had like a hundred percent success rate every time, then perhaps I'd go for it but it's not guaranteed, it's not a cure.

Hannah Jones, interview by Liz Hayes, *60 Minutes Australia*, April 11, 2009

Question for Discussion

Would Hannah be allowed to refuse treatment due to the fact that some risk is involved? Provide the reason for your answer.

Text 8

Every human being of adult years and sound mind has a right to determine what shall be done with his own body.

Benjamin N. Cardozo, *Schloendorff v. Society of New York Hospital,* 105 N.E. 2nd 92, 93 (1914)

Text 9

Secular ethics is primarily concerned with who gets to make a decision. Courts and legislatures are thus preoccupied with advance directives, surrogate decision-making, ethics committees, IRB's, etc. This is so because the primary value the law seeks to enshrine is the autonomy of the individual. Thus, once we identify the "who," we essentially have no interest in the "what." By contrast, Jewish law is far more interested in the substance of what the decision should be and in theory, the resolution should not depend on the identity/personal predilections of the decider. Secular law asks who decides; Jewish law asks what is to be decided.

Rabbi Yitzchok A. Breitowitz, "How A Rabbi Decides A Medical Halacha Issue," Jlaw.com

Old Enough to Decide?

Text 10

"That's the million-dollar question, isn't it? To start with, because it's Hannah's choice, that's the main thing in all of this. Hannah doesn't have much choice or control over her life, but she does have control over when she's going to die."

Kristy Jones, interview by Liz Hayes, *60 Minutes Australia*, April 11, 2009

Medical Coercion

Text 11a

רק בחולי ומכה שבגלוי שביש לרופא ידיעה ודאית והכרה ברורה בהם, ועוסק בתרופה בדוקה וגמורה, ודאי לעולם כופין לחולה המסרב במקום סכנה . . . כל כהאי גוונא ודאי עושין לו ומעשין אותו בעל כרחו משום הצלת נפש. ואין משגיחין בו אם הוא אינו רוצה ביסורין ובוחר מות מחיים, אלא חותכין לו אפילו אבר שלם, אם הוצרך לכך למלטו ממות . . . וכל אדם מוזהר על כך משום ולא תעמוד על דם רעך (ויקרא יט,טז).

מור וקציעה, אורח חיים שכח

In the case of an illness or wound which is exposed, about which the physician has definite knowledge and clear recognition, and which has a proven and complete course of treatment, it is certain that we always impose the treatment on a patient who refuses, if his life is in danger. . . . In all such cases, we certainly perform [the procedure upon] him and we [even] force him against his will because of [the value of] saving a life. We pay no attention to the fact that he doesn't want to suffer and prefers death to life, and we are even willing to amputate an entire limb if this is needed to spare him from death . . . This is incumbent on every individual because of the command to "not stand by the shedding of your fellow's blood" (Leviticus 19:16).

Rabbi Ya'akov Emden, Mor Uketsiah, Orach Chayim 328

Learning Activity 3

Based on Text 11a, what prerequisites are necessary before coercing a patient to accept treatment? Write down your answer.

Text **11b**

ובדבר כשהחולה אינו רוצה ליקח הרפואה . . . אם הוא מחמת שאינו מאמין לרופאים
אלו צריכין למצא רופא שמאמין בו, ואם ליכא רופא כזה ואי אפשר לפניו מצד המחלה
לחכות עד שיבין שהוא לטובתו וגם לא לשלחו כשרוצה בבית חולים וברופאים שהם
בעיר אחרת מוכרחין הרופאים שבכאן לעשות בעל כורחיה אם כל הרופאים שבבית
חולים זה סוברים שזהו רפואתו.

וגם יהיה באופן שלא יתבעת מזה שאם יתבעת מזה אפילו שהוא ענין שטות אין
לעשות כי הביעתותא אפשר שיזיקהו וגם ימיתהו ויהיה זה כהמיתוהו בידים ולכן יותר
טוב שלא לעשות בעל כורחיה אף שהקרובים רוצים שיעשו לו גם בעל כרחיה, וצריכין
הרופאים להתיישב בזה הרבה כשנזדמן חולה שאינו רוצה בהרפואה שעושין לו אם
לכפותו כשהוא גדול שקרוב שלא תהא לתועלת כל כך, ולעשות בזה לשם שמים.

ובאם יש בהרפואה עצמה איזו סכנה אבל הרופאים נוהגין ליתן רפואה זו להחולה שיש
לו מחלה מסוכנת שמדת סכנה של הרפואה פחותה הרבה מסכנת המחלה
אין ליתן בעל כרחיה בכל אופן.

אגרות משה, חושן משפט ב, עג,ה

Rabbi Moshe Feinstein (1895–1986). Rabbi and leading halachic authority of the 20th century. Born near Minsk, Belarus; became rabbi of Luban in 1921; immigrated to the U.S. in 1937 and became the dean of Metivta Tiferet Yerushalayim in New York. Rabbi Feinstein became the leading halachic authority of his time and his rulings are always considered. His halachic decisions have been published in a multi-volume collection titled *Igrot Moshe*. He also published works on the Talmud and was known for his fine character traits.

Regarding a patient that refuses to take a treatment . . . If the patient's refusal is because he does not trust his physicians, then we must find him a physician that he trusts. If there is no such physician, and because of the illness there is no time to wait until he realizes that the treatment is needed for his wellbeing, or [there is no time] for him to be sent to a hospital and physicians in another city, then his physicians must coerce the treatment, so long as all the physicians of that hospital agree that this is indeed what will heal him.

But this must be in a way that will not scare the patient. If he is scared, even if his fright is foolish, the treatment should not be administered, since the fright could harm him and maybe even kill him, and it would be as if the physicians murdered him directly. Therefore, it is better not to coerce him, even if the relatives want the physicians to force him. The doctors must act in good faith and carefully consider the case of an adult that refuses the treatment, since it is very likely that coercion will not bring about much benefit.

If the treatment contains some risk, although physicians administer it to patients whose illness is of greater danger to them than the danger of the treatment, such a treatment cannot be coerced in any manner.

Rabbi Moshe Feinstein, *Igrot Moshe, Choshen Mishpat*, vol. 2, 73:5

Learning Activity 4

Based on Text 11b, what prerequisites are necessary before coercing a patient to accept treatment? Write down your answer.

Postscript

Text **12**

A terminally ill girl who refused life saving heart surgery in 2007 and 2008 has returned to school after changing her mind and undergoing a transplant.

Hannah Jones, 14 . . . had the operation in London's Great Ormond Street Hospital in July. . . .

Hannah had various health complications after the transplant but went back to St Mary's High School, in Lugwardine, on Monday. . . .

Her mother Kirsty said: "She spent ten days in the intensive care unit unconscious with her chest open because they couldn't close it up."

She developed chest infections that twice turned into pneumonia and then caught swine flu, she added.

"It's been a bit of a rollercoaster but that is nothing compared to what we experienced previously," Mrs Jones said.

Hannah said she found it "difficult" at first going back to school but added that it was "nice to get back to normal." . . .

"I changed my mind because the way I was going I wasn't going to get much of a longer life and I wanted to see the world a bit and do more things.

"I think if I had said no again to the operation I would have regretted it because I would not have been well enough to do those things," she added.

Hannah said one of the greatest benefits of her new heart was that she could run around and "chase her brothers and sisters."

She said she was also looking forward to going on two family holidays this year to celebrate her improved health.

"Heart Refusal Girl Back at School," BBC.co.uk, January 5, 2010

Key Points

1. Judaism imposes an obligation for us to guard our lives by living safely and healthily.

2. There is an obligation for patients to seek medical intervention to cure illness.

3. The obligation to seek treatment in no way diminishes the role played by G-d in our lives. In every dimension of living, G-d gives us the opportunity to partner with Him in developing and perfecting the world we live in.

4. An important part of healing is realizing that G-d is the one that cures through the agency of nature and physicians. Thus, prayer is an important part of healing.

5. The physical body and the spiritual soul are intertwined and depend on each other. When the spirit is healthy, it aids in bringing about physical cure.

6. If the patient is terminally ill and the chances for success are greater than the risks, the obligation to seek treatment will apply even to risky treatments.

7. In principle, it is an obligation to do everything possible to save others from death, even to the point of forcing them to accept treatment. However, in many cases, compulsion may not be practical or advised.

Additional Readings

The Morality of Coercion

Shimon M Glick
Ben Gurion University, Beer Sheva, Israel

Abstract

The author congratulates Dr Brian Hurwitz, who recently reported the successful "intimidation" of an elderly competent widow into accepting badly needed therapy for a huge ulcerated carcinoma. He reports approvingly of the Israeli Patients' Rights Law, enacted in 1996, which demands detailed informed consent from competent patients before permitting treatment.

But the law also provides an escape clause which permits coercing a competent patient into accepting life-saving therapy if an ethics committee feels that if treatment is imposed the patient will give his/her consent retroactively. He suggests this approach as an appropriate middle road between overbearing paternalism and untrammelled autonomy.

Dr Brian Hurwitz, in a recent issue of the journal,[1] almost apologetically reported the successful intimidation of an elderly competent widow into accepting badly needed therapy for a huge ulcerated basal cell carcinoma. He placed great emphasis on the unreasonable wasting of valuable scarce resources, and these considerations pushed him into what ultimately spared this woman much suffering and possibly death. Yet in spite of this courageous step on his part, Dr Hurwitz, in his reflection, still is agonising: "Did I apply undue pressure upon Mrs Thomas?"

Dr Hurwitz's hesitation is indeed justified, if looked at in light of the priority placed upon autonomy in today's Western medical ethics.[2] He might well be accused by many ethicists of paternalistically violating this woman's precious autonomy.

I would like to suggest rather that Dr Hurwitz is to be congratulated for his courage, and that it is high time that the pendulum which has swung from overbearing, autocratic and insensitive paternalism to an often cruel and dangerous autonomy, be allowed to swing back to a more moderate and sensible balance between autonomy and beneficence.

I would like to use the current Israeli patients' rights law, as perhaps one possible example of a sensible, sensitive and nuanced middle-of-the-road position.

Israel, in 1996, became one of the few nations to enact national patients' rights legislation.[3] The law covers a wide variety of patient rights, but I shall focus here only on the issue of informed consent. The law specifies quite explicitly that prior to any treatment, a competent patient's consent must be obtained, and that in the process of obtaining such consent the physician must provide the patient with information about:

Diagnosis and prognosis of his/her condition.

Description of the nature, the process, the goal, the expected benefit and the chances of success of the proposed treatment.

The dangers of the treatment, including side effects, pain and discomfort.

Risks and benefits of alternate forms of therapy or of no therapy at all.

[1] Hurwitz B. Pressuring Mrs Thomas to accept treatment: a case history. *Journal of Medical Ethics* 1998;24:320-1.

[2] Wolpe PR. The triumph of autonomy in American bioethics: a sociological view. In: Devries R, Subedi J, eds. *Bioethics and society.* Upper Saddle River, New Jersey: Prentice Hall, 1998.

[3] Patients' Rights Law 1996. Laws of State of Israel. Jerusalem: Israel Government Printing Office, 1996: 327.

In this legislation the Israeli legislators clearly came down firmly in favour of the American courts' standard of the "reasonable patient",[4] rather than the British standard of the "reasonable physician".[5]

Yet when the issue of the possibility of treatment of a competent patient against his/her will was considered the Israeli law-makers hesitated. On the one hand there is virtual unanimity in the West that no competent patient may be forced to accept even life-saving therapy. But here the strong "sanctity of life" Jewish tradition could not accept so lightly permitting a salvageable patient to die.

Faced with this dilemma, the attorney general of the state of Israel convened a meeting of some 30 experts, including physicians, lawyers, rabbis and philosophers, to advise him on this vexing dilemma. As might be expected, the civil libertarians argued vigorously for the Western view that no competent person could ever be treated against his/her will. On the other hand religious leaders spoke out against permitting a patient to die, even if this was his/her express wish. One of Israel's leading philosophers characterised his own dilemma by stating: "I have a conflict between my head and my heart. The former tells me not to treat the patient, but my heart does not permit me to let him die. I am unable to stand by and watch a man who wants to commit suicide by lying on the railroad tracks, to remain there, without pushing him off even against his will". At the end of a long discussion period, a compromise was reached. The law now reads that if there is serious risk of death or permanent major disability in the absence of treatment, the treatment is clearly beneficial, the patient refuses therapy, and the hospital ethics committee feels that if treatment is imposed the patient will later give his consent retroactively, treatment may be imposed.

I must confess that my initial reaction to the compromise was one of derision. While the Holy Land has a long tradition of prophecy, it seemed, on first thought, to be unreasonable to expect an ethics committee to exercise such powers.

But on further thought, and stimulated by an actual case, I have come to conclude that the Israeli compromise has Solomonic wisdom, and indeed merits consideration by other societies as well.

In a recent case at one of Israel's hospitals a young Bedouin man was admitted with pneumococcal pneumonia (generally a highly treatable disease in this age group, with reasonable expectation of complete recovery). He was having trouble with adequate oxygenation and was tiring. Intubation and mechanical respiration were medically indicated. The patient, fully "competent" by the usual standards, was adamant in his refusal to be intubated. The physicians attempted to persuade the patient, using family members as well as interpreters, but to no avail. The physicians did not take advantage of the clause in the law permitting the possible imposition of treatment in this case, but accepted the patient's refusal and treated him without intubation. The patient died.

Surprising ending

Ironically a recent article by a physician in a nonmedical magazine[6] describes an almost identical case in the United States, with an opposite, and surprising ending. A man, in his late thirties, with bacterial pneumonia, in serious respiratory distress, refused intubation in spite of all efforts to persuade him. The physicians in this case also honoured his refusal, but immediately upon the patient's loss of consciousness intubated him, attached him to a respirator and sedated him. When his condition improved, some 24 hours later, the sedation was stopped, and the tube removed. The patient's first words were "Thank you".

The Israeli patient's death would be considered perfectly acceptable by many Western ethicists. But I would disagree strongly, and consider the death an unnecessary and preventable tragedy. Here was a patient, acutely ill, with a curable disease. The physicians were not dealing with a patient who was suffering with a terminal illness, who was looking forward to death as a salvation and about whom I would agree that imposition of mechanical respiration to prolong his suffering would be unconscionable. This patient, while technically and

---

[4] Canterbury and Spence. 464 F2d 772 (DC Cir 1972).

[5] Sidaway v The Board of Governors of the Bethlem Royal Hospital and the Maudsley Hospital. Argued in the House of Lords 1984 Dec 3-6, 1984. Reported at [1985] 2WLR 480.

[6] Gawande A. Whose body is it, anyway? *New Yorker Magazine* 1999 Oct 4: 84-91.

legally competent, obviously feared the intubation. But had his life been saved by several hours of mechanical respiration, he would have undoubtedly been eternally grateful to a Dr Hurwitz, who might have had the courage to act decisively. Under the new Israeli law, such a step would have been perfectly legal, and Dr Hurwitz would not have had to feel guilty about his actions. But the Western influence of autonomy, reigning supreme, influenced this man's physicians to accept his tragic choice.

The American physicians who violated American legal and ethical norms, I believe acted appropriately, in accord with the spirit of the Israeli law.

I believe that a more careful examination of the specific cases in the casuistic tradition,[7] and a more nuanced application of terms such as competence and autonomy are indicated. If competence is regarded as an all or none phenomenon and autonomy as an absolute trump over all other values, obviously the Israeli law is unethical. But in evaluating a specific case, even according to the "four principles" method, which in its original form, does not necessarily give automatic priority of one principle over another, the relative magnitude of each principle should be taken into consideration.

The degree of competence of patients, all of whom are certified as "competent" by a psychiatrist, may vary from patient to patient. Autonomy is predicated on a rational determination free of coercion, not just coercion by a physician but also by the overall circumstances. The reasoned, repeated, well thought out decision by a chronically ill cancer patient should be given greater weight than a hasty decision by an acutely ill frightened, although technically competent, patient.

On the other hand the refusal to submit to a major operation with great risk, pain and suffering or to a dangerous treatment should carry greater weight than the refusal of a procedure with relatively trivial risk and with virtually guaranteed certainty of life-saving.

Retroactive consent is not automatically superior to proactive consent and indeed it is often identical in its

conclusion. But oftentimes individuals under acute stress may make hasty tragic decisions which they subsequently, under more careful consideration, regret. Hindsight, or the "retrospectoscope", using additional data, beyond those present at the time of the original decision, may result in a decision more acceptable *to the patient himself/herself*. It is perhaps equivalent to the decision of an appeals court which reverses the decision of a lower court after considering it in light of additional evidence.

The ethics committee is called upon to weigh the quality of the competence of the patient, the degree of his/her autonomy, the potential for risk and suffering in the procedure, the likelihood of its success, the danger of refusal and the likelihood of the patient's subsequent reversal of his earlier refusal. If on balance the scales tip towards imposing treatment on a currently unwilling patient they may so decide.

'Escape clause'
This "escape clause" is not intended for frequent or routine use. Far from it, and as the case of the Bedouin patient indicates, it may be underused. But when the magnitude of the beneficence is huge, and the weight of the autonomy consideration weak, why not let beneficence "override" autonomy?

I would hope that even the most devoted advocates of autonomy might accept the premise that a patient who is frightened and stressed, may not be fully autonomous; his/her refusal should therefore be assigned less weight.

It is tragic to accept such a patient's refusal automatically at face value, even if a team of psychiatrists and lawyers judge that person legally competent. Competence and autonomy must be evaluated on a continuum and not as simplistic all-or-none phenomena.

In addition, autonomy is of no value to a dead person. By permitting a patient to die avoidably, when it is virtually certain that were he saved against his present protest he would be grateful, one is granting that person his short term "autonomous" wish while depriving him of his long term autonomy. The Israeli law's line of reasoning is similar to J Stuart Mill's refusal to permit

---

[7] Jonsen AR, Toulmin S. *The abuse of casuistry—a history of moral reasoning*. Berkeley: University of California Press, 1988.

an individual to sell himself into slavery,[8] because he thereby uses his freedom, to deprive himself of freedom which is the ultimate raison d'etre of autonomy.

Obviously the present situation is not identical to Mill's example. Nor do I contend that in keeping with the analogy one should never accept a patient's autonomous decision to let him die. But the analogy does emphasise the principle that autonomy is not the ultimate end and that it does not always "trump" all other values. It must be considered in the context of its broader goals and evaluated on a case by case basis.

If the ethics committee errs in coercing the patient who subsequently persists in his/her withholding consent the patient's autonomy has been violated, which is not a matter to be taken lightly. On the other hand if the ethics committee errs in the other direction and permits the patient to die, in a situation where the patient might in retrospect have wanted to live, the damage would seem to be infinitely greater; there is no reversal of death.

I am not advocating a return to insensitive, arrogant paternalism, which places little or no value on individual patients' opinions and values, and arrogates to the physician the absolute right to select therapy, under the guise of always knowing what is best for the patient. But when a thoughtful ethics committee listens carefully to a patient's viewpoint, and is convinced that the patient's welfare demands a particular treatment, and that the patient, too, will subsequently be grateful for such intervention, I believe it to be ethically appropriate to overrule the patient's objections.

The proposed position would obviously be opposed by the most militant exponents of autonomy such as Robert Veatch[9] who states categorically that he knows of no case in which patient welfare is so weighty that it could outweigh autonomy, and who claims that "no competent patient in the United States has ever been forced to undergo medical treatment for his or her own good. No matter how tragic, autonomy should always win if its only competitor is the paternalistic form of beneficence."

There have been several more moderate voices[10] [11] [12] suggesting that there are situations, particularly in the area of public policy, where the common good should override personal autonomy. However, they have not publicly crossed the Rubicon to suggest that treatment be imposed on an unwilling, competent individual patient for his or her own good.

But in the moving exchange between Dax Stewart and Robert Burt[13] about the imposition of therapy on the devastatingly burnt Dax and in the subsequent article[14] commenting on the exchange, a view similar to the one expressed here comes to the fore. For even Dax who has fought so eloquently and vigorously and helped create the famous "Please Let Me Die" and "Dax's Case" videos, accepted the possibility of not acquiescing immediately to an acutely ill patient's request to die, but entering into negotiations on the matter.

I believe there are sound ethical and humanitarian grounds for a retreat from the absolutism of autonomy, and I congratulate Dr Hurwitz for acting bravely and for raising the issue publicly.

Shimon M Glick, MD, is Chairman of the Moshe Prywes Center for Medical Education, Ben Gurion University, Beer Sheva, Israel.

Journal of Medical Ethics 26, no 5 (October 2000): 393–395. Reprinted with permission by publisher

---

[8] Mill JS. *On liberty*. Cambridge: Hackett, 1978.

[9] Veatch RM. Which grounds for overriding autonomy are legitimate? *Hastings Center Report* 1996:26:42-3.

[10] Callahan D. Autonomy: a moral good, not a moral obsession. *Hastings Center Report* 1984;14:40-2.

[11] Gaylin W. Worshipping autonomy. *Hastings Center Report* 1996; 26:43-5.

[12] Leeman CP. Patient autonomy and undertreatment of critical disease. *Hospital Practice* 1998; Feb 15: 177-83.

[13] Anonymous. Confronting death: who chooses, who controls? A dialogue between Dax Cowart and Robert Burt. *Hastings Center Report* 1998;28:14-24.

[14] Arnold DG, Menzel PT. When comes "the end of the day"? *Hastings Center Report* 1998;28:25-7.

Autonomy Should Chair, Not Rule

Charles Foster

During a recent conversation among medical ethicists in an Oxford pub, one person suggested that: "Medical ethics is really a very straightforward subject these days." He went on to explain: "In most cases there's only one relevant principle: autonomy. All that you ever have to do is to decide what the patient's autonomous wishes are. And then do them in a way that won't affront the lawyers. True, there are sometimes debates about resource allocation, and then other issues might come into play. But even then autonomy gives you the solution. The right allocation of resources will be the one that maximises the autonomy of the greatest number."

This was in deadly earnest. It was an expression of the ruling orthodoxy in medicine. At medical school, students learn about the four classic principles of medical ethics: autonomy, justice, non-maleficence ("do no harm") and beneficence ("do good"). But as soon as they start practising they will thumb nervously through the guidelines of the professional bodies, and there they will find that the shrill voice of autonomy drowns out the modest protestations of the other principles.

This is, of course, far preferable to the bluff, arrogant paternalism of yesteryear—to which it is a reaction. Medicine has rightly committed those attitudes to the dustcart of history, along with the white coat that was their emblem. But other things were slung out too: notably the patient's ancient right to say: "You know best, doctor", and the peace of mind that comes from it.

There are many models of autonomy, but the one almost universally adopted in discussing medical ethics is the straightforward libertarianism of John Stuart Mill, Peter Singer, and Julian Savulescu. It says that everyone has (or should have) a consciously drafted "life plan"—a sort of ontological road map—and it assumes that the patient and nobody but the patient will want to steer along it. It's a terribly middle-class philosophy, which

is why it has been repeatedly and uncritically endorsed in the courts by middle-class judges.

But that's not how most people live. To force them to adopt this model is a sort of philosophical imperialism. Onora O'Neill has proposed that our ability to make health-care choices for ourselves is well down our list of health-care priorities. What patients want most in their doctors is to be able to trust them. Patients don't necessarily want to be told everything about their condition and prognosis, or about the side-effects of their medication reported just last week in an obscure medical journal. They want to know that there is a medically qualified human being on their side who'll play fair with them. Of course, autonomy is right to insist that if a patient wants to know the full story, they should be told, and that for a patient to trust a doctor, the patient must know that nothing is being withheld that should be spoken.

But don't I have a basic right not to be told things? The answer is a complex one. Suppose that I undergo genetic testing for condition X. The test will also indicate whether or not I have condition Y. If I do have Y, it will certainly manifest itself in a terrible way. I ask my doctor not to tell me the results of the testing for Y. Let's assume that I am single and have had a vasectomy and, therefore, that no actual or potential person will be very directly affected by my decision not to know about condition Y. What should the doctor do?

The answer is clear enough. He should not disclose the information. There does seem to be a generally recognised right not to have collected health information forced on you. The big international instruments are emphatic. "Everyone is entitled to know any information collected about his or her health. However, the wishes of individuals not to be so informed shall be observed", says the European Convention on Human Rights and Biomedicine. Similar provisions are found elsewhere, and are enshrined in some national laws. "The person's will to remain ignorant of diagnostic and prognostic information should be respected, except where third parties are exposed to a risk of transmission", says the French Law on Patients' Rights. It is echoed in Hungary, Belgium, the Netherlands, and elsewhere.

But the situation is rather different when it comes to consent to treatment. If you don't want to know the risks associated with a particular procedure, it is harder to remain comfortably ignorant. Most of the national regulatory and guiding bodies are terse and clear. They don't seem to think that there's anything to discuss. "Informed consent is a basic policy in both ethics and law that physicians must honor", says the American Medical Association (2006). A doctor must ensure "that patients are informed of the material risks associated with any part of the proposed management plan", insists the Australian Medical Council (2009). The Medical Council of New Zealand is rather more generous, but the result is an unhelpful fudge: "Give patients all the information they want or need to know about their condition and its likely progression/treatment options, including expected risks, side-effects, costs and benefits" (2008).

When they come off the fence, the regulators show their true colours. This is what the UK General Medical Council says (2008):

"If a patient asks you to make decisions on their behalf or wants to leave decisions to a relative, partner, friend, carer or another person close to them, you should explain that it is still important that they understand the options open to them, and what the treatment will involve. If they do not want this information, you should try to find out why.

"If, after discussion, a patient still does not want to know in detail about their condition or the treatment, you should respect their wishes, as far as possible. But you must still give them the information they need in order to give their consent to a proposed investigation or treatment . . .

"If a patient insists that they do not want even this basic information, you must explain the potential consequences of them not having it, particularly if it might mean that their consent is not valid. You must record the fact that the patient has declined this information. You must also make it clear that they can change their mind and have more information at any time."

Here's my paraphrase: "If a frightened patient comes to you and says: 'I trust you to do the right thing, doctor.

But I don't want to know any of the details, thank you. You know what I'm like: they would just make me worried sick', you must do your best to give them the information anyway. It's good for them really. But if you really can't give them any of it, make sure your medico-legal back is covered."

Why should anyone insist that the patient needs this information? Well, partly because of the lawyers licking their lips in the hospital reception, of course; but more fundamentally because of the patronising presumption that a patient is not really acting rationally unless they share the ruling "life-plan" view of autonomy. And so, in an almost amusing irony, autonomy becomes tyrannous. "You will be autonomous whether you like it or not", it shrieks. Autonomy has taken away the right autonomously to delegate one's autonomy. You cannot autonomously opt for your doctor to act in a benevolently paternalistic way. And that's a shame.

Philosophically the roots of this irony are to be found in Immanuel Kant. True freedom, for Kant, consisted in obedience to the "Universal Law"—which in his case was more or less identical with the norms of orthodox Christianity. So for him, someone who sought to have sexual intercourse outside marriage was not acting truly freely, and there was accordingly nothing offensive about stopping them. Something similar is going on in modern medical ethics. The new Universal Law is that autonomy trumps all other considerations, and therefore all truly free people will want to make all their decisions entirely themselves, with the benefit of all relevant information.

If someone doesn't agree, then they are not in their right mind. You should treat them as you would treat any other patient who lacks capacity; you should act in their "best interests". And what are those best interests? To be made to grasp the tiller of their own life, even if it's the last thing they want.

Note something else. The Kantian man was icy and grey. He lacked the three-dimensionality and the sympathy necessary in a good doctor. You would shudder to see him striding across the ward to you, however impeccable his clinical skills. It is the same with anyone who thinks that philosophical principles, rather than human need, should write ethics guidelines. Ethics were made for the patient, not the patient for the ethics. If guidelines make an old, frightened man cry, it is time to rip them up.

A world in which autonomy did not have a prominent place would be monstrous. Autonomy should, indeed, have the casting vote. The revolution against the Lancelot Spratts was urgent and necessary. But, as so often, the revolution was over-zealous. It killed off all the perceived opposition, and grew arrogant in power. It forgot the people (the patients) who put it on the throne.

No bloody counter-revolution is needed. Autonomy just needs to be content to chair the discussions, listen respectfully to the contributions made by justice, non-maleficence, and beneficence, trim its own arguments in the light of what they say, and be prepared to accept graciously the occasional possibility of being outvoted. Humility becomes a man, and humility becomes a principle.

One of the things that I love about the discipline of medical ethics is the tolerance and niceness of almost all its serious practitioners. The stridency of its key principle is a bemusing anomaly. This is the conversation I would like to hear:

"Medical ethics is a really fascinating subject, isn't it?"

"I quite agree, but why do you think so?"

"For me, it's the discourse between the governing principles. Their conversation is like a human conversation. A skilful ethicist simply eavesdrops and transcribes."

The Lancet 375, no. 9712 (30 January 2010): 368–369.
Reprinted with permission by publisher

SATZ v. PERLMUTTER

MICHAEL J. SATZ, State Attorney for Broward County, Florida, Appellant, v. ABE PERLMUTTER, Appellee No. 78-1486 District Court of Appeal of Florida, Fourth District 362 So. 2d 160; 1978 Fla. App. LEXIS 16354

OPINION

The State here appeals a trial court order permitting the removal of an artificial life sustaining device from a competent, but terminally ill adult. We affirm.

Seventy-three year old Abe Perlmutter lies mortally sick in a hospital, suffering from amyotrophic lateral sclerosis (Lou Gehrig's disease) diagnosed in January 1977. There is no cure and normal life expectancy, from time of diagnosis, is but two years. In Mr. Perlmutter, the affliction has progressed to the point of virtual incapability of movement, inability to breathe without a mechanical respirator and his very speech is an extreme effort. Even with the respirator, the prognosis is death within a short time. Notwithstanding, he remains in command of his mental faculties and legally competent. He seeks, with full approval of his adult family, to have the respirator removed from his trachea, which act, according to his physician, based upon medical probability, would result in "a reasonable life expectancy of less than one hour." Mr. Perlmutter is fully aware of the inevitable result of such removal, yet has attempted to remove it for himself (hospital personnel, activated by an alarm, reconnected it). He has repeatedly stated to his family, "I'm miserable take it out" and at a bedside hearing, told the obviously concerned trial judge that whatever would be in store for him if the respirator were removed, "it can't be worse than what I'm going through now."

Pursuant to all of the foregoing, and upon the petition of Mr. Perlmutter himself, the trial judge entered a detailed and thoughtful final judgment which included the following language:

ORDERED AND ADJUDGED that Abe Perlmutter, in the

exercise of his right of privacy, may remain in defendant hospital or leave said hospital, free of the mechanical respirator now attached to his body and all defendants and their staffs are restrained from interfering with Plaintiff's decision.

We agree with the trial judge.

The State's position is that it (1) has an overriding duty to preserve life, and (2) that termination of supportive care, whether it be by the patient, his family or medical personnel, is an unlawful killing of a human being under the Florida Murder Statute *Section 782.04, Florida Statutes (1977)* or Manslaughter under Section 782.08. The hospital, and its doctors, while not insensitive to this tragedy, fear not only criminal prosecution if they aid in removal of the mechanical device, but also civil liability. In the absence of prior Florida law on the subject, their fears cannot be discounted.

The pros and cons involved in such tragedies which bedevil contemporary society, mainly because of incredible advancement in scientific medicine, are all exhaustively discussed in *Superintendent of Belchertown v. Saikewicz, Mass., 373 Mass. 728, 370 N.E.2d 417 (1977).* As *Saikewicz* points out, the right of an individual to refuse medical treatment is tempered by the State's:

1. Interest in the preservation of life.

2. Need to protect innocent third parties.

3. Duty to prevent suicide.

4. Requirement that it help maintain the ethical integrity of medical practice.

In the case at bar, none of these four considerations surmount the individual wishes of Abe Perlmutter. Thus we adopt the view of the line of cases discussed in *Saikewicz* which would allow Abe Perlmutter the right to refuse or discontinue treatment based upon "the constitutional right to privacy . . . an expression of the sanctity of individual free choice and self-determination." (*Id. 426.*) We would stress that this adoption is limited to the specific facts now before us, involving a competent adult patient. The problem is less easy of solution when the patient is incapable of understanding and we, therefore, postpone a crossing of that more complex bridge until such time as we are required to do so.

PRESERVATION OF LIFE

There can be no doubt that the State *does* have an interest in preserving life, but we again agree with *Saikewicz* that "there is a substantial distinction in the State's insistence that human life be saved where the affliction is curable, as opposed to the State interest where, as here, the issue is not whether, but when, for how long, and at what cost to the individual [his] life may be briefly extended." (*Id. 425-426.*) In the case at bar the condition is terminal, the patient's situation wretched, and the continuation of his life temporary and totally artificial.

Accordingly, we see no compelling State interest to interfere with Mr. Perlmutter's expressed wishes.

PROTECTION OF THIRD PARTIES

Classically, this protection is exemplified in the case *Application of the President and Directors of Georgetown College, Inc., 118 U.S.App.D.C. 80, 331 F.2d 1000, cert. denied, 377 U.S. 978, 84 S. Ct. 1883, 12 L. Ed. 2d 746 (1964),* where the patient, by refusing treatment, is said to be abandoning his minor child, which abandonment the State as *parens patriae* sought to prevent. We point out that Abe Perlmutter is 73, his family adult and all in agreement with his wishes. The facts do not support abandonment.

PREVENTION OF SUICIDE

As to suicide, the facts here unarguably reveal that Mr. Perlmutter would die, but for the respirator. The disconnecting of it, far from causing his unnatural death by means of a "death producing agent" in fact will merely result in his death, if at all, from natural causes, *Saikewicz, Id., 426, fn. 11.* The testimony of Mr. Perlmutter, like the victim in the *Georgetown College* case, *supra*, is that he really wants to live, but do so, God and Mother Nature willing, under his own power. This basic wish to live, plus the fact that he did not self-induce his horrible affliction, precludes his further refusal of treatment being classed as attempted suicide.

Moreover we find no requirement in the law that a competent, but otherwise mortally sick, patient undergo the surgery or treatment which constitutes the only hope for temporary prolongation of his life. This being so, we see little difference between a cancer ridden patient who declines surgery, or chemotherapy, necessary for his temporary survival and the hopeless predicament which tragically afflicts Abe Perlmutter. It is true that the latter appears more drastic because affirmatively, a mechanical device must be disconnected, as distinct from mere inaction. Notwithstanding, the principle is the same, for in both instances the hapless, but mentally competent, victim is choosing not to avail himself of one of the expensive marvels of modern medical science.

The State argues that a patient has *no right* to refuse treatment and cites several of the familiar blood transfusion cases.[1] However, a reading of these reveal substantial distinctions between them and the case at bar. In the blood transfusion cases, the patient is either incompetent to make a medical decision, equivocal about making it ("he would not agree to be transfused but would not resist a court order permitting it because it, because it would be the court's will and not his own."[2]), or it is a family member making the decision for an inert or minor third party patient. By contrast, we find, and agree with, several cases upholding the right of a competent adult patient to refuse treatment for himself.[3] From this agreement, we reach our conclusion that, because Abe Perlmutter has a right to refuse treatment in the first instance, he has a concomitant right to discontinue it.

ETHICS OF MEDICAL PRACTICE

Lastly, as to the ethical integrity of medical practice, we again adopt the language of *Saikewicz*:

 The last State interest requiring discussion is that of the maintenance of the ethical integrity of the medical profession as well as allowing hospitals the full opportunity to care for people under their control. *See Georgetown, supra*; *United States v. George, supra*; *John F. Kennedy Memorial Hosp. v. Heston, supra* [58 N.J. 576, 279 A.2d 670]. The force and impact of this interest is lessened by the prevailing medical ethical standards, *see Byrn, supra* at 31. Prevailing medical ethical practice does not, without exception, demand that all efforts toward life prolongation be made in all circumstances. Rather, as indicated in *Quinlan*, the prevailing ethical practice seems to be to recognize that the dying are more often in need of comfort than treatment. Recognition of the right to refuse necessary treatment in appropriate circumstances is consistent with existing medical mores; such a doctrine does not threaten either the integrity of the medical profession, the proper role of hospitals in caring for such patients or the State's interest in protecting the same. It is not necessary to deny a right of self-determination to a patient in order to recognize the interests of doctors, hospitals, and medical personnel in attendance on the patient. Also, if the doctrines of informed consent and right of privacy have as their foundations the right to bodily integrity, *see Union Pac. Ry. v. Botsford, 141 U.S. 250, 11 S. Ct. 1000, 35 L. Ed. 734 (1891)*, and control of one's own fate, then those rights are superior to the institutional considerations. (*Id.* 426-427, footnotes omitted)

It is our conclusion, therefore, under the facts before us, that when these several public policy interests are weighed against the rights of Mr. Perlmutter, the latter must and should prevail. Abe Perlmutter should be allowed to make his choice to die with dignity, notwithstanding over a dozen legislative failures in this state to adopt suitable legislation in this field. It is all very convenient to insist on continuing Mr. Perlmutter's life so that there can be no question of foul play, no resulting civil liability and no possible trespass on medical ethics. However, It Is qulte another matter to do so at the patient's sole expense and against his competent will, thus inflicting never ending physical torture on his body

---

[1] *Application of the President and Directors of Georgetown College, Inc., 118 U.S.App.D.C. 80, 331 F.2d 1000 (D.C.Cir. 1964) cert. den., 377 U.S. 978, 84 S. Ct. 1883, 12 L. Ed. 2d 746 (1964); U. S. v. George, 239 F. Supp. 752 (D.Conn. 1965); Powell v. Columbian Presbyterian Medical Center, 49 Misc.2d 215, 267 N.Y.S.2d 450 (Sup.Ct. 1965).*

[2] *U. S. v. George, supra, at 753.*

[3] *Superintendent of Belchertown v. Saikewicz, Mass., 373 Mass. 728, 370 N.E.2d 417 (1977). In the Matter of Schiller, 148 N.J.Super. 168, 372 A.2d 360 (1977); In the Matter of Melideo, 88 Misc.2d 974, 390 N.Y.S.2d 523 (Sup.Ct. 1976); In re Quinlan, 70 N.J. 10, 355 A.2d 647 (1976); In re Osborne, 294 A.2d 372 (D.C.App. 1972); In re Estate of Brooks, 32 Ill.2d 361, 205 N.E.2d 435 (1965); Erickson v. Dilgard, 44 Misc.2d 27, 252 N.Y.S.2d 705 (1962); see Roe v. Wade, 410 U.S. 113, 153, 93 S. Ct. 705, 35 L. Ed. 2d 147 (1973).*

until the inevitable, but artificially suspended, moment of death. Such a course of conduct invades the patient's constitutional right of privacy, removes his freedom of choice and invades his right to self-determine.

The judgment of the trial court is hereby affirmed. In addition, all time periods having hitherto been waived, it is required that any petition for rehearing be actually received by this court no later than noon on Tuesday, September 19, 1978. Copies of any such petition shall likewise be simultaneously hand delivered to all parties entitled thereto. As to response, any such shall be delivered to this court no later than noon on Friday, September 22, 1978.

This is unquestionably a matter of great public interest and we have considered certification to our Supreme Court. Although we here carry an unusually heavy burden, and it would be a relief to share it, we feel that the exigencies of this situation dictate our conclusion without certification.

AFFIRMED.

MOORE, J., concurs.

ANSTEAD, J., concurs specially with opinion.

CONCUR

ANSTEAD, Judge, specially concurring

I am in complete agreement with the majority opinion, but I am also of the firm opinion that the question decided today is one of great public interest that should be certified for review to the Florida Supreme Court under the provisions of *Article V, Section 3(b)(3), of the Florida Constitution*, and *I* must note my disagreement with my colleagues to the extent that they decline to certify the question for consideration by the Supreme Court.

Without such a certification it is doubtful whether the Supreme Court will have jurisdiction to review this decision. The Supreme Court's jurisdiction is limited by Article V, Section 3 of the Constitution. Everyone agrees that this is a case of first impression in the appellate courts of Florida. Hence, there is no case in conflict with this decision that would give rise to conflict certiorari jurisdiction in the Supreme Court. It may be that jurisdiction would vest under the provisions of Section 3(b)(1) whereby decisions construing a provision of the state or federal constitution are made reviewable. Our decision today rests primarily on a recognition of a constitutional right of privacy. However, the question presented is a question of great public interest and the framers of our state constitution surely had such questions in mind when providing for review by the Supreme Court of questions so certified by the District Courts of Appeal. While convinced of the soundness of our decision today, I am concerned that the decision may not receive the full review intended under the terms of the Constitution.

Whose Body is it, Anyway? What Doctors Should Do When Patients Make Bad Decisions.

Atul Gawande

The first time I saw the patient, it was the day before his surgery and I thought he might be dead. Joseph Lazaroff, as I'll call him, lay in bed, eyes closed, a sheet pulled up over his thin, birdlike chest. When people are asleep—or even when they are anesthetized and not breathing by themselves—it does not occur to you to question whether they are alive. They exude life as if it were heat. It's visible in the tone of an arm muscle, the supple curve of their lips, the flush of their skin. But as I bent forward to tap Lazaroff on the shoulder I found myself stopping short with that instinctive apprehension of touching the dead. His color was all wrong—pallid, fading. His cheeks, eyes, and temples were sunken, and his skin was stretched over his face like a mask. Strangest of all, his head was suspended two inches above his pillow, as if rigor mortis had set in.

"Mr. Lazaroff." I called out, and his eyes opened. He looked at me without interest, silent and motionless.

I was in my first year of surgical residency and was working on the neurosurgery team at the time. Lazaroff had a cancer that had spread throughout his body, and he had been scheduled for surgery to excise a tumor from his spine. The senior resident had sent me to "consent" him—that is, to get Lazaroff's signature giving final permission for the operation. No problem, I had said. But now, looking at this frail, withered man, I had to wonder if we were right to operate on him.

His patient chart told me the story. Eight months earlier, he had seen his doctor about a backache. The doctor initially found nothing suspicious, but three months later the pain had worsened and he ordered a scan. It revealed extensive cancer—multiple tumors in Lazaroff's liver, bowel, and up and down his spine. A biopsy showed an untreatable cancer.

Lazaroff was only in his early sixties, a longtime city administrator who had a touch of diabetes, the occasional angina, and the hardened manner of a man who had lost his wife a few years earlier and learned to live alone. His condition deteriorated rapidly. In a matter of months, he lost more than fifty poinds. As the tumors in his abdomen grew, his belly, scrotum, and legs filled up with fluid. The pain and debility eventually made it impossible for him to keep working. His thirty-something son moved in to care for him. Lazaroff went on around-the-clock morphine to control his pain. His doctors told him that he might have only weeks to live. Lazaroff wasn't ready to hear it, though. He still talked about the day he'd go back to work.

Then he took several bad falls; his legs had become unaccountably weak. He also became incontinent. He went back to his oncologist. A scan showed that a metastasis was compressing his thoracic spinal cord. The oncologist admitted him to the hospital and tried a round of radiation, but it had no effect. Indeed, he became unable to move his right leg; his lower body was becoming paralyzed.

He had two options left. He could undergo spinal surgery. It wouldn't cure him—surgery or not, he had at the most a few months left—but it offered a last-ditch chance of halting the progression of the spinal-cord damage and possibly restoring some strength to his legs and sphincters. The risks, however, were severe. We'd have go through his chest and collapse his lung just to get at his spine. He'd face a long, difficult, and painful recovery. And given his frail condition—not to mention the previous history of heart disease—his chance of surviving the procedure and getting back home was slim.

The alternative was to do nothing. He'd go home and continue with hospice care, which would keep him comfortable and help him maintain a measure of control over his life. The immobility and incontinence would certainly worsen. But it was his best chance of dying peacefully, in his own bed, and being able to say goodbye to his loved ones.

The decision was Lazaroff's.

That, in itself, is a remarkable fact. Only decades ago, doctors made the decisions; patients did what they were told. Doctors did not consult patients about their desires and priorities, and routinely withheld information—sometimes crucial information, such as what drugs they were on, what treatments they were being given, and what their diagnosis was. Patients were even forbidden to look at their own medical records: it wasn't their property, doctors said. They were regarded as children: too fragile and simpleminded to handle the truth, let alone to make decisions. And they suffered for it. People were put on machines, given drugs, and subjected to operations they would not have chosen. And they missed out on treatments that they might have preferred.

My father, a urologist who practices in Ohio, recounts that, through the seventies and much of the eighties, when men came to him seeking vasectomies it was accepted that *he* would judge whether the surgery was not only medically appropriate but also personally appropriate for them. He routinely refused to do the operation if the men were unmarried, married but without children, or "too young." In retrospect, he's not sure he did right by all these patients, and, he says, he'd never do things this way today. In fact, he can't even think of a patient in the last few years whom he has turned down for a vasectomy.

One of the reasons for this dramatic shift in how decisions are made in medicine was a 1984 book, "The Silent World of Doctor and Patient," by a Yale doctor and ethicist named Jay Katz. It was a devastating critique of traditional medical decision-making, and it had wide influence. In the book, Katz argued that medical decisions could and should be made by the patients involved. And he made his case using the stories of actual patients.

One was that of "Iphigenia Jones," a twenty-one-year-old woman who was found to have a malignancy in one of her breasts. Then, as now, she had two options: mastectomy (which would mean removing the breast and the lymph notes of the nearby axilla) or radiation with minimal surgery (removing just the lump and the lymph nodes). Survival rates were equal, although in a spared breast the tumor can recur and ultimately make a mastectomy necessary. This surgeon preferred doing mastectomies, and that's what he told her he'd do. In the days leading up to the operation, however, the surgeon developed misgivings about removing the breast of someone that young. So the night before the operation he did an unusual thing: he discussed the treatment options with her and let her choose. She chose the breast-preserving treatment.

Sometime later, both patient and surgeon appeared on a panel discussing treatment options for breast cancer. Their story drew a heated response. Surgeons almost uniformly attacked the idea that patients should be allowed to choose. As one surgeon asked, "If doctors have such trouble deciding which treatment is best, how can patients decide?" But, as Katz wrote, the decision involved not technical but personal issues: Which was more important to Iphigenia—the preservation of her breast or the security of living without a significant chance that the lump would grow back? No doctor was the authority on these matters. Only Iphigenia was. Yet in such situations doctors did step in, often not even asking about a patient's concerns, and make their own decisions—decisions perhaps influenced by money, professional bias (for example, surgeons tend to favor surgery), and personal idiosyncrasy.

Eventually, medical schools came around to Katz's position. By the time I attended, in the early nineties, we were taught to see patients as autonomous decision-makers. "You work for them," I was often reminded. There are still many old-school doctors who try to dictate from on high, but they are finding that patients won't put up with that anymore. Most doctors, taking seriously the idea that patients should control their own fates, lat out the options and the risks involved. A few even refuse to make recommendations, for fear of improperly influencing patients. Patients ask questions, look up information on the Internet, seek second opinions. And they decide.

In practice, however, matters aren't so straightforward. Patients, it turns out, make bad decisions, too. Sometimes, of course, the difference between one option and another isn't especially significant. But when you see your patient making a grave mistake, should you simply do what the patient wants? The current medical orthodoxy says yes. After all, whose body is it, anyway?

Lazaroff wanted surgery. The oncologist was dubious about the choice, but she called in a neurosurgeon. The neurosurgeon, a trim man in his forties with a stellar reputation and fondness for bow ties, saw Lazroff and his son that afternoon. He warned them at length about how terrible the risks were and how limited the potential benefit. Sometimes, he told me later, patients just don't seem to hear the dangers, and in those cases he tends to be especially explicit about them—getting stuck on a ventilator because of poor lung function, having a stroke, dying. But Lazaroff wasn't to be dissuaded. The surgeon put him on the schedule.

"Mr. Lazaroff, I'm a surgical intern, and I'm here to talk to you about your surgery tomorrow," I said. "You're going to be having a thoracic spine corpectomy and fusion." He looked at me blankly. "This means that we will be removing the tumor compressing your spine," I said. His expression did not change. "The hope is that it will keep your paralysis from worsening."

"I'm not paralyzed," he said at last. "The surgery is so I *won't* become paralyzed."

I quickly retreated. "I'm sorry—I meant, keep you from becoming paralyzed." Perhaps this was just semantics—he could still move his left leg some. "I just need you to sign a permission form so you can have the surgery tomorrow."

The "informed-consent form" is a relatively recent development. It lists as many complications as we doctors can think of—everything from a mild allergic reaction to death—and, in signing it, you indicate that you have accepted these risks. It has the mark of law-yerdom and bureaucracy, and I doubt that patients feel any better informed after reading it. It does, however, provide an occasion to review the risks involved.

The neurosurgeon had already gone over them in detail. So I hit the highlights. "We ask for your signature so we're sure you understand the risks," I said. "Although you're having this done to preserve your abilities, the operation could fail or leave you paralyzed." I tried to sound firm without being harsh. "You could have a stroke or heart attack or could even die." I held the form and a pen out to him.

"No one said you could die from this," he said, tremu-lously. "It's my last hope. Are you saying I'm going to die?"

I froze, not knowing quite what to say. Just then, Lazroff's son, whom I'll call David, arrived, with his wrinkled clothes, scraggly beard, and slight paunch. The father's mood changed abruptly, and I remem-bered from notes in the medical chart that David had recently raised the question with him of whether heroic measures were still appropriate. "Don't give up on me," Lazaroff now rasped at his son. "You give me every chance I've got." He snatched the form and the pen from my hand. We stood, chastised and silent, as Lazaroff made a slow, illegible scrawl near the line for his signature.

Outside the room, David told me that he wasn't sure this was the right move. His mother had spent a long time in intensive care on the ventilator before dying of emphysema, and since then his father had often said that he did not want anything like that to happen to him. But now he was adamant about doing "every-thing." David did not dare argue with him.

Lazaroff had his surgery the next day. Once under anesthesia, he was rolled onto his left side. A thoracic surgeon made a long incision, opening onto the chest cavity from the front around to the back along the eighth rib, cranked it own, slipped in a rib spreader, cranked it open, and then fixed in place a retractor to hold the deflated lung out of the way. You could see right down into the back of the chest to the spi-nal column. A fleshy, tennis-ball size mass enveloped the tenth vertebra. The neurosurgeon took over and meticulously dissected around and under the tumor. It took a couple of hours, but eventually the tumor was attached only where it invaded the bony vertebral body. He then used a rongeur—a rigid, jawed instrument—to take small, painstaking bites in the vertebral body, like a beaver gnawing slowly through a tree trunk, ulti-mately removing the vertebra and, with it, the mass. To rebuild the spine, he filled the space left behind with a doughy plug of methacrylate, an acrylic cement, and let it slowly harden in place. He slipped a probe in behind the new artificial vertebra. There was plenty of space. It had taken more than four hours, but the pressure on the spinal cord was gone. The thoracic surgeon closed Lazaroff's chest, leaving a rubber chest tube jutting out to reinflate his lung, and he was wheeled into inten-sive care.

The operation was a technical success. Lazaroff's lungs wouldn't recover, however, and we struggled to get him off the ventilator. Over the next few days, they gradu-ally became stiff and fibrotic, requiring higher ventilator pressures. We tried to keep him under sedation, but he frequently broke through and woke up wild-eyed and thrashing. David kept a despondent bedside vigil. Successive chest X-rays showed worsening lung dam-age. Small blood clots lodged in Lazaroff's lungs, and we put him on a blood thinner to prevent more clots from forming. Then some slow bleeding started—we weren't sure from where—and we had to give him blood trans-fusions almost daily. After a week, he began spiking fevers, but we couldn't find where the infection was. On the ninth day after the operation, the high ventila-tor pressures blew small holes in his lungs. We had to cut into his chest and insert an extra tube to keep his lungs from collapsing. The effort and expense it took to keep him going were enormous, the results dispir-iting. It became apparent that our efforts were futile.

It was exactly the way Lazaroff hadn't wanted to die—
strapped down and sedated, tubes in every natural
orifice and in several new ones, and on a ventilator. On
the fourteenth day, David told the neurosurgeon that
we should stop.

The neurosurgeon came to me with the news. I went to
Lazaroff's I.C.U. room, one of the eight bays arrayed in
a semicircle around a nursing station, each with a tile
floor, a window, and a sliding glass door that closed it
off from the noise but not from the eyes of the nurses.
A nurse and I slipped in. I checked to make sure that
Lazaroff's morphine drip was turned up high. Taking
my place at the bedside, I leaned close to him and, in
case he could hear me, told him I was going to take
the breathing tube out of his mouth. I snipped the ties
securing the tube and deflated the balloon cuff holding
it in his trachea. Then I pulled the tube out. He coughed
a couple of times, opened his eyes briefly, and then
closed them. The nurse suctioned out phlegm from his
mouth. I turned the ventilator off, and suddenly the
room was quiet except for the sound of his labored,
gasping breaths. We watched as he tired out. His
breathing slowed down until he took only occasional,
agonal breaths, and then he stopped. I put my stethoscope on his chest and listened to his heart fade away.
Thirteen minutes after I took him off the ventilator, I
told the nurse to record that Joseph Lazaroff had died.

Lazaroff, I thought, chose badly. Not, however, because
he died so violently and appallingly. Good decisions can
have bad results (sometimes people must take terrible chances), and bad decisions can have good results
("Better lucky than good," surgeons like to say). I
thought Lazaroff chose badly because his choice ran
against his deepest interests—interests not as I or anyone else conceived them but as he conceived them.
Above all, it was clear that he wanted to live. He would
take any risk—even death—to live. But, as we explained
to him, life was not what we had to offer. We could offer
only a chance of preserving minimal lower-body functioning for his brief remaining time—at a cost of severe
violence to him and against extreme odds of a miserable death. But he did not hear us: in staving off paralysis,
he seemed to believe that he might stave off death.
There are people who will look clear0eyes at such odds
and take their chances with surgery. But, knowing how

much Lazaroff had dreaded dying the way his wife had,
I do not believe he is one of them.

Could it have been a mistake, then, even to have told
him about the surgical option? Our contemporary
medical credo has made us exquisitely attuned to the
requirements of patient autonomy. But there are still
times—and they are more frequent than we readily admit—when a doctor has to steer patients to do
what's right for themselves. This is a controversial suggestion. People are rightly suspicious of those claiming
to know better than they do what's best for them. But a
good physician cannot simply stand aside when patients
make bad or self-defeating decisions—decisions that go
against their deepest goals.

I remember a case from my first weeks of internship.
I was on the general surgical service, and among the
patients I was responsible for was a woman in her fif-
ties—I'll call her Mrs. McLaughlin—who had a big
abdominal operation just two days before. An incision
ran the entire length of her belly. Fluids and pain medication dripped through an intravenous line into her
arm. She was recovering according to schedule, but she
wouldn't get out of bed. I explained why it was essential
for her to get up and around: it cuts the risk of pneumonia, clot formation in leg veins, and other complications.
She wasn't swayed. She was tired, she said, and didn't
feel up to it. Did she understand that she was risking
serious problems? Yes, she said. Just leave me be.

During rounds that afternoon, the chief resident asked
me if the patient had gone out of bed. Well, no, I said—
she had refused. That's no excuse, the chief said, and
she marched me back to Mrs. McLaughlin by the hand,
and then said, "It's time to get out of bed now." And I
watched Mrs. McLaughlin get up without a moment's
hesitation, shuffle over to a chair, plot herself down, and
say, "You know, that wasn't so bad after all."

I had come into residency to learn how to be a surgeon.
I had thought that meant simply learning the repertoire
of moves and techniques involved in doing an operation
or making a diagnosis. In fact, there was also the new
and delicate matter of talking patients through their
decisions—something that entailed its own repertoire
of moves and techniques.

Suppose you're a doctor. You're in an examination room of your clinic—one of those cramped spaces with fluorescent lights, a Matisse posted on the wall, a box of latex gloves on the counter, and a cold, padded patient table as a centerpiece—seeing a female patient in her forties. She's a mother of two and a partner in a downtown law firm. Despite the circumstances, and the flimsy paper gown she's in, she manages to maintain her composure. You feel no mass or abnormality in her breasts. She had a mammogram before seeing you, and now you review the radiologist's report, which reads, "There is a faint group of punctate, clustered calcifications in the upper outer quadrant of the left breast that were not clearly present on the prior examination. Biopsy may be considered to exclude the possibility of malignancy." Translation: Worrisome features have appeared; they could mean breast cancer.

You tell her the news. Given the findings, you say, you think she ought to have a biopsy. She groans, and then stiffens. "Every time I see one of you people, you find something that you want biopsied," she says. Three times in the past five years, her annual mammogram has revealed an area of "suspicious" classifications. Three times a surgeon has taken her to the operating room and removed the tissue in question. And three times, under the pathologist's microscope, it has proven to be benign. "You just don't know when enough is enough," she says. "Whatever these specks are that keep turning up, they've proved to be normal." She pauses, and decides. "I'm not getting another goddam biopsy," she says, and she stands up to get dressed.

Do you let her go? It's not an unreasonable thing to do. She's an adult, after all. And a biopsy is not a small thing. Scattered across her left breast are three raised scars—one almost three inches long. Enough tissue has already been taken out that the left breast is distinctly smaller than the right one. And, yes, there are doctors who biopsy too much, who take out breast tissue on the most equivocal of findings. Patients are often right to push for explanations and second opinions.

Still, these calcifications are not equivocal findings. Now, if having control over one's life is to mean anything, people have to be permitted to make their own mistakes. But when the stakes are high, and the bad

choice may be irreversible, doctors are reluctant to sit back. This is when they tend to push.

So push. Your patient is getting ready to walk out the door. You could stop her in her tracks and tell her she's making a big mistake. Give her a heavy speech about cancer. Point out the fallacy in supposing that three negative biopsies prove she's different. And in all likelihood you'll lose her. The aim isn't to show her how wrong she is. The aim is to win her over.

Notice what good doctors do. They don't jump right in. they step out for a minute and give her time to get dressed. Then they take her down to the office. It's more congenial there—comfortable chairs, a throw rug, family pictures all around. They sit her down. And, typically, they don't stand or assume the throng behind the big oak desk but pull up a chair and sit close beside her. As one surgical professor told me, when you sit close by, on the same level as your patients, you're no longer the rushed, bossy doctor with no time for them; patients feel less imposed upon and more inclined to think you're both on the same side of the issue.

The curious thing is that the doctors I've observed wont fuss or debate, even at this point. Instead, they have these strange, almost formulaic conversations with the patient, repeating, virtually word for word, what she tells them. "I see your point," they might say. "Every time you come in, we find something to biopsy. The specks keep coming up normal, but we never stop biopsying." Beyond this, these doctors say almost nothing until they're asked to. Oddly enough, nine times out of ten this approach works. People feel as if they've been heard, and have had the opportunity to vent. At this point, they finally begin to ask questions, voice doubts, even work through the logic themselves. And they come around.

A few still resist, and doctors will turn to other tactics. They enlist reinforcements. "Should we call the radiologist and see what he really thinks?" they might ask, or "Your husband's been out in the waiting room. Why don't we ask him to come in?" They might give her time "to think it over," knowing that people commonly waver and come around (though they don't let it go on too long). Sometimes they resort to subtler dynamics.

When she says she's sticking to her decision, they might simply fall silent, letting their disappointment show. The seconds become a full minute. Then two. Before a thoughtful, sympathetic, and, yes, crafty physician, few patients will not eventually "choose" what the physician desires.

But it's misleading to view all this simply as the art of doctorly manipulation: when you see patients cede authority to the doctor, something else may be going on. The new orthodoxy about patient autonomy has a hard time acknowledging the awkward truth: patients frequently don't want the freedom we've given to them. That is, they're glad to have their autonomy respected, but the exercise of autonomy means being able to relinquish it.

That's something I came to understand earlier this year. My youngest child, Hunter, was born five weeks early, weighing barely four pounds, and when she was eleven days old she stopped breathing. She had been home a week and doing well. That morning, however, she seemed irritable and fussy, and her nose ran. Thirty minutes after her feeding, her respiration became rapid, and she began making little grunting noises with each breath. Suddenly, Hunter stopped breathing. My wife, panicked, leaped up and shook Hunter awake, and the baby started breathing again. We rushed her to the hospital.

Fifteen minutes later, we were in a large, bright emergency-department examination room. With an oxygen mask on, Hunter didn't quite stabilize—she was still taking over sixty breaths a minute and expending all her energy to do it—but she regained normal oxygen levels in her blood and held her own. The doctors weren't sure what the cause of her troubles was. It could have been a heart defect, a bacterial infection, a virus. They took X-rays, blood, and urine, did an electrocardiogram, and tapped her spinal fluid. They suspected—correctly, as it turned out—that the problem was a simple respiratory virus that her lungs were too little and immature to handle. But the results from the cultures wouldn't be back for a couple of days. They admitted her to the intensive-care unit. That night, she began to tire out. She had several spells of apnea—periods of up to sixty seconds in which she stopped breathing, her heartbeat slowed, and she became pale and ominously still—but each time she came back, all by herself.

A decision needs to be made. Should she be intubated and put on a ventilator? Or should the doctors wait to see if she could recover without it? There were risks either way. If the team didn't intubate her now, under controlled circumstances, and she "crashed"—maybe the next time she would not wake up from an apneic spell—they would have to perform an emergency intubation, a tricky thing to do in a child so small. Delays could occur, the breathing tube could go down the wrong pipe, the doctors could inadvertently traumatize the airway and cause it to shut down, and then she might suffer brain damage or even die from lack of oxygen. The likelihood of any such disaster was slim but real. I myself had seen it happen. On the other hand, you don't want to put someone on a ventilator if you don't have to. Serious complications, such as pneumonia or the sort of lung blowout that Lazaroff experienced, happen frequently. And, as people who have been hooked up to one of these contraptions can tell you, the machine shoots air into and out of you with terrifying, uncomfortable force; your mouth becomes sore; your lips crack. Sedation is given, but the drugs bring complications, too.

So who should have made the choice? In many ways, I was the ideal candidate to decide what was best. I was the father, so I cared more than any hospital staffer ever could about which risks were taken. And I was the doctor, so I understood the issues involved. I also knew how often problems like miscommunication, overwork, and plain hubris could lead physicians to make bad choices.

Any yet when the team of doctors came to talk to me about whether to intubate Hunter I wanted *them* to decide—doctors I had never met before. The ethicist Jay Katz and others have disparaged this kind of desire as "childlike regression." But that judgment seems heartless to me. The uncertainties were savage, and I could not bear the possibility of making the wrong call. Even if I made what I was sure was the right choice for her, I could not live with the guilt if something went wrong. People like Katz believe that patients should be pushed to take responsibility for major decisions. But that would have seemed like a kind of harsh paternalism in itself. I needed Hunter's physicians to bear the responsibility: they could live with the consequences, good or bad.

I let the doctors make the call, and they did so on the spot. They would keep Hunter off the ventilator, they told me. And, with that, the bleary-eyed stethoscope-collared pack shuffled onward to their next patient.

It turns out that patients commonly prefer to have others make their medical decisions. One study found that although sixty-four percent of the general public thought they'd want to select their own treatment if they developed cancer, only twelve percent of newly diagnosed cancer patients actually did want to do so.

Still, there was the nagging question: If I wanted the best decision for Hunter, was relinquishing my hard-won autonomy really the right thing to do? Carl Schneider, a professor of law and medicine at the University of Michigan, recently published a book called "The Practice of Autonomy," in which he sorted through a welter of studies and data on medical decision-making, even undertaking a systematic analysis of patients' memoirs. He found that the ill were often in a poor position to make good choices: they were frequently exhausted, irritable, shattered, or despondent. Often, they were just trying to get through their immediate pain, nausea, and fatigue; they could hardly think about major decisions. This rang true to me. I wasn't even the patient, and all I could do was sit and watch Hunter, worry, or distract myself with busywork. I did not have the concentration or the energy to weigh the treatment options properly.

Schneider found that the physicians, being less emotionally engaged, are able to reason through the uncertainties without the distortions of fear and attachment. They work in a scientific culture that disciplines the way they make decisions. They have the benefit of "group rationality"—norms based on scholarly literature and refined practice. And they have the key relevant experience. Even though I am a doctor, I did not have the experience that Hunter's doctors had with her specific condition.

In the end, Hunter managed to stay off the ventilator, although she had a slow and sometimes scary recovery. At one point, less than twenty-four hours after the doctors had transferred her to a regular floor, her condition deteriorated and they had to rush her back to the I.C.U. She spent ten days in intensive care and two weeks in the hospital. But she went home in fine shape.

Just as there is an art to being a doctor, there is an art to being a patient. You must choose wisely when to submit and when to assert yourself. Even when patients decide not to decide, they should still question their physicians and insist on explanations. I may have let Hunter's doctors take control, but I pressed them for a clear plan in the event that she should crash. Later, I worried that they were being too slow to feed her—she wasn't being given anything to eat for more than a week, and I pestered them with questions as to why. When they took her off the oxygen monitor on her eleventh day at the hospital, I got nervous. What harm was there in keeping it on, I asked. I'm sure I was obstinate, even wrongheaded, at times. You do the best you can, taking the measure of your doctors and nurses and your own situation, trying to be neither too passive not too pushy for your own good.

But the conundrum remains: If both doctors and patients are fallible, who should decide? We want a rule. And so we've decided that patients should be the ultimate arbiter. But such hard-and-fast rules seem ill-suited both to a caring relationship between doctor and patient and to the reality of medical care, where a hundred decisions have to be made quickly. A mother is in labor: Should the doctor give her hormones to stimulate stronger contractions? Should he or she break the bag of water? Should an epidural anesthetic be given? If so, at what point in labor? Are antibiotics needed? How often should the mother's blood pressure be checked? Should the doctor use forceps? Should the doctor perform an episiotomy? If things don't progress quickly, should the doctor perform a cesarean section? The doctor should not make all the decisions, and neither should the patient. Something must be worked out between them, one on one—a personal modus operandi.

Where many ethicists go wrong is in promoting patient autonomy as a kind of ultimate value in medicine rather than recognizing it as one value among others. Schneider found that what patients want most from doctors isn't autonomy per se; it's competence and kindness. Now, kindness will often involve respecting patients' autonomy, assuring that they have control over vital decisions. But it may also mean taking on burdensome decisions when patients don't want them, or guiding patients in the right direction when they do. Even when patients do want to make their own decisions, there are times when the compassionate thing to do is to press, hard: to steer them to accept an operation or treatment that they fear, or forgo one that they'd pinned their hopes on. Many ethicists find this line of reasoning disturbing, and medicine will continue to struggle with how patients and doctors ought to make decisions. But, as the field grows ever more complex and technological, the real task isn't to banish paternalism; the real task is to preserve kindness.

One more case, again from my internship year. The patient—I'll call him Mr. Howe—was in his late thirties, stout, bald, and with a muted, awkward manner. I wanted to turn the sound up when he spoke, and pictured him as someone who worked alone, perhaps as an accountant or a computer programmer. He was in the hospital following an operation for a badly infected gallbladder. Whenever I saw him, he wore the sad look of someone caged and he asked no questions. He could not wait to leave the hospital.

Late Sunday afternoon, maybe three days after his surgery, his nurse paged me. he had spiked a high fever and became short of breath. He didn't look well, she said.

I found him sweating profusely, his face flushed, eyes wide. He was sitting bent forward, proper up on his thick arms, panting. He had an oxygen mask on, and, even with the flow turned up to the maximum, the pulse-oximer readings showed barely adequate oxygen levels in his blood. His heart was racing at well over a hundred beats a minute, his blood pressure was much too low.

His wife, a small, thin, pale woman with lank black hair, stood to the side, rocking on her feet and hugging herself. I put on my decisive, confident-surgeon look, examined him, drew blood for rests and cultures, and

asked the nurse to give him a bolus of intravenous fluid. Then I went out into the hall and paged S., one of the chief residents, for help.

When she called back, I filled her in on the details. I think he's septic, I said. Sometimes a bacterial infection gets into the bloodstream and triggers a massive system-wide response: high fevers ad dilation of the body's peripheral blood vessels, causing the skin to flush, the blood pressure to drop, and the heart to speed up. After abdominal surgery, a common cause of this is an infection of the surgical wound. But his incision was not red or hot or tender, and he had no pain in his belly. His lungs, however, had sounded like a washing machine when I listened with my stethoscope. Perhaps a pneumonia had started this disaster.

S. came right over. She was just past thirty, almost six feet tall, with short blond hair, athletic, exhaustibly energetic, and relentlessly can-do. She took one look at Howe and then murmured to the nurse to keep an intubation kit available at the bedside. I ahd started antibiotics, and the fluids had improved his blood pressure a bit, but he was still on maximal oxygen and working hard to maintain his breathing. She went over to him, put a hand on his shoulder, and asked how he was doing. It took a moment before he managed to reply. "Fine," he said—a silly answer to a silly question, but a conversation starter. She explained the situation: the sepsis, the likely pneumonia, and the probability that he would get worse before he got better. The antibiotics would fix the problem, but not instantly, she said, and he was tiring out quickly. To get him through it, she would need to put him to sleep, intubate him, and place him on a breathing machine.

"*No*," he gasped and sat straight up. "Don't... put me... on a... machine."

It would not be for long, she said. Maybe a couple of days. We'd give him sedatives so he'd be as comfortable as possible the whole time. And—she wanted to be sure he understood—without the ventilator he would die.

He shook his head. "No... machine!"

He was, we believed, making a bad decision—out of

fear, maybe incomprehension. With antibiotics and some high-tech support, we had every reason to believe he'd recover fully. Howe had a lot to live for—he was young and otherwise healthy, and he had a wife and a child. Apparently, he thought so too, for he had cared enough about his well-being to accept the initial operation. If not for the terror of the moment, we thought, he would have accepted the treatment. Could we be certain we were right? No, but if we *were* right, could we really just let him die?

S. looked over at Howe's wife, who was stricken with fear and, in an effort to enlist her in the case, asked what she thought her husband should do. She burst into tears. "I don't know, I don't know," she cried. "Can't you save him?" She couldn't take it anymore, and left the room. For the next few minutes, S. kept trying to persuade Howe. When it was clear that she was making no headway, she left to phone his attending surgeon at home, and then returned to the bedside. Soon Howe did tire out. He leaned back in his bed, pale, sweaty strands of hair sticking to his pate, oxygen levels dropping on the monitor. He closed his eyes, and he gradually fell into unconsciousness.

That was when S. went into action. She lowered the head of Howe's bed until he lay flat. She had a nurse draw up a tranquilizing agent and administer it in his I.V. She pressed a bag mask to his face and squeezed breaths of oxygen down into his lungs. Then I handed her the intubation equipment, and she slipped a long, clear plastic breathing tube down into his trachea on the first try. We wheeled Howe in his bed to the elevator and took him down a few floors to the intensive-care unit.

Later, I found his wife and explained that he was now on a ventilator in the I.C.U. She said nothing and went to see him.

Over the next twenty-four hours, his lungs improved markedly. We lightened up on the sedation and let him take over breathing from the machine. He woke up and opened his eyes, the breathing tube sticking out of his mouth. He did not struggle.

"I'm going to take this tube out of your mouth now,

O.K.?" I said. He nodded. I cut the ties and deflated the balloon cuff holding the tube in place. Then I pulled it out, and he coughed violently a few times. "You had pneumonia," I told him, "but you're doing just fine now."

I stood there, silent and anxious for a moment, waiting to see what he would say. He swallowed hard, wincing from the soreness. Then he looked at me, and, in a hoarse but steady voice, he said, "Thank you."

The New Yorker, October 4, 1999.
Reprinted with permission by publisher

Lesson 2

Flesh of My Flesh:
Organ Transplants in Jewish Law
Introduction

Someone, somewhere needs something that only you can give. But to give them what they need, you will have to cut away from your own flesh.

What are the ethics of organ donation? Are you violated—cannibalized—when you give away a part of your body? Or does your selfless giving make you more complete?

Case **Study**

The dilemma began in 1996 when David Patterson, serving a 13-year sentence for burglary and heroin possession, donated a kidney to Renada Daniel, the 13-year-old daughter he had abandoned as an infant. Renada was born with congenital renal anomalies and underwent cadaveric renal transplant at age 5. When that transplant failed, she had dialysis for 7 years. In 1996, her father underwent compatibility testing and was found to be the best transplant match. He donated his kidney and thereby renewed his relationship with his daughter. This altruistic donation received national media attention because it required the permission and financial support of prison authorities.

Fast forward to December 1998. Sixteen-year-old Renada was hospitalized at UCSF with an acute rejection episode. During this hospitalization, her father made the unprecedented offer to replace her failing kidney with his remaining one. Transplant surgeons at UCSF refused to consider the offer, but the family insisted. The matter was referred to the hospital's ethics committee.

Deborah Josefson, "The Kidney Dilemma," *Western Journal of Medicine* 170 (June 1999): 373–374

Learning **Activity 1**

What would Jewish law say about these transplants? Which, if any, do you think Jewish law would permit? Take a moment to explain your reasoning.

Kidney #1, from a cadaver, is permitted/forbidden/obligated by Jewish law because

____

____

____

____

Kidney #2, from a live donor, leaving the donor with a remaining kidney, is permitted/forbidden/obligated by Jewish law because

____

____

____

Kidney #3, from a live donor, leaving the donor without any kidney, is permitted/forbidden/obligated by Jewish law because

____

____

____

Life or Self preservation.

Sanctity of the Body. If Body.

Halacha?

"if organ Donor can Save a life immediatley — it can be done.

Cadaveric Donation
Non-Heartbeating Donation

Text 1

Rabbi Moshe Sofer (1762–1839). Also known by the title of his main work, *Chatam Sofer,* a collection of responsa literature. One of the leading rabbinical authorities of the 19th century, his policies and decisions helped shape Austro-Hungarian Jewry. Born in Frankfurt am Main, Germany, he entered the yeshivah of Rabbi Natan Adler at the age of nine. After declining various offers for the rabbinate, he ultimately accepted a position in Pressburg (now Bratislava), Slovakia. Serving as rabbi, and head of the yeshivah he established, Rabbi Sofer maintained a strong traditionalist perspective, fighting all deviations from tradition.

אך בני ישראל מאמינים גם אדם כי ימות באהל (במדבר יט,יד) עדיין במותו נקרא אדם פנימי ולא פגר (קערפער) כי גם בגופו שהיה נרתיק לנשמה נשאר בו לחלוחית קדושה ונוהגים בו כבוד.

חתם סופר, יורה דעה שלו

Jews, however, believe that even after death the deceased is still called "a person" and not a corpse, [as the verse states] "A person that has died in a tent" (Numbers 19:14). Even after death, there remains residual holiness in the body which served as a receptacle for the soul, and therefore, we treat it with respect.

Rabbi Moshe Sofer, Chatam Sofer, Yoreh De'ah 336

אם צוה שלא יקבר אין שומעין לו, שהקבורה מצוה שנאמר כי קבור תקברנו
(דברים כא,כג).

רמב״ם, הלכות אבל יב,א

f [the deceased] had instructed that he not be buried after his death, we do not listen to him, because burial is a mitzvah, as it states, "You shall bury him [on that same day]" (Deuteronomy 21:23).

Maimonides, *Mishneh Torah*, Laws of Mourning 12:1

Rabbi Moshe ben Maimon (1135–1204). Better known as Maimonides or by the acronym Rambam; born in Córdoba, Spain. After the conquest of Córdoba by the Almohads, he fled Spain and eventually settled in Cairo, Egypt. There, he became the leader of the Jewish community and served as court physician to the vizier of Egypt. His rulings on Jewish law are considered integral to the formation of halachic consensus. He is most noted for authoring the *Mishneh Torah*, an encyclopedic arrangement of Jewish law, and for his philosophical work, *Guide for the Perplexed*.

Text **2b**

וכל המלין את מתו עובר בלא תעשה אלא אם כן הלינו לכבודו ולהשלים צרכיו.

רמב״ם, הלכות אבל ז,ח

ne who delays the burial of a dead person overnight is in violation of a negative commandment, unless the delay is for the honor of the deceased and to complete preparation of the [burial] needs of the deceased.

Maimonides, *Mishneh Torah*, Laws of Mourning 4:8

Text 2c

המת אסור בהנאה כולו, חוץ משערו שהוא מותר בהנאה מפני שאינו גופו, וכן ארונו
וכל תכריכיו אסורין בהנאה.
רמב״ם, הלכות אבל יד,כא

It is forbidden to derive benefit from any part of the dead except for the hair, which one may derive benefit from since it is not part of the body. It is also forbidden to derive benefit from the coffin or any of the shrouds.

Maimonides, *Mishneh Torah*, Laws of Mourning 14:21

Text 2d

מעשה בבני ברק באחד שמכר בנכסי אביו ומת, ובאו בני משפחה וערערו לומר קטן
היה בשעת מיתה, ובאו ושאלו את רבי עקיבא: מהו לבודקו.
אמר להם: אי אתם רשאים לנוולו.
תלמוד בבלי, בבא בתרא קנד,א

An incident occurred in Bnei Brak in which a son sold property that he had inherited from his father and subsequently died. Other family members came [to the court] and argued that the seller was a minor at the time of his death [and therefore, they had the right to annul the sale and recover the property from the buyers]. They asked Rabbi Akiva for permission to check the body

[for physiological evidence that he had not matured].
Rabbi Akiva responded, "You are not permitted to disgrace the body."

Talmud, Bava Batra 154a

Text 3a

וּשְׁמַרְתֶּם אֶת חֻקֹּתַי וְאֶת מִשְׁפָּטַי אֲשֶׁר יַעֲשֶׂה אֹתָם הָאָדָם וָחַי בָּהֶם אֲנִי ה׳.
ויקרא יח,ה

ou shall observe My laws and ordinances, which a person shall perform and live by them. I am the Lord.

Leviticus 18:5

Text 3b

וחי בהם ולא שימות בהם.
תלמוד בבלי, יומא פה,ב

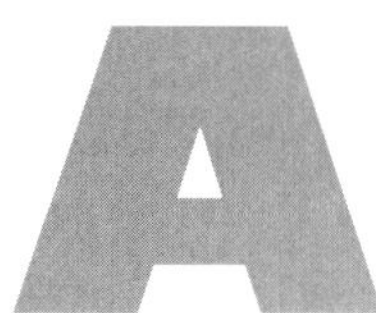nd live by them—and not die by them.

Talmud, Yoma 85b

מי שחלה ונטה למות ואמרו הרופאים שרפואתו בדבר פלוני מאיסורין שבתורה עושין
ומתרפאין בכל איסורין שבתורה במקום סכנה חוץ מעבודת כוכבים וגילוי עריות
ושפיכת דמים שאפילו במקום סכנה אין מתרפאין בהן.

רמב״ם, הלכות יסודי התורה ה,ו

If one took ill and was about to die, and the doctors advise that he can only be cured by doing something forbidden by Torah law, then we should follow the physician's counsel. In cases of danger, we violate any of the commandments of the Torah should this bring a cure, except for idolatry, forbidden sexual relations, and murder, which are prohibited even in the face of danger.

Maimonides, *Mishneh Torah*, Laws of the Foundation of the Torah 5:6

Learning **Activity 2**

Using the mitzvah of Shabbat as an example, in which of the following cases would we be required to violate Shabbat in order to save a life? Circle the appropriate numbers.

1. You are required to attend a CPR course offered on Shabbat because at some point, you may have the opportunity to use this knowledge to save a life.

2. You are required to replace the smoke alarm batteries in a public building on Shabbat because it is dangerous for people to be in a building without a working smoke alarm.

3. You are required to go out in your boat on Shabbat to save a drowning person.

4. You are required to call an ambulance on Shabbat for a person suffering a severe attack of asthma that makes breathing almost impossible.

Text **4a**

פשוט הדבר שחייבים להקריב אבר מן המת עבור ספק הצלה של חי מסוכן לפנינו מבלי להתחשב כלל עם רצון המת או קרוביו.

מנחת שלמה ב, פג,א

I t is obvious that we are obligated to donate an organ from the deceased for the sake of a possible rescue of a living person that is in danger in front of us, without regard for the desires of the deceased or his relatives.

Rabbi Shlomoh Zalman Auerbach, *Minchat Shlomoh*, vol. 2, 83:1

Rabbi Shlomoh Zalman Auerbach (1910–1995). Born in Jerusalem, Israel; served as the dean of Yeshivah Kol Torah. He is recognized as one of the prominent halachic authorities of the 20th century. Many of Rabbi Auerbach's decisions and works are related to issues of medical ethics and the halachic problems that arose with the introduction of modern technology.

Text **4b**

שעל הבא לישאל אם יתרום אבר מאבריו לאחר מותו לשם מטרה כזאת, היו גם כן מיעצים לו שלא לעשות כזאת . . . ובמתים חפשי כתיב (תהלים פח,ו) ואין עליו כל חיוב לעשות מצוות בגופו לאחר מותו אפילו משום פיקוח נפש. ועם מותו עליו לתת להחזיר את גופו בשלימותו אל המקום אשר ממנו לוקח בראשונה כפי אשר עלתה ונגזר מלפניו יתברך שמו . . . מפני שההכרה העמוקה של האדם מישראל המאמין [ומושרש עמוק באמונתו] היא, דכשם שלאחר המות הרוח תשוב אל האלקים אשר נתנה (קהלת יב,ז), כך גזירת הצו האלקי בזה כי כי גם הגוף בשלימותו יקוים בו, כי ישוב העפר על הארץ כשהיה (שם). ולא להתחכם להחזיר לתחיה חלקים ממנו, ויהיה

הנימוק מה שיהיה . . . דכך גזרה התורה על מת דכי קבור· תקברנו. ולכן אינו רשאי לבטל ממנו חיוב זה אפילו זה משום הצלת נפש. וגם אחרים מוזהרים על כך, דקיום המצוה דכי קבור תקברנו כמאמרה ובשלימותה הכתובה במת נאמרה על החיים. ציץ אליעזר יג,צא

If someone would ask whether to donate an organ after death for the purpose of transplantation, we would recommend against this . . . It states, "The dead are free" (Psalms 88:6), [meaning that] there is no obligation for a deceased person to engage in *mitzvot,* even for the purpose of saving a life. Upon death, one should return the whole body to the earth from which it came, as deemed proper by G-d. . . . For the deep rooted recognition of the believing Jew is that just as after death, "the spirit is returned to G-d Who gave it" (Ecclesiastes 12:7), likewise, it is the divine decree that the body in its complete form shall "return to the earth as it once was" (ibid.). One should not be overly clever and return parts of it to life, regardless of the result. . . . This is the command of the Torah: that the dead shall be buried. Thus, it is not proper to annul this mitzvah even in order to save lives. Others as well [beside for the deceased] are commanded regarding this, for the mitz-vah of burial was said to the living.

Rabbi Eliezer Waldenburg, *Tsits Eliezer* 13:91

האמת שליכא חיוב . . . אבל מצוה ודאי איכא שאף שטבע האדם להצטער טובא על
מתו יותר מעל כל ממונו מסתבר שחיוב ליכא על זה
ולכן מצוה שלא יצטער טובא ויציל נפש באבר של מתו.

אגרות משה, יורה דעה ב,קעד

The truth is that there is no obligation [for family members to donate organs from the deceased. This is because of the distress associated with losing part of the corpse]. . . . But it is certainly a mitzvah, for even though it is natural to be pained by the loss of the corpse more than the loss of all one's fortune, there is no obligation to feel this way. Therefore, there is a mitzvah not to be pained to this extent, and to allow a life to be saved with an organ of the deceased.

Rabbi Moshe Feinstein, *Igrot Moshe, Yoreh De'ah* 2:174

Rabbi Moshe Feinstein (1895–1986). Rabbi and leading halachic authority of the 20th century. Born near Minsk, Belarus; he became rabbi of Luban in 1921; immigrated to the U.S. in 1937 and became the dean of Metivta Tiferet Yerushalayim in New York. Rabbi Feinstein became the leading halachic authority of his epoch and his rulings are always considered. His halachic decisions have been published in a multi-volume collection titled *Igrot Moshe*. He also published works on the Talmud and was known for his fine character traits.

Heartbeating Donation

Text 5a

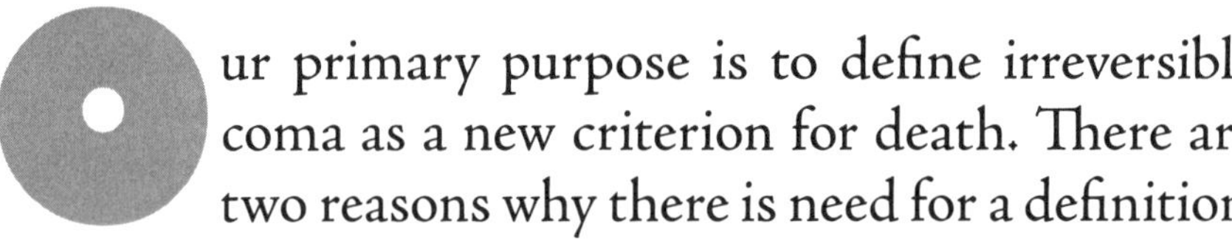

ur primary purpose is to define irreversible coma as a new criterion for death. There are two reasons why there is need for a definition:

(1) Improvements in resuscitative and supportive measures have led to increased efforts to save those who are desperately injured. Sometimes these efforts have only partial success so that the result is an individual whose heart continues to beat but whose brain is irreversibly damaged. The burden is great on patients who suffer permanent loss of intellect, on their families, on the hospitals, and on those in need of hospital beds already occupied by these comatose patients.

(2) Obsolete criteria for the definition of death can lead to controversy in obtaining organs for transplantation.

"A Definition of Irreversible Coma: Report of the Ad Hoc Committee of the Harvard Medical School to Examine the Definition of Brain Death," *Journal of the American Medical Association* 205, no. 6 (1968): 337

Text 5b

We contend that the proposition that brain death constitutes death of the human being is incoherent and, therefore, not credible. To be sure, brain death is a valid diagnosis of irreversible coma. No one who satisfies the criteria for brain death regains consciousness. Contrary, however, to the Uniform Determination of Death Act developed by a president's commission in 1981, many patients properly diagnosed as dead under whole brain death criteria do not have "irreversible cessation of all functions of the entire brain." For example, the brains of many patients retain a variety of homeostatic functions, from regulation of temperature to control over salt and water balance.

James Bernat and colleagues have responded that brain death should not require the loss of literally *all* functions of the entire brain, but only those that preserve the "functioning of the organism as a whole." According to Bernat, the diagnosis of brain death signifies the loss of those *critical* brain functions that maintain the integrity of the body as a living organism. The loss of these functions causes the body to "disintegrate," leading over a period of days to cardiac arrest. This deterioration is claimed to be inevitable, regardless of whether the patient is on life support.

With both theoretical analysis and empirical data, Alan Shewmon has seriously challenged Bernat's defense of brain death. Shewmon has shown, for example, that some patients who fulfill all of the diagnostic criteria of

Franklin G. Miller, Ph.D. is a member of the senior faculty in the Department of Bioethics, National Institutes of Health in Bethesda Maryland. He serves on the Neuroscience Institutional Review Board of the NIH Intramural Research Program and the Ethics Committee for its clinical center. Dr. Miller has written numerous published articles in medical and bioethics journals on the ethical issues concerning death and dying as well as other issues.

Dr. Robert D. Truog is professor of medical ethics, anesthesiology & pediatrics at Harvard Medical School and a senior associate in Critical Care Medicine at Children's Hospital, Boston. Dr. Truog has published more than 200 articles in bioethics and related disciplines, including recent national guidelines for providing end-of-life care in the intensive care unit. His writings on the subject of brain death have been translated into several languages, and in 1997 he provided expert testimony on this subject to the German Parliament.

brain death can "survive" for many years. With life support systems no more complex than home mechanical ventilation, these patients maintain an array of integrative functions including circulation, digestion and metabolism of food, excretion of wastes, hormonal balance, wound healing, growth and sexual maturation, and even gestation of a fetus.

Based on meta-analytic data of brain dead patients maintained on ventilators for one week or more, Shewmon argues that the human body does not need the brain to integrate homeostatic functions, and that integration of these activities is possible even in the absence of these supposedly critical brain functions. In sum, patients who fulfill all of the diagnostic criteria for brain death remain alive in virtually every sense except for the fact that they have permanently lost the capacity for consciousness.

Franklin G. Miller and Robert D. Truog, "Rethinking the Ethics of Vital Organ Donation," *Hastings Center Report*, November–December 2008, p. 39

The Case of Live Donation

Most organs for transplantation come from cadavers, but as these have failed to meet the growing need for organs, attention has turned to organs from living donors. Organ donation by living donors presents a unique ethical dilemma, in that physicians must risk the life of a healthy person to save or improve the life of a patient. Transplantation surgeons have therefore been cautious in tapping this source. As surgical techniques and outcomes have improved, however, this practice has slowly expanded.

Robert D. Truog, M.D., "The Ethics of Organ Donation by Living Donors," *New England Journal of Medicine* 353, no. 5 (August 4, 2005): 444

Text **7**

מניין לרואה את חברו שהוא טובע בנהר או חיה גוררתו או לסטין באין עליו שהוא
חייב להצילו תלמוד לומר לא תעמוד על דם רעך (ויקרא יט,טז).
והא מהכא נפקא מהתם נפקא: אבדת גופו מניין תלמוד לומר והשבותו לו (דברים
כב,ב). אי מהתם הוה אמינא הני מילי בנפשיה אבל מיטרח ומיגר אגורי
אימא לא קא משמע לן.
תלמוד בבלי, סנהדרין עג,א

How do we know that if someone sees his friend drowning in the river, or being dragged by a wild animal, or attacked by robbers that he is obligated to save him? Because it says,

"You shall not stand by the shedding of your fellow's blood" (Leviticus 19:16).

But do we learn it from this verse? Don't we learn this from another place in the Torah? As we have learned: How do we know that one has an obligation to restore another's life [saving him in case of danger]? Because it says: "You shall return [his lost property] to him" (Deuteronomy 22:2).

[The Talmud explains:] From this verse ("You shall return it to him) alone, one would have concluded that one must only save another's life with one's own bodily efforts, but there is no requirement to spend money to hire others to save another's life [just as one is not required to spend one's money to save someone else's property].

That is why we need [the verse "You shall not stand by the shedding of your fellow's blood," to teach that one is required to spend one's own financial resources to save a life].

Talmud, Sanhedrin 73a

Question **for Discussion**

Analyze Text 7. What does it tell you about an instance where the rescue involves risk to life? Is one obligated to risk one's life to save someone else?

Text **8a**

אין לחייב לאדם ליכנס בספק סכנה להצלת חברו מודאי סכנה . . . אבל מסתבר שיהיה
חלוק לאו דלא תעמוד על דם רעך משאר לאוין לענין איסור דבשאר לאוין הא אסור
להכניס עצמו לספק סכנה כדי שלא יעבור אלאו . . . אבל להציל נפש חברו . . .
יהיה מותר להכניס עצמו בספק מאחר דעל כל פנים יוצל נפש מישראל.

אגרות משה, יורה דעה ב,קעד

t is not obligatory for one to take on a possible risk in order to save another from certain danger. . . . However, it is reasonable that there should be a difference between the commandment "You shall not stand by the shedding of your fellow's blood" and all other commandments, in that for all other commandments it would be forbidden to assume risk in order to keep the commandment . . . whereas to save another . . . it would be allowed to put yourself in possible danger since in this case, a life will be saved as a result.

Rabbi Moshe Feinstein, *Igrot Moshe, Yoreh De'ah* 2:174

Text **8b**

ומכל מקום אם יש סכנה אין לו לסכן עצמו כדי להציל את חבירו מאחר שהוא חוץ מן

הסכנה ואף שרואה במיתת חבירו ואף על פי שהוא ספק וחבירו ודאי מכל מקום הרי

נאמר וחי בהם ולא שיבא לידי ספק מיתה

על ידי שיקיים מה שנאמר לא תעמוד על דם רעך.

שולחן ערוך הרב, אורח חיים שכט,ח

Rabbi Shne'ur Zalman of Liadi (1745–1812). Known as "the Alter Rebbe" and "the Rav." Born in Liozna, Belarus and buried in Hadich, Ukraine. Chasidic rebbe and founder of the Chabad movement, he was among the principle students of the Magid of Mezeritch. His numerous works include the *Tanya,* an early classic of Chasidism, *Torah Or* and *Likutei Torah*, and *Shulchan Aruch Harav,* a rewritten code of Jewish law. He was succeeded by his son, Rabbi Dovber of Lubavitch.

If a rescue effort is dangerous, then it is forbidden to risk one's life in order to save a companion, since the rescuer is not in danger. Although [this means that] one will witness the death of one's companion, and an attempt at rescue is only a possible danger, whereas one's companion is in certain danger, [the Torah] states "And you should live by them," which implies that one should not risk possible death by fulfilling the mitzvah of "You shall not stand by the shedding of your fellow's blood."

Rabbi Shne'ur Zalman of Liadi, *Shulchan Aruch Harav, Orach Chayim* 329:8

Learning **Activity 3**

1. Together with your neighbor, review and summarize Texts 7, 8a, 8b, and Text 9 in the table below.

Text 7 What must we be willing to do in order to save a person who is in danger?

Text 8a According to Rabbi Moshe Feinstein, may you risk your life to save someone who is danger?

Text 8b According to R. Shne'ur Zalman of Liadi, may you risk your life to save someone who is in danger?

Text 9 Must you risk a limb to save someone who is in danger?

Text 9

אם אמר השלטון לישראל

הנח לי לקצץ אבר אחד שאינך מת ממנו או אמית ישראל חבירך . . .

דכתיב דרכיה דרכי נועם (משלי ג,יז) וצריך שמשפטי תורתינו

יהיו מסכימים אל השכל והסברא ואיך יעלה על דעתנו שיניח אדם

לסמא את עינו או לחתוך את ידו או רגלו כדי שלא ימיתו את חבירו הלכך איני רואה

טעם לדין זה אלא מדת חסידות ואשרי חלקו מי שיוכל לעמוד בזה.

שאלות ותשובות רדב״ז ג,תרכז

Rabbi David ben Shlomo ibn Zimra (1479–1573). Born in Spain; emigrated to Safed, Israel upon the expulsion of the Jews from Spain in 1492. In 1513, he moved to Egypt and served as rabbi, judge and head of the yeshivah in Cairo. He also ran many successful business ventures and was independently wealthy. In 1553, he returned to Safed where he would later be buried. He authored what would later become a classic commentary to Maimonides' code of law, and wrote many halachic responsa, of which more than ten thousand are still extant.

If the government told a Jew, "Allow one of your limbs to be amputated—one which will not endanger your life—or we will kill your friend," [what should he do]? . . .

It states "Her ways are the ways of pleasantness" (Proverbs 3:17), and it is necessary that the laws of our Torah will accord with reason and rational thought.

How could it occur to us that a person should allow his eyes to be blinded or his hands or feet to be cut off so that his friend should not be killed?

Therefore, I find no basis for such a ruling [that obligates one to suffer the loss of limb] other than as an act of outstanding piety; blessed is the portion of one who can withstand this.

Rabbi David ibn Zimra, responsa 3:627

2. Based on the above sources (Texts 7–9), if a member of your immediate community required the following life-saving procedures and you were the only person available to serve as a donor, would you be required, permitted, or obligated to undergo the following procedures? Discuss the reasons for your answer with your neighbor. (If there is more than one possible answer for a question, depending on the halachic opinion followed, mark both answers.)

Procedure	Required	Permitted	Forbidden
Blood Donation	✓		
Bone Marrow Donation	✓		
First Kidney Donation		✓	
Lobe of Liver Donation			
Second Kidney Donation			✓

incindiary

אולם באמת שנמסר לנו מפי רופאים מומחים ויראי שמים שדרגת הסיכון בהוצאת
הכליה לאדם התורם, היא מועטת מאד, וכתשעים ותשעה אחוזים מהתורמים חוזרים
לבריאותם התקינה . . . לכן נראה שהעיקר להלכה שמותר וגם מצוה לתרום כליה
אחת מכליותיו להצלת חייו של אדם מישראל השרוי בסכנה במחלת הכליות.
וראויה מצוה זו להגן על התורם אלף המגן.

יחווה דעת ג,פד

Rabbi Ovadiah Yosef (1920–). Born in Basra, Iraq; talmudic scholar and former Sephardic chief rabbi of Israel. Rabbi Yosef is recognized as a modern authority in Halachah. His responsa are highly regarded within rabbinic circles and are considered binding in many Sephardic communities. He has also become a major political figure in Israel, serving as the spiritual leader of the Shas party. Among his most popular works are *Yabi'a Omer* and *Yechaveh Da'at*.

However the truth is that we have been informed by expert and G-d fearing physicians that the level of risk to a kidney donor is extremely low, and that ninety-nine percent of the donors return to normal health. . . . Thus, it appears that the standard rule is that it is permitted and also a mitzvah to donate one of his kidneys to save the life of an endangered fellow who suffers from renal failure. And this mitzvah is worthy of protecting the donor like a thousand shields.

Rabbi Ovadiah Yosef, *Yechaveh Da'at* 3:84

Resolution of Case Study and Postscript

Renada Daniel-Patterson, who gained public attention 11 years ago when her incarcerated father gave her one of his kidneys, died Sunday, exactly a week before she would have turned 25.

"I was home with her. I was with her when she died. I felt her spirit leave," said her mother, Vicki Daniel, her longtime caretaker, in a phone conversation from Atlanta.

"She had been living on dialysis, and she was really ill."

Daniel and Daniel-Patterson, formerly of Oakland, had been living in Atlanta for the past two years.

Daniel-Patterson was born with one unhealthy kidney and underwent her first unsuccessful transplant at the age of 5, when she received a kidney from a cadaver. She captured national attention in 1996, when she received a replacement kidney from her estranged father, a convict at Folsom Prison whom she had never met. David Patterson reached out to his daughter with a letter offering the organ.

Daniel-Patterson returned to the headlines three years later, after her father's kidney failed and she needed another transplant. Patterson offered his remaining organ, but an ethics panel at UCSF Medical Center refused the request, arguing it would shorten his life.

Daniel-Patterson received a kidney from an uncle in that crisis, but that organ also failed within a few years, said Daniel, because her daughter could not physically handle the rigorous anti-rejection medicine and steroids necessary—the same problem that had contributed to the failure of the kidney donated by her father.

Marisa Lagos, "Woman Whose Inmate Dad Donated Kidney to Her Dies," *San Francisco Chronicle*, March 20, 2007

Key Points

1. Judaism teaches that we ought to respect a dead body. This is reflected in the obligation to bury it, the prohibition against deriving benefit from it, and the prohibition against unnecessary desecration of the body.

2. The importance of life in Jewish law is reflected in the fact that all *mitzvot* are suspended when life is in danger, except for idolatry, prohibited sexual relationships, and murder.

3. There are grounds to say that it is permissible and even obligatory to donate an organ after death has been confirmed according to Jewish law, if it can save a life.

4. It is forbidden to harvest organs from a person who has not been certified dead according to Jewish law.

5. One is obligated to save someone else that is in danger. This obligation includes making a physical and financial effort but not the assumption of risk.

6. One is never obligated to lose a limb to save another.

7. A person who is the only available match may be obligated to donate blood and bone marrow.

8. According to many halachic authorities, the risks of live kidney donation are low enough for us to permit and encourage donation.

9. It is an important Jewish value to think about the needs and wants of other people.

Additional Readings

The Search for Organs: *Halachic* Perspectives on Altruistic Giving and the Selling of Organs

J.D. Kunin

Abstract

Altruistic donation of organs from living donors is widely accepted as a virtue and even encouraged as a duty. Selling organs, on the other hand, is highly controversial and banned in most countries. What is the Jewish legal (halachic) position on these issues? In this review it is explained that altruistic donation is praiseworthy but in no way obligatory. Selling organs is a subject of rabbinic dispute among contemporary authorities.

Organ transplantation has now evolved to be standard and life saving therapy for a wide variety of illnesses. One of its major limitations, however, is a shortage of donor organs. Over the last ten years, the need for organs has grown nearly five times faster than the number of available donors. The number of patients dying while awaiting transplantation in the United States alone is estimated to be 6000 annually.[1] Although brain stem dead donors are a critical source of donation, the donor pool is insufficient and other means of procuring organs are continually being sought. These sources include organ harvesting from non-beating heart donors and from living healthy adults. The latter is the subject of this paper.

Organ procurement from the healthy donor may be divided into two categories: 1) altruistic giving in which there is no monetary reward, and 2) selling organs for profit. In the ethical literature, altruistic donation is universally accepted and widely praised as a virtue. Healthy persons, usually relatives of end stage renal failure patients, have been donating kidneys for decades. This is well accepted medically because it entails extremely low risk to the donor and has a high success rate for the recipient. Although donation of a lobe of a liver or lung carry higher risk to the donor than does a donor nephrectomy, advances in surgical care have resulted in sufficiently low risk to make donation of these partial organs from living volunteers medically acceptable. Unlike altruistic donation, however, the practice of selling organs is banned in the vast majority of countries and its ethical status is very much open to question.

In Jewish law (*halacha*), these methods are of particular interest because donation from brain dead patients is highly controversial. (Publication is pending of a paper by myself on this subject entitled: *Brain death: reconsidering the rabbinic opinions in light of current medical knowledge.*) From the viewpoint of *halacha* the acceptability of either type of giving is not a simple question. Is altruistic giving a proper course that should be encouraged? As well, does *halacha* prohibit the sale of organs? In the following pages both of these ethical dilemmas will be examined from a *halachic* perspective.

ALTRUISTIC DONATION

It is widely assumed that saving human life is an absolute value in Jewish law. Saving another life is indeed a mitzvah (commandment) of the Torah as Maimonides states: "Anybody who is able to save someone else and fails to do so transgresses the mitzvah of 'Do not stand idly by the blood of your brother' ".[2] This being so, perhaps it would not only be allowed to give an organ to save a fellow human being but would be mandatory to do so to fulfil this Torah commandment. The problem is that in the case of donating an organ, there may be conflicting obligations that would overrule the mitzvah to save another's life. One such potential conflict is the

---

[1] *Sade RM, Kay H, Pitzer S, et al. Increasing organ donation: a successful new concept. Transplantation 2002;47:1142–8.*

[2] *Maimonides. Mishnah Torah, Laws of murder.*

mitzvah to preserve one's own life (Maimonides,[3] ch 11 p 4).[4] Inclusive in this mitzvah is the prohibition of placing oneself in danger. With this potential conflict, which mitzvah takes precedence? The Talmud records a dispute between Ben Peturah and Rabbi Akiva.[5] A case of two men dying of thirst in the desert is brought before the sages. One of them has a jug of water that is sufficient to get him alone to safety. If they share the water, however, they will each live a little longer, but they will both eventually die in the desert. Ben Peturah rules that the owner of the jug should share his water because otherwise he would be denying his friend temporary life, and thus he will be hastening, albeit indirectly, the death of his friend. Rabbi Akiva rules that the owner may drink it all himself, stating "one's own life takes precedence over his friend". The Talmud leaves the dispute unresolved, but one of the major medieval codifiers of *halacha* (Rosh,[6] *Bava Metzia* 62a) rules according to Rabbi Akiva.[7] Rabbi Moshe Feinstein of the modern era rules that the *halacha* unequivocally follows Rabbi Akiva.[8]

If this is so, however, what of the policeman or fireman or soldier who risks himself for the sake of another? In fact, there are clear examples of self sacrifice in the Bible and the Talmud that seem to contradict this prohibition on sacrificing one's own life for another. The most famous example of sacrificing one's own life is the suicide of King Saul. Suicide is considered a subcategory of murder by *halacha* and is unequivocally prohibited. There is considerable controversy among the authorities whether King Saul was acting properly in committing suicide. One authority concludes that King Saul may have committed suicide in order to save the lives of his fellow Jews.[9] What emerges from this debate is a principle that self sacrifice may be permissible if it is for the sake of saving one's country, or, in practical terms, even the saving of a community—that is, many lives.

The question with regard to organ donation is, however, much more restrictive. Here, the issue is not sacrificing one for the many, but one individual sacrificing for the sake of another individual. It is in such a circumstance that the above quoted talmudic rule, "Your life takes precedence over your friend's," might apply and one would not be permitted to donate the organ. This principle was codified into law in the modern era by the well accepted 16th century responsum of Radbaz who wrote on the question of placing oneself in danger to save another: "[In trying to save another life,] if there is any doubt of threat to [your] life, [saving another's life over your own] is piety of idiocy because your possible danger takes precedence over your fellow man's definite danger".[10]

While this responsum may apply to a case where there is a high probability of danger to one's life, the *halacha* is not so clear cut on the question of placing oneself in possible but unlikely danger in order to save another person. The majority of opinions hold that when danger to oneself is unlikely there is permission but no obligation for self sacrifice. On the other hand, there are two notable opinions that mandate saving a person who is in definite danger, even if one must put oneself in possible, although unlikely, danger. Radbaz himself, in another responsum, states that so long as one's likelihood of dying is less than 50% one is obligated to save a person in definite danger (Ben Zimra,[11] 1582). The *Jerusalem Talmud* also teaches that it is incumbent upon someone who is only in possible danger to proceed and save somebody in definite danger (Maimonides,[12] ch 1 p 4).

Fortunately, the concern of danger to the life of the organ donor is not much of a *halachic* problem today. In the current state of medicine, operations to harvest a kidney are of minimal risk of mortality and long term morbidity. Such procedures cannot even be considered "possible danger" in a *halachic* sense. This is supported by studies of perioperative mortality and long term morbidity. In a US national survey, the mortality rate was measured to be a mere 0.03%. In a 20 year follow up of patients who had donated kidneys, all criteria measur-

---

[3] Ibid.

[4] *Caro Y*. Shulchan Aruch, Yoreh de'ah.116:5.

[5] *Babylonian Talmud: tractate Bava metzia 62a.*

[6] Ibid.

[7] Ibid.

[8] *Feinstein M*. Igrot Moshe, yoreh de'ah: part I :145.

[9] *Luria S*. Yam shel Shlomo. Bava kamma: ch 8: 91a: s 59.

[10] *Ben Zimra D*. Responsas of Radbaz :1052.

[11] Ibid.

[12] *Maimonides*. Mishnah Torah, Laws of murder.

ing possible renal disease, including abnormal creatinine clearance, hypertension, and proteinuria, were similar compared to siblings.[13] Therefore, even going by the opinion that one may not place oneself in any substantial danger, in the current state of extremely low mortality from organ donation, the concern over one's own danger is not sufficiently strong to exempt one from the obligation of saving another life by donating an organ. It would appear then that *halacha* would mandate somebody to donate an organ to save another life.

There is, however, another potential *halachic* conflict when considering the mitzvah of saving another's life. This is the prohibition on injuring oneself. Donating an organ is by definition self injury. Is this permissible? Again, here is a conflict between two Torah obligations. On the one hand there is an obligation to save another life. On the other hand, one is prohibited from self injury. In resolving this conflict it is important to appreciate the unique strength of the mitzvah of saving a life. The commandment of saving a life is a higher priority mitzvah than almost all other *mitzvot* of the Torah. This is emphasised by the many areas in *halacha* where "*pikuach nefesh*," (the saving of a life) overrides even stringent prohibitions such as Sabbath observance and the fast of Yom Kippur. By this reasoning the prohibition of wounding oneself should probably be deferred for the sake of *pikuach nefesh* (Feinstein,[14] Part II, ch 174, s 4). However, the obligations of *pikuach nefesh* also have limitations. Exactly how much one needs to sacrifice to fulfil the mitzvah of saving somebody else's life, be it monetary loss or pain and suffering, is a matter of considerable *halachic* controversy. All agree, however, that there are limits to the obligation. No authority suggests—for example, that one would be required to sacrifice an organ to save another life. This is above and beyond what is mandated. (Likewise, one is not mandated to spend all of one's wealth to save another's life.) Therefore, the *halachic* conclusion is that because of the force of the mitzvah of saving another life, it is *permissible* to injure oneself but is not *obligatory*. So too it is permissible but not obligatory to donate an organ.

Indeed, Radbaz in his responsum cited above permits self injury to save another life. His emphasis is, however, telling. In no uncertain terms he states that there is no *obligation* to sacrifice an organ, even for the saving of another life. Writing on the question of a sadistic murderer who gives an ultimatum, "give me your arm or I will kill your friend," he writes "The law of the Torah must agree with reason and logic. How is it possible to make a person blind, or cut off his hand so another doesn't die? Therefore, I see no reason to rule that this sacrifice is anything but an act of piety, and praiseworthy is his lot, who is able to perform them".[15]

This widely accepted responsum is the basis for the permission to donate an organ to save another person.

It is worth mentioning that in discussing the permissibility of donating an organ to save another person, Rabbi M S Klein, a senior judge of the influential rabbinic court of Rabbi S H Wosner of Bnei Brak, Israel, downplayed the wording of Radbaz that it is "an act of piety". He said the *halacha* is simply that it is permissible. Period. In current ethical trends it is considered a great virtue to donate an organ. This attitude is so pervasive that one could conclude that if someone chooses not to donate an organ he or she could be considered negligent in their duty. There could well be an expectation by family members that one should donate an organ and refusal would be a great shame. Therefore, says Rabbi Klein, the *halacha* says only that organ donation is permissible and should not be construed in any way as obligatory. In other words, such donation, even to save a life, is above and beyond what is necessary to fulfil the law of the Torah.

Selling organs

The ethical literature is quite divided on the permissibility of selling organs. The arguments against selling organs include the concern that the possibility of selling an organ may undermine a poor person's status as an autonomous individual—that is, given the opportunity to sell an organ, a desperately poor person may be compelled to sell. The permissibility to sell an organ raises the concern that the wealthy may exploit and coerce the desperately poor.[16]

---

[13] *Najarian JS, Chavers BM, McHugh LE, et al. 20 years or more of follow up of living kidney donors. Lancet1992;340:807–9.*

[14] *Feinstein M.* Igrot Moshe, yoreh de'ah: part I:145.

[15] *Ben Zimra D. Responsas of Radbaz :1052.*

[16] *Demonico FL, Arnold R, Scheper-Hughes N, et al. Ethical*

Deontological principles play substantial roles in the arguments against the sale of organs. One such line of reasoning is that by permitting the sale of organs, society would make the parts of human beings and, by extension, people themselves, commodities. This may dehumanise society.[17] It is argued that donation should be limited to altruistic giving because altruism is a value that ought to be encouraged in society. By legalising the sale of organs and establishing a commercial market, altruism may be undermined.[18] Arguments that have been put forward in favour of selling organs tend to be more utilitarian. The most obvious is that selling organs may be a strategy to increase supply.[19] While it may be argued that permitting organ sales is exploitation of the poor, the opposite can be cogently argued: prohibiting the selling of organs is depriving a poor person of a legitimate means of achieving a financial goal. Finally, if the purpose of banning the sale of organs is to preserve the principle of autonomy, is there ever true autonomy? Is not altruistic giving also fraught with the risk of pressure from family members, thus also compromising personal autonomy?[20]

From a *halachic* perspective, selling organs presents similar questions to those mentioned above in connection with altruistic giving. Here again, the primary problem is the prohibition on injuring oneself. As was stated, the prohibition on injuring oneself may be lifted when fulfilling the mitzvah of saving another life. Here, however, in selling for financial gain, one does not have the countervailing force of the mitzvah of saving a life because this is in no way the intent of the action.

When a new question arises, *halachic* authorities, much like secular courts, rely upon related precedents and prior rulings. Deriving a precedent from the Talmud is ideal because this great tome is by the far most authoritative source for all of Jewish law and thought.

The source for adjudicating the problem of self injury is in the talmudic tractate *Bava kamma*, (*Babylonian Talmud*,[21] tractate *Bava kamma* 90a, 91b), which must be studied in detail to understand the problems involved in the *halachic* question of selling organs. It states there directly that one is prohibited from injuring oneself. The Tosafot, the classic mediaeval school of talmudic commentary, teaches that even if one wishes to injure oneself because of a material need such as preventing monetary loss, one is still prohibited from doing so. The Talmud itself, however, subsequently discusses a case that seems to take exception to the prohibition on wounding oneself for financial considerations. It relates an incident where Rabbi Chisda, one of the sages of the Talmud, needed to pass through a field of thorns. He lifted his clothing in order to avoid irreparably damaging it. In so doing he allowed his legs to be wounded. Rabbi Chisda in explaining his actions, stated: "My wounds will heal, my clothes will not". This incident seems to contradict the previous ruling of the Talmud that one may not injure oneself. Tosafot unfortunately does not directly comment on this obvious contradiction of the Talmud. The exact understanding of the story of Rabbi Chisda is pivotal in rendering a *halachic* decision as to whether one may sell an organ for profit.

The important 18th century commentator, P'nei Yehoshua, resolves the paradox by arguing that Tosafot's prohibition on self injury was for a small need, whereas the case of Rabbi Chisda, not directly commented on by Tosafot, was for a relatively great need.[22] The degree of need is determined by comparing the loss and gain in any particular circumstance. In the case of Rabbi Chisda, as he himself argues, his property would be irreparably damaged and the reversible wounding of his legs was worth the relatively small suffering in order to save his clothes. In other words, the self injury was justified because of the greater loss of his

incentives—not payment—for organ donation. *N Eng J Med* 2002;346:2002–5.

17 *Joralemon D, Cox P. Body values.* Hastings Cent Rep 2003;33:27–33.

18 *Matas AJ, Garvey CA, Jacobs CL, et al. Non-directed donation of kidneys from living donors. N Eng J Med* 2000;343:433–6.

19 *Council on Ethical and Judicial Affairs of AMA. Financial incentives for organ procurement. Arch Int Med* 1995;155:581–8.

20 *Sade RM. Cadaveric organ donation. Arch Int Med* 1999;159:438–42; *Cameron JS, Hoffenberg R. Ethics of organ transplantation. Kidney Int* 1999;55:725–32; *Radcliffe Richards J, Daar AS, Guttmann RD, et al. The case for allowing kidney sales. Lancet* 1998;352:1950–2.

21 *Babylonian Talmud: tractate Bava metzia 62a.*

22 *P'nei Yehoshua: tractate Bava kamma :91b.*

clothing. Following this line of logic a general principle may be derived—that is, the prohibition on self injury is relative and depends on the particular circumstance. Understanding the Talmud in this way, we may rule that for a poor person with a dire need and who can substantially profit from selling an organ, perhaps the self injury is worth the resulting reward and may be *halachically* acceptable.

The P'nei Yehoshua's understanding of the Talmud seems to be accepted by Rabbi Yosef Shalom Elyashiv of Jerusalem, the pre-eminent living *halachic* authority, who allows selling of organs under restricted circumstances. Rabbi Yaakov Weiner of the Jerusalem Center of Research in *Halachah* and Medicine recently asked Rabbi Elyashiv this specific question and relayed this answer to me. He rules that the need must be great and the sale must accomplish the financial goal, otherwise it cannot be considered of sufficient value to override the prohibition of injuring oneself. For example, if one has a $10000 debt that if not paid would result in imprisonment, and the sale of the kidney would result in a net profit of $10000, then it may be authorised. If, however, the debt is $100000 then a sale for only $10000 would not be permitted, as the self injury could not be justified by the partial benefit. In a case that was recorded by Cameron and Hoffenberg, an impoverished man sold his kidney in order to provide medicine for his sick daughter.[23] According to the reasoning of Rabbi Elyashiv, there would be an even stronger argument here for approving the sale because there is an additional factor of saving another life.

Other authorities, however, do not come to the same conclusion. Rabbi Wosner does not permit the sale of organs. His understanding of the story of Rabbi Chisda is that he did not lift his garments for the express purpose of injuring himself but rather only to avoid damaging the garments. Moreover, it was not absolutely certain he would even be injured—that is, it was only an anticipated possibility. His goal was only to avoid damaging his garments and it was not *necessary* that he be injured in order to fulfil that goal. Quite the opposite is true with the sale of an organ where the benefit of the

action only comes from the injury itself, and therefore the injury was wholly intended. Thus, in selling an organ there is a direct, intentional violation of the prohibition against injuring oneself. This is not permissible, argues Rabbi Wosner. It may be noted that this approach is in conflict with the opinion of P'nei Yehoshua who explicitly allows for intentional self injury so long as the need is great.

The late Rabbi Moshe Feinstein, another of the great contemporary *halachic* authorities, seems to take a third approach. While he wrote extensively on *halachic* questions in medicine, he did not directly rule on the sale of organs. Some indication of his thinking, however, can be appreciated from a related responsum on the question of the permissibility of cosmetic surgery (Feinstein,[24] part II: 66). At first glance, cosmetic surgery seems also to be a violation of the prohibition on injuring oneself. In understanding the story of Rabbi Chisda, Rabbi Feinstein also disagrees with Pnei Yehoshua. He writes that it is distorting the plain meaning of the Talmud and the accompanying Tosafot teaching "to distinguish between a small need and a great need. This distinction was never written explicitly". So, Rabbi Feinstein asks: "How is it permissible for Rabbi Chisda to go through the field of thorns?". In trying to explain the Talmud he explicitly rejects the idea that the injury was not certain—that is, he disagrees with Rabbi Wosner on this point, and says: "Therefore, one needs to say that the prohibition of injuring oneself is only when [the injury] is to degrade oneself . . . He walked [through the field] for a need and this [in itself] was not degrading and there is no prohibition. One needs to say that [the actions that] are prohibited . . . are things that are done for the purpose of causing distress, like [a mourner] wounding himself [which is done for the express] purpose of causing pain. This is prohibited because the will and the need is the distress [itself] and this is degrading."

In this responsum, Rabbi Feinstein permits cosmetic surgery because it is not the type of injury intended in the *halachic* prohibition on self injury—that is, it is not an injury intended to degrade, but rather to improve oneself. Of course, what Rabbi Feinstein would have ruled in the question of selling an organ is speculative.

---

[23] *Cameron JS, Hoffenberg R*. Ethics of organ transplantation. Kidney Int 1999;55:725–32;

[24] **Caro Y.** *Shulchan Aruch, Yoreh de'ah.116:5*

It would seem, though, that by following his reasoning, he would have argued that a person who submits to an operation to sell an organ is definitely intending to injury himself and gain benefit from the injury itself, as in the case of the mourner, which is clearly prohibited. In this sense it is not comparable to Rabbi Chisda who did not *require* the injury to achieve his intended result of avoiding injury to his garments. From this perspective, he seems to agree with Rabbi Wosner. Also, organ donation is not similar to cosmetic surgery where the injury itself is for the good of the person undergoing the cosmetic surgery. With organ donation, while a person may profit monetarily, the injury itself cannot be construed in any way as benefiting him. After all, it results in the loss of an organ, pain from the surgery, scarring, etc. I would conclude, with trepidation, that Rabbi Feinstein would also prohibit organ donation for profit.

There remains another potential argument in favour of selling organs. When all is said and done, lives are saved by selling organs. So the question may be posed, if the sale of an organ results in saving of a life, even if that is not the intention of the donor, would it not be permissible? That is to say, just as with altruistic giving where the prohibition on self injury may be lifted for the sake of *pikuach nefesh*, why should it not be lifted here too if it results in saving a life? Does the intention of the donor really matter when in the end a life is saved? As mentioned above, this question is also debated in the secular literature, with some saying that maintaining the spirit of altruism is important and others, adopting a more utilitarian perspective, saying the intent of the donor should not matter.

This question of profit affects many areas of *halacha*. Does a mitzvah remain a mitzvah even if one profits from its performance? One example offered by the Code of Jewish law is the question of whether a scribe who writes sacred documents such as a Torah scroll, but is also making his livelihood from this, is considered to be involved in a mitzvah. If the scribe writes when no money is involved this is unquestionably considered a mitzvah. This is true to the extent that so long as he is writing he is released from any other daily obligation such as praying. Is the same true if he is earning money for his writing? The Code of Jewish law rules that so long as he has some intention that he is performing a

mitzvah, the fact that he may also be profiting from his action does not nullify the mitzvah. If, however, he is writing with no substantive intention of performing a mitzvah, then his motivation for profit may well cancel the mitzvah (Caro, *Shulchan Aruch, Orech chaim* 33.8). So too, if someone wishes to donate an organ and get some monetary compensation, the mere fact that he requests some remuneration may not cancel the mitzvah of saving a life. Indeed, even by the more stringent standards of Rabbi Wosner, this may be permissible. According to the decision of Rabbi Wosner, however, and in keeping with the analogous case of the scribe writing, if his intention is purely for profit, it would be problematic and perhaps forbidden.

In summary, there is a difference of opinion among the great *halachic* authorities on the permissibility of selling organs. Certainly, a major figure in the person of Rabbi Elyashiv allows sale under specific circumstances and one is surely on solid footing in relying on this opinion. As is recorded by A S Abraham, the late Rabbi Shlomo Zalman Auerbach, another of the great contemporary authorities, seems to agree. He writes that even if a donor's primary motive is for profit, the donation is permissible because it saves a life.[25] It cannot be overemphasised, however, that in Jewish law even if this more lenient opinion is used, in practice, a legislated policy permitting organ sale would not obviate the need for an individual to obtain a rabbinic approval, making certain that the need was sufficiently great; that the goal was achievable in order to justify the prohibition against injuring oneself, and that the person was physically fit so there would be no concern about any health consequences. Moreover, as Grazi and Wolowelsky have written, the ultimate permissibility of selling organs "is inextricably connected to solving a series of pragmatic problems, such as creating a system that ensures that potential vendors and donors are properly informed and not exploited . . . [and] regulation of payments so they reasonably reflect compensation for pain and suffering".[26] One such system has recently been

---

25 **Abraham AS**. *Nishmat Avraham 4 :213.*

26 *Grazi RV, Wolowelsky JB. Non-altruistic kidney donations in contemporary Jewish law and ethics. Transplantation2003;75:250–2.*

proposed in Israel[27] where there would be a central registry in which people could sell organs, and where direct purchase of organs would be illegal. In this proposed system priority would be given to medical need rather than ability to pay. Again, it is worth emphasising that even if such a policy is instituted, while in principle it would be permissible by some rabbinic authorities, from a *halachic* perspective it would nevertheless require adjudication on a case by case basis, as is true in all areas of Jewish jurisprudence. In this way potential abuse of such a public policy could be averted.

Journal of Medical Ethics 31, no. 5 (2005): 269–272.
Reprinted with permission by publisher

Organs in the American Marketplace: Paying for Kidneys Increases the Supply, But at What Cost?

Courtney Hutchison
ABC News Medical Unit

Would you give up your kidney to save a strangers life?

How about if you were paid you handsomely to do so?

A former transplant official says it's time to pay people for their organs. That is the crucial question tackled by a recent study from the University of Pennsylvania on living organ donation.

In a world where thousands of people die each year waiting for a donated organ to become available, researchers sought to tease out the factors that impact decisions to donate.

They found that the higher the payment, the more people are willing to go under the knife.

The concept of selling one's organs to pay the bills is fraught with disconcerting implications, but if the study's findings hold true, an organ market may be a particularly effective way of boosting donation rates and, consequently, saving lives.

"If someone were to design an [organ donation] system, they would never design a system [like the current one] that allowed thousands to die each year while costing the government $33 billion in medical costs," says Dr. Scott Halpern, the lead author on the study and senior fellow at the University of Pennsylvania's Center for Bioethics.

A market-based solution, in which the government compensated donors a fixed sum for their organs and regulated allocation of the organs, "could easily bridge the gap."

The study, published in the Annals of Internal Medicine, hopes to dispel some of the concerns most commonly voiced against offering payment for organs.

Halpern is not the only voice calling for a drastic change in the way organ exchange is regulated. But whether for theoretical concerns or ethical ones, his call for an organ market is met with apprehension and opposition by medical ethicists and policymakers.

The Proof Is in the Polling

In surveying 342 Philadelphians on their morning commute, Halpern and colleagues found several surprising trends among who would donate and why.

For instance, those living below the poverty line were nearly twice as likely to report that they would give up their kidney to a stranger than those who make $100,000 plus a year—a trend that plays into the concern that an organ market would exploit the poor.

But contrary to expectation, researchers found that the

---

[27] *Friedlaender MM*. *A protocol for paid kidney donation in Israel. IMAJ2003;5:611–14.*

bias is not affected by providing monetary reward. The poor consistently donated more than the rich at every compensation level, including none. Their willingness to donate didn't increase with compensation any more than that of their richer counterparts.

"This paper takes away the non-proven claim of exploitation of the poor," says Dr. David Cronin, associate professor of surgery at the Medical College of Wisconsin. "The poor have an opportunity to be compensated for donation. Why should they be further exploited by taking the opportunity and decision away from them?"

But the bias, in and of itself, "raises concerns about justice," says David Magnus, a professor of medicine at Stanford University and a co-author of the study's editorial.

An imbalance of the poor disproportionately providing organs to the rich has caused problems in other countries that have tried organ markets such as Iran and the Philippines, he says.

Another concern about offering compensation is that it would decrease the amount of people willing to donate for free. The study, however, and a growing body of research on the subject, suggests otherwise, Halpern says.

Researchers compared the responses of those who were given the money option up front with those that were given altruistic-only scenarios to start and found that the "specter of payment did not affect whether they responded 'yes' to doing it for free."

What this data cannot predict, however, is what percentage of people would actually donate, Halpern warns.

"The study has been misinterpreted by some," he says. "They'll cite that 30 percent of people are willing to donate an organ to a stranger, but the study was not designed to gauge this. The study offers a number for this, but I don't believe that number."

Instead, he warns, the study can suggest how changes in incentive structures change an individual's decision to donate. But at the end of the day, these were hypothetical questions.

The equality or success of the incentive aside, the question to ask in this debate may be: As a nation, are we OK with the idea of making a profit off of our organs?

Up until 2008, the letter of the law was that no compensation whatsoever—short of the joy of giving—could be given in exchange for organs, according to the National Organ Transplant Act of 1984.

But the Charlie Norwood amendment, passed two years ago, provided a tiny window in the legislation that allowed for paired organ donation.

That is a system whereby an organ swap, sometimes with up to 26 people involved, takes people who would give a kidney to their loved ones but are not matches for them and allows them to give their organs to strangers in return for the organ of other strangers who match their loved ones. Thirteen patients in the Washington, D.C. area were given a new lease on life last Christmas by just such a swap.

But is there a difference between payment in kind and payment in cash? This organ quid pro quo was passed by Congress with overwhelming approval, but other forms of compensation are seen as unethical, Harlan Abraham, lawyer and co-author of "On the List: Fixing America's Failing Organ Transplant System," points out.

Isn't a wife who donates a kidney for her husband, on whom she relies for income, also donating for compensation in a way? Cronin asks.

Halpern goes even further, arguing that while kidney donation is an extremely low-risk transaction, another form of selling the body, prostitution, brings great risk to the seller. Even readily acceptable trades such as stunt doubling and playing for the NFL are ways of selling the body by incurring bodily risks, he says.

So where do should the line be drawn when it comes to putting bodies on the market?

That is an unanswerable question, Abraham says.

"If only religion ruled the day, we'd get one answer," he says. "And if only politics ruled the day, we'd get another. And if only economics ruled, we'd get yet another.

"Eighteen people will die today on an organ donation wait list, and 18 tomorrow," he adds. "Right now, there is a disincentive to donate because health insurance doesn't always cover post surgery."

But, Abraham argued, an organ market is not the way to meet the need.

He prefers non-monetary compensation, such as 20 years of health care or life insurance, or even tax credits, as a way to "give donors an incentive that isn't bargaining for their flesh."

"There is a reason that selling organs is illegal in almost every country of the world," he says. "I believe it's unethical."

But Halpern sees no ethical difference between this kind of compensation and money in your pocket, and he argues that swapping systems and tax breaks will not be nearly as effective.

"Small payments won't do it; we know the magnitude of the payment is intrinsically related to its effectiveness," he says.

So should the guiding hand of the marketplace be brought to bear on whether or not Americans sell their organs?

An experiment in this approach, at least, is long overdue, Cronin says.

"If we test this . . . in a small, highly monitored, government regulated, geographically limited way, . . . and the outcomes are poor, I'll be at the head of the line to end the program," says Halpern. "My concern is that we not leap to the theoretical conclusion that using it *won't* work."

ABCnews.go.com, April 2, 2010.
Reprinted with permission

Are Alcoholics Less Deserving of Liver Transplants?

Daniel Brudney

Abstract

When does behavior trigger a lesser claim to medical resources? When does chronic drinking, for example, mean that one has a lesser claim to a liver transplant? Only when one's behavior becomes a callous indifference to others' needs—when one knows the consequences of heavy drinking and knows that by drinking one may end up depriving someone else of a liver.

As many studies show, Americans tend to think that an illness has a morally weaker claim to medical care when it is caused by personal conduct that is known to put health at risk. More specifically, many Americans believe that health-risky conduct can make for a significantly weaker claim to scarce medical resources. According to one study, for example, "respondents were 10 to 17 times more likely to allocate liver transplants or asthma treatment to patients they deemed not responsible for their illnesses than to patients they deemed responsible for their conditions."[1] My goal in this essay is to see if there are conditions under which this belief may be justified. I want to see where—if anywhere—this belief touches defensible moral ground.

Broadly speaking, one could examine two different issues. When, if ever, is it morally appropriate to make some agents pay at least part of the extra cost of medical care for illness that is due to their voluntary, health-risky

---

[1] E. Wittenberg et al., "Rationing Decisions and Individual Responsibility for Illness: Are All Lives Equal?" *Medical Decision Making* 23, no. 3 (2003): 194. For a discussion of this general attitude toward the sick, see R. Galvin, "Disturbing Notions of Chronic Illness and Individual Responsibility: Towards a Genealogy of Morals," *Health: An Interdisciplinary Journal for the Social Study of Health, Illness and Medicine* 6, no. 2 (2002): 107-137. See also P. Ubel et al., "Allocation of Transplantable Organs: Do People Want to Punish Patients for Causing Their Illness?" *Liver Transplantation* 7, no. 7 (2001): 600-607.

conduct? And when, if ever, is it morally appropriate to make it more difficult to gain access to medical resources—and so in effect sometimes to deny access—for illness that is due to an agent's voluntary, health-risky conduct?

The question of when to impose financial costs on health-risky conduct is important, and will become increasingly so as we learn more about our own role in our own ailments. However, rather than try to find criteria for when it would be proper to impose financial costs on agents—a task likely to be burdened by citizens' conflicting beliefs about which activities have significant social value—I will focus on the perhaps more dramatic issue of when voluntary conduct should trigger a lesser claim to medical resources. As my paradigm example, I will look at alcoholics and liver transplants. This sort of case is widespread and presents comparatively few epistemic problems—it occurs reasonably frequently, and frequently it is sufficiently clear that the patient's liver disease is in fact due to drinking.[2]

My analysis will suggest that there are indeed conditions under which it would be justified to give an alcoholic a lesser claim to a transplant, but that at present very few cases would satisfy those conditions. I don't want to blink the fact that when those conditions are satisfied, my claim is that we are justified in putting a desperately ill person in an even graver medical position on the ground that his past conduct was morally lacking. This may seem to border on the cruel, yet in some cases it will be justified. Nevertheless, the central claim of this essay is that in the great majority of cases, at least at present, it will *not* be justified.

An agent's conduct can make him morally vulnerable only if that conduct is in fact voluntary. Throughout, my analysis assumes that the conduct in question is sufficiently voluntary. I leave to others the task of determining what that amounts to.[3]

Conduct and Responsibility

Let's take Jane as our first example. Let's assume that her long-term drinking was sufficiently voluntary (whatever we decide that means).[4] And assume, too, that it is sufficiently clear that her drinking ruined her liver. It might be urged, now, that Jane should bear the consequences of her conduct, meaning that she should be penalized by moving her lower down on the waiting list for liver transplants. This claim has in fact been made by a number of writers.[5] I quote from Walter Glannon's formulation:

"[The alcoholic] will have a weaker claim to receive a liver than someone whose end-stage liver failure is beyond his control and thus contracted through no fault of his own. . . . [The] moral judgment of lower or higher priority for claims to medical treatment . . . [is made] on grounds of the control of their behavior which they reasonably can be expected to exercise. This control makes them either more or less responsible for their condition and in turn determines the strength of their claims to receive treatment."[6]

---

[2] IV drug use might also cause liver disease. However, the issue of holding someone responsible is more complicated here because it is possible to contract liver disease from one dirty needle. The impulse to penalize the alcoholic comes in part from the fact that her disease is a consequence of long-term, repeated conduct.

[3] For a fine discussion of the conditions for holding an alcoholic responsible for her alcoholism, see W. Glannon, "Responsibility, Alcoholism, and Liver Transplantation," *Journal of Medicine and Philosophy* 23, no. 1 (1998): 31-49. The issue of what follows from saying that the alcoholic is responsible for her condition fits in with the extensive philosophical debate on distributive justice and luck. Canonical texts in that debate include R. Arneson, "Equality and Equal Opportunity for Welfare," *Philosophical Studies* 56 (1989): 77-93, and "Liberalism, Distributive Subjectivism, and Equal Opportunity for Welfare," *Philosophy and Public Affairs* 19 (1990): 158-94; G.A. Cohen, "On the Currency of Egalitarian Justice," *Ethics* 99 (1989): 906-944; and R. Dworkin, *Sovereign Virtue: The Theory and Practice of Equality* (Cambridge, Mass.: Harvard University Press, 2000).

[4] Perhaps it would be sufficient that there was a point, prior to her liver disease, at which we could reasonably have expected Jane to get herself into treatment. For this suggestion, see A.H. Moss and M. Siegler, "Should Alcoholics Compete Equally for Liver Transplantation?" *Journal of the American Medical Association* 265 (1991): 1295-98.

[5] Moss and Siegler make the proposal as early as 1991. See Moss and Siegler, "Should Alcoholics Compete Equally for Liver Transplantation?"

[6] Glannon, "Responsibility, Alcoholism, and Liver Transplantation," 41 and 43.

Robert Veatch asserts something similar: "[I]f one is free to engage in these risky behaviors," he writes, "one must be prepared to take the consequences, even if that should happen to result in a lower position on the organ waiting list."[7]

Here, then, is the principle that Glannon and Veatch advocate, which I will just call "the Principle":

"An agent is responsible for knowingly, voluntarily, and repeatedly engaging in easily avoidable conduct that might significantly contribute to that agent's needing a scarce, lifesaving resource. An agent who is responsible for such conduct may legitimately be given a weaker claim on scarce, lifesaving resources if her need for such resources is due to such conduct."

The point of "knowingly" and "voluntarily" should be clear even if the standards for knowing enough or being sufficiently voluntary may sometimes be disputable. I include "repeatedly" because it is not clear whether it is suspect to engage in a few instances of health-risky conduct.

A decent life is likely to involve some health risks, and it might be thought that penalties for risky conduct should begin beyond a threshold of "normal" or "acceptable" risky conduct. We might even think that a very occasional step over that threshold should be ignored, that each of us should get a mulligan or two of this kind.[8] Our model cases, then, will be those of conduct repeated over a long period of time. This ties into the "easily avoidable" condition. It is but a small crimp in one's lifestyle not to do unprotected class five rock climbs every weekend or to drink until the bar closes four times a week for a decade.

It is important to note that the Principle does not assert that drinking is *malum in se*. Its focus is on the consequences of Jane's conduct, not on whether that conduct was intrinsically good or bad.[9] If drinking did not destroy livers, Jane's drinking would not trigger the Principle. Moreover, we should not confuse the question of whether an agent is responsible for her medical condition with the quite separate question of what institutions should do. That Jane is responsible for her condition does not, of itself, entail any specific institutional response.[10]

Assume now that Jane asks to be put on the transplant list. Assume that, medically speaking, her chance of successful surgery and good longterm outcome is the

---

[7] R. Veatch, *Transplantation Ethics* (Washington, D.C.: Georgetown University Press, 2000), 315. See also Moss and Siegler, "Should Alcoholics Compete Equally for Liver Transplantation?" 1297.

[8] Readers inclined toward a stricter standard should simply remove "repeatedly" from the Principle and have the relevant phrase read, "knowingly and voluntarily."

[9] The fact that one is responsible for one's health-risky conduct does not entail that such conduct is morally wrong. It might even be praiseworthy (imagine Alice, who rushes into the toxic waste pit to pull out the baby who has fallen in). Failure to make the distinction between prima facie and all-things-considered assessments vitiates Peter Ubel's example of a person who risks his health (and so needs scarce medical resources) by excessive work helping others.

See P. Ubel, "Transplantation in Alcoholics: Separating Prognosis and Responsibility from Social Biases," *Liver Transplantation and Surgery* 3 (1997): 343-46. Ubel says January-February 2007 HASTINGS CENTER REPORT 47 that if one would not criticize such a person but would criticize the alcoholic, then one must be criticizing the alcoholic because one thinks drinking is morally wrong. The inference is invalid. If the hard worker ruins hishealth (and so needs scarce medical resources) as part of an activity that produces significant benefits (for a few other people, for society generally—it may not matter), then on balance his conduct might be permissible or even praiseworthy.

[10] We are responsible for voluntarily and repeatedly engaging in (easily avoidable) conduct that a reasonable person would know holds a high risk of generating severe health problems. This applies to the smoker and the overeater as much as to the alcoholic. It applies as well to the habitual rock climber and hang glider. In a straightforward sense, certain kinds of repeated voluntary conduct *do* make me responsible for my medical condition. But how medical institutions should respond to that fact is a separate matter. Here, many considerations are relevant. A partial list would include the epistemic question of how easy it is to ascertain that the agent's voluntary conduct was in fact the cause of her medical condition, the administrative question of how costly such a determination would be, and the moral question of how invasive it would be. One could accept that in many cases agents might be responsible for their conduct but that, for one or another reason, institutions should ignore that fact.

same as that of many of the nonalcoholics on the list. Of course, in real life a large number of factors will go into ranking Jane versus other candidates. Our question is whether Jane's place on the list should be affected by a particular consideration—namely, the fact that she brought her liver disease on herself.

The Principle says, Yes, it should.

Before turning to the Principle's major problem, I want to note some minor ones. To begin with, the Principle leaves unclear the *moral weight* of the fact that Jane brought her disease on herself. This issue would be relevant if we remove the stipulation that all other factors are equal between Jane and her transplant competitors. At one extreme, the moral weight of her conduct could be so heavy that Jane would lose out to any at least minimally viable competing candidate. At the other extreme, the moral weight might be so modest that she would lose out only when all other criteria were equal—the fact that she ruined her liver would be merely a tiebreaker.[11] But then how should the degree of moral weight be determined? By how voluntary Jane's conduct was (as Glannon seems to suggest)?[12] Now, it is no easy task to determine whether conduct is voluntary or involuntary, and it is surely *much* harder (is it even really possible?) to determine the degree of voluntariness. So to begin with, there is important unclarity about the Principle's practical consequences.

A different minor problem concerns moral luck. The underlying intuition in favor of penalizing Jane is that her disease is due to her voluntary conduct while Jack's is due to his bad luck. The thought is that it is unfair for Jack to die due to bad luck but not unfair for Jane to die due to voluntary, health-risky conduct. Surrounding this thought are some puzzles familiar to philosophers. For instance, imagine Jill, who drank as much as Jane

but whose liver is unaffected by her drinking. However, through no fault of her own and apart from her drinking, Jill contracts liver disease and now needs a new liver. Jill's conduct was as risky as Jane's, but most people would not penalize Jill by moving her lower on the transplant list. Yet if we don't think people should be penalized just for having bad luck, then why should Jane, who had the bad luck not to have a strong liver like Jill's, be penalized for doing exactly what Jill did? If the idea is to minimize the effect of bad luck on Jack, then why is it fair *not* to minimize the effect of bad luck in the comparison of Jane and Jill? But as I say, most people would feel uneasy about penalizing Jill for conduct that did not ruin her liver.[13]

Yet another worry concerns the value of reform. Is Jane a recovering alcoholic? For our purposes, the question is relevant only if outcomes with nonrecovering alcoholics are poor enough that there is a good medical reason to put nonrecovering alcoholics lower down on the transplant list. If that is in fact the case, then Jane should be assumed to be a former alcoholic who is now in recovery. If there is no medical outcome issue, then the question of whether she is in recovery can be left open. The point is to keep our focus on the moral question, not the medical one. Still, the issue of recovery might be thought to have some moral resonance.

Consider Kate, who is a recovering alcoholic. Recovery presumably involves taking responsibility for one's past conduct. But another part of what recovery involves is to see oneself, and to be seen by others, as a new person, as having had a change of heart. Precisely how to calibrate sanctions for the past conduct of the now reformed person is a vexed question in the theory of punishment. It strikes me as more vexing when, as here, Kate's prior conduct harmed no one but herself. From

---

[11] Moss and Siegler simply say that Jane should be given a "lower priority." See Moss and Siegler, "Should Alcoholics Compete Equally for Liver Transplantation?" 1298.

[12] See Glannon, "Responsibility, Alcoholism, and Liver Transplantation," 43, where he says that alcoholics' control of their conduct makes them "either more or less responsible for their condition and in turn determines the strength of their claims to receive treatment."

[13] And of course there are moral luck cases in which alcoholism is only the *indirect* cause of organ damage. Susan repeatedly drives drunk and as a result has an accident in which she suffers liver damage. Should she be penalized with respect to her place on the transplant list? And what about Frank who also drives drunk, never has an accident, but simply contracts liver disease? Should he be penalized? I thank John Lantos for pointing out this class of cases.

the standpoint of her claim on the supply of available livers, Kate's recovery seems morally relevant.

Death Is Different

The above considerations are not trivial. Still, the most important worry about the Principle is something else, namely, proportionality—the "death is different" problem. So we return to Jane.

Jane has brought her liver disease on herself. As Elizabeth Anderson has pointed out, however, we do not necessarily abandon those who have brought their ills on themselves.[14] Suppose Paul is starving to death in the street. He is in this condition because he made foolish investments and refused several job offers. My car is filled with bread, mine to disburse as I wish. Clearly, I should give Paul bread. Clearly, I have an obligation to do so.

The Principle holds that the reason to put Jane lower on the transplant list, and so perhaps to deny her an opportunity for a longer life, is that she has brought her disease on herself. The question is why this is *sufficient* reason to dramatically increase Jane's chance of dying. The answer is not that Jane's conduct has been so intrinsically immoral as to deserve death. If that were the answer, then Jane would not receive a liver even if she were the only claimant—and no one has suggested *that*. It seems odd to impose a drastic consequence for not-intrinsically-immoral conduct. Dramatically increasing the likelihood that Jane will die does not seem a proportional response to her drinking.

It is true that life sometimes imposes draconian penalties for our missteps, even our minor ones. Suppose I fail to look as I cross the street and am hit by a car—killed or crippled. Even if the accident was due to my own carelessness, the consequence is wildly disproportionate. Still, one might say that's how the world works. Yet it needn't be how our public institutions work. It is important to remember that at issue are the decisions of institutions, specifically of institutions directly or indirectly supported by the public purse. The choice of which consequences

they impose is up to us. And that decision should not be hostage to the thought that life is unfair.[15]

What Kind of Justice?

But what of Jack, the person displaced if Jane goes on the list? Surely his need is relevant. Consider a transplant list of ten people in need of a liver. Assume that all are serious candidates in the sense both of desperately needing one *and* of having a good chance of long-term success with one. Suppose both Jane and Jack are candidates for the #1 slot and are essentially equal candidates, except that Jane's liver disease is due to her alcoholism. By whatever other criteria you choose, assume that each is a better candidate than Roy, the #3 candidate—but that Roy is still a *good* candidate for a transplant. If the sanction against Jane is merely the tiebreaker sanction, then Jack goes to #1 and Jane to #2. But had Jane not ruined her liver by her voluntary conduct, Roy would instead be at #2, and so on with the remainder of the list. And of course, if enough livers do not become available, this might mean death for Roy (or for someone else lower down the list). So now—to return to the question of the moral weight of Jane's drinking—the tiebreaker sanction might seem too weak. Shouldn't Jane be put *further* down the list? Shouldn't the fact that she ruined her own liver mean that she should go behind candidates who, measured by other criteria, are worse candidates than Jane but are still viable and, but for the fact that Jane ruined her liver, would be closer to getting a new liver and at least a chance for a longer life?

From one angle, penalizing Jane with the only penalty available seems grossly out of proportion to her conduct; from another, it seems unfair to others not to put them (or at least many of them) before Jane. We are pulled both ways.[16]

---

[14] See E.S. Anderson, "What Is the Point of Equality?" *Ethics* 109, no. 2 (1999): 295-300; and S. Scheffler, "What Is Egalitarianism?" *Philosophy and Public Affairs* 31, no 1 (2003): 18-19.

[15] This is one of John Rawls's themes. See J. Rawls, *A Theory of Justice* (Cambridge, Mass.: Harvard University Press, 1971), 102, where Rawls remarks on the tendency to rationalize unjust political arrangements on the ground that the natural distribution of talents is unjust. His point is that just institutions alter or at least mitigate natural injustice.

[16] That may be why someone like Veatch, whose analysis ought to entail a severe sanction for Jane, ends up in fact recommending only the most modest sanction, the

It is time to ask what kind of question the transplant question is. Let's go through some possibilities.

Is the issue one of *retributive* justice? Well, with retributive justice, an offender is punished—retribution is exacted—because the offender has done something bad to someone else.[17] But let's assume that so far, Jane's drinking has harmed only Jane and done nothing bad to anyone else.[18] This must be kept in mind when asking whether, in light of her voluntary conduct, an alcoholic is deserving of the potential death sentence that being put well down the transplant list might involve. The issue of harm to others is relevant, but the harm in question is the harm that would occur *if* we transplant Jane, not any harm that Jane has caused *prior to* a transplant.

Is the issue one of *compensatory* justice? Does it concern compensation for a harm done to someone? But again, Jane's drinking, taken by itself, has harmed no one but Jane.

Is the issue one of *distributive* justice? In a sense, it is. There is a scarce good to be distributed, and we are determining what considerations establish stronger or weaker claims. So we might be looking for a justifiable distributive policy to handle this case.

Consider, then, a distributive policy to be applied to future cases. Such a policy would penalize alcoholics, putting them lower on the transplant list. The thought is this: the knowledge that they will be put lower on the list will deter some people from excessive drinking and so from ruining their livers, thus reducing the overall demand for donor livers and so saving lives. One might be skeptical about the likely efficacy of such a policy, of course, but put that aside. In principle, such a policy might be defensible. Still, it would be unfair to apply it

to current alcoholics. The proposed policy is supposed to induce people in the future—once the policy is in effect—to drink less. But obviously it can have no incentive effect for Jane, who has already ruined her liver.[19]

Of course, many things that institutions do involve retroactive consequences. Perhaps I have invested in Acme Tool and Dye because I expected to receive a tax break for doing so. Before I can recoup my investment, the government repeals the tax break and my money is lost. Nevertheless, I have no basis for complaint. That is how public policy works.[20] By contrast, however, when the severe sanctions of the criminal law are at stake, we think things should be different. When the consequences are prison or execution, we think citizens should be put on clear, advance notice. There should be no retroactive penal sanction.

Here, the severity of the consequences to be imposed on Jane is relevant. Her situation does not involve the criminal law, but the impact of penalizing her with respect to the transplant list could turn out be as harsh as any consequence that the criminal law imposes. This is crucial. Although the distribution of a scarce resource—donor livers—makes the case seem to be one of distributive justice, the imposition of a severe sanction for the agent's conduct turns the institutional response into something analogous to the treatment of a criminal. Despite the fact that Jane has done nothing intrinsically immoral, the institutional decision is functionally equivalent to an instance of punishment. And if that is the case, then fairness requires adequate notice to Jane.

I want to belabor this point. If the institutionally mandated consequences to Jane were minor, the issue might be different. What would in effect count as a

---

tiebreaker. See Veatch, *Transplantation Ethics*, 320-21.

[17] Or at the very least the offender has taken steps toward doing something bad to someone else.

[18] This is of course an idealization. Most serious drinking leads to harm of some kind to the drinker, her family, and so forth. However, as J.S. Mill noted, these are not harms directly from drinking (see J.S. Mill, *On Liberty* Indianapolis, Ind.: Hackett Publishing, 1978], chapter 5). My point is that Jane's drinking directly harms nobody but herself.

[19] Note, incidentally, that the ultimate justification for the proposed policy need not be consequentialist. It might be chosen behind Rawls's veil of ignorance, or it might be chosen for its consequentialist benefits. Either way, however, it seems unfair to impose it on Jane.

[20] Sometimes a new law grandfathers in those who have relied on the earlier law. But this is done precisely to mitigate what is thought to be an unfair hardship for those suddenly subject to new rules. And if some financial losses are thought to be an unfair hardship, then clearly a dramatic increase in the likelihood of near term death is unfair.

retroactive penalty might be permissible. But when, as here, the institutionally imposed consequences are very grave, the case seems sufficiently analogous to punishment that considerations relevant to fairness in punishing need to be brought to bear.

Now, some readers may balk at the term "punishment." One doesn't want to see medical institutions in a punitive role. And the analogy is admittedly imperfect. Most importantly, and in contrast to the criminal law, there is no thought of sanctioning Jane as an end in itself.[21] If there are enough livers for all, Jane gets one. On the other hand, we must acknowledge the gravity of what might be done to Jane via the procedures of a publicly funded medical institution. If, in purely medical terms, Jane is no worse a candidate than Jack, but she is to go lower down the transplant list due to her past voluntary conduct, then we are in fact judging that her conduct has been sufficiently morally problematic to warrant imposing a grave, possibly fatal consequence on her. This sort of institutional action should surely trigger at least some of the usual safeguards surrounding punishment. Adequate notice is the most obvious one.

Conceding this point, we might decide to make the proposed policy applicable only to future cases. We could make it purely prospective. Moreover, suppose we promulgate it widely, educating children in schools, buying television ads, putting signs in every bar and labels on every bottle. Imagine that in five or ten years an alcoholic comes to us with a ruined liver. Would it *then* be appropriate to put her further down the transplant list?

Perhaps—on the premise that our new policy has an adequate justification. As noted, one justification might be that given such a policy, some people will drink less and not ruin their livers, and so, on balance, there will be a smaller gap between the supply and demand for livers.

However, there is also another relevant consideration. Maybe Jane is simply less *deserving* of that last available liver than Jack. After all, she has brought her disease on herself. Quite apart from other issues, one might think that makes a moral difference.

In fact, it does make a moral difference, but only in a particular context. Suppose livers were plentiful and cheap (perhaps a well-functioning artificial liver has been invented). In that context, helping Jane would hurt no one. No issue of comparative desert would arise. But that is not our context. In our world, helping Jane often means hurting Jack. And that prompts the thought that Jane is less deserving.

Yet even here, a condition must be met before this thought can be justified, and that condition goes beyond the Principle's focus on the fact that Jane's conduct has been voluntary. *Jane must also have known or be culpable for not knowing certain things*—namely, that if she destroys her liver, she will need a transplant, that donor livers are scarce, and that providing her with a liver will deny one to someone else, and so make that person's death more likely.

Imagine case 1, in which Jane is nonculpably ignorant of the potential consequences of her drinking for others such as Jack. She knows the likely impact of her drinking on herself, but she does not know and is not culpable for not knowing about transplant lists and organ shortages. In case 1, Jane is nonculpably ignorant of the fact that her conduct could have negative consequences for anyone but herself. From her perspective, her conduct is entirely self-regarding. In case 1, Jane does not knowingly create a situation in which saving her life might mean death for Jack. Here, Jane neither intends to harm anyone nor displays negligence with respect to her conduct's impact on others. On the stipulated premise, her conduct is not morally suspect, and so she is not morally deserving of what, by any standard, counts as severe punishment.

By contrast, in case 2, Jane is aware of the likely consequences for others of her drinking. She knows that what she does might create a state of affairs in which she will live only if someone else does not. In case 2, her readiness to drink away her liver can plausibly be seen as expressing a callous disregard for the wellbeing of whoever will *not* receive a liver should she receive one. Knowingly to drink away one's liver and then to ask for

---

[21] See Feinberg: "It is an essential and intended element of punishment, however, that the victim be made to suffer." J. Feinberg, *Doing and Deserving* (Princeton, N.J.: Princeton University Press, 1970), 67. That is not the situation with case 2 Jane.

a transplant is to act with reckless disregard for the consequences of your conduct for another person's life chances. To do *that* is in fact highly immoral.[22]

The basis for thinking Jane less deserving of a liver, then, is not merely that she is responsible for her voluntary conduct. That is a necessary but not a sufficient condition. When information has been adequately distributed, Jane's voluntary conduct becomes a form of callous disregard for and indifference to others' dire needs. The harm of her conduct is negligently to make herself a competitor for a scarce, lifesaving resource. Under those circumstances, it is appropriate for a publicly funded institution to judge that Jane is morally less deserving than Jack of receiving that last liver.[23] This is where the widespread belief from which we started does touch defensible ground.

The situation might be thought similar to other forms of negligence. If I drive recklessly but no one is hurt and I am not caught, I have acted immorally but I am lucky and go unsanctioned. If Jane negligently drinks away her liver but an available donor liver has no other claimant, then Jane, too, has acted immorally but is lucky and goes unsanctioned. The thought behind imposing the sanction when we must choose between Jack and case 2 Jane is that she, not he, should be the person vulnerable to luck.[24]

––––––––––––––

[22] I suspect that this claim could be justified in many ways, but my hope is that the basic thought will be common ground for diverse moral views. For instance, the maxim to engage in such conduct could surely not be universalized (Kant); a rule permitting such conduct could be reasonably rejected, say, by Jack (Scanlon's contractualism); and engaging in such conduct is almost certainly utility-reducing.

[23] There is also a third possibility. Suppose Jane knows of liver shortages and so on, but as yet there is no promulgated rule announcing the consequences for bringing one's liver disease on oneself. In this case, Jane is morally guilty, but whether she should be institutionally sanctioned is not clear. I would say that in such a case, moral guilt is both a necessary and a sufficient condition for a severe sanction, but different views about this seem likely.

[24] This may also explain why it is fair to sanction a case 2 Jane but not a case 2 Jill. Their conduct has been equally immoral and places them equally at the mercy of luck. Case 2 Jill simply has better luck than case 2 Jane. I thank Walter Glannon for pressing this point and urging that here might be a case in

The Conditions of Sanction

So there are circumstances under which it is proper to impose a severe sanction on Jane—but those circumstances must obtain. Jane must know (or ought to know) basic facts about liver scarcity and transplant lists. And it may be a long time before such knowledge is sufficiently widespread that this condition is satisfied, at least for a first transplant. This is the key point. Case 2 Jane's conduct is, morally speaking, highly suspect— but we can say this *only* of case 2 Jane. And hers is, at least at the moment, a rare condition.

For now, the practical outcome of my analysis is something like this: Anyone who is currently a candidate for a first liver transplant due to her own health-risky conduct probably did not know enough (nonculpably) soon enough about donor lists and so forth to count as having negligently disregarded her conduct's consequences for others. But I assume that the process of receiving a transplant is educative, and, in any event, it could be made educative. We could then assume that thereafter the agent knew enough or ought to have known enough. Thus if she comes to need a second transplant because of subsequent voluntary, health-risky conduct, it would be proper to sanction her by putting her lower, perhaps much lower, on the transplant list. Indeed, I think that anyone who has received a transplant, regardless of the original cause of his liver disease, can be assumed thereafter to know enough that subsequent voluntary, health-risky conduct, perhaps including noncompliance with postoperative treatment, makes that person morally vulnerable.[25]

Many issues remain to be explored. For instance, how does the act/omission distinction apply here? That is, is there a morally significant difference between causing one's illness and not preventing it? Consider Allen, whose liver disease is due to a repeated failure to get an easily available and medically recommended hepatitis B shot. If he knew of transplant shortages and so

––––––––––––––

which leaving someone exposed to luck is morally proper.

[25] I thank Mary Simmerling for pointing out the need to make explicit these practical consequences of my analysis.

forth, is he as culpable as case 2 Jane, so that he should also be sanctioned on the transplant list?[26]

Moreover, on my analysis, there will be a question about the process for determining that the agent did or should have had the requisite knowledge. If the justification for a severe sanction bears on claims about what the agent knew or should have known, then there must be an adequate basis for those claims. Having already had a transplant is a useful proxy here. But in the longer term, some other standard for determining what the agent knew or should have known must be worked out.

I leave such issues for another day. My claim here is that there are circumstances under which we may justifiably make it significantly less likely that an agent will obtain a scarce, lifesaving resource—namely, if the agent has engaged in conduct that *deliberately* or *negligently* puts her in competition for the resource in question with others who have *not* engaged in conduct that deliberately or negligently puts them in competition for the resource in question. So there could come a time when we could rightly say that due to their voluntary, health-risky conduct, some agents are less deserving than others of receiving a scarce, lifesaving resource. However, except in rare cases, that time is not now.

Acknowledgment

I am very grateful to Walter Glannon, John Lantos, Mark Siegler, and Mary Simmerling for their helpful comments on earlier drafts of this article.

Hastings Center Report 37, no. 1 (January–February 2007): 41–47.
Reprinted with permission by publisher

---

[26] I thank John Lantos for bringing up this case.

Lesson 3

Rolling the Dice:
Risky and Experimental Treatments

Introduction

Are you a gambler? Do you like to play the odds? Are you willing to risk everything for the chance at a big win?

Or do you prefer to play it safe, passing up the chance to live life's lottery for the comfort of avoiding unexpected losses?

When life asks you to place your bets on the unknown, how will you play the game? And does Judaism have advice for those making decisions under conditions of uncertainty? What guidelines can it offer for those considering experimental and risky treatment?

Risky Treatments

Case Study I

Tom is a fifty-year-old heavy drinker and smoker. He is told that he has serious heart disease that will lead to his death in the near future. A quadruple bypass, together with a dramatic change in lifestyle, will alleviate his illness and allow him many more years of life. Tom is aware that all such surgeries are risky, but his case is complex. Tom's underlying health issues mean that the chances of success are not great. His doctors sensitively inform him that his chances for surviving the surgery are not higher than the chances for failure. Tom wants the surgery. He wants a chance at living long enough to see his grandchildren grow up. His wife, however, prefers he let nature take its course. Her sister went in for surgery for heart problems just last year and died on the operating table.

Questions for Discussion

1. What are the arguments for and against the operation?

2. In light of what we have learned so far, do you think Jewish law would a) prohibit, b) permit, or c) require Tom to undergo the operation? Explain your reasoning.

Chaé Olam (eternal life)

Chaé Shaa (hourly life)
short
or limited

The Value of a Single Moment

Text **1a**

מי שנפלה עליו מפולת ספק הוא שם ספק אינו שם מפקחין עליו, מצאוהו חי אף על פי שנתרוצץ ואי אפשר שיבריא מפקחין עליו ומוציאין אותו לחיי אותה שעה.

רמב״ם הלכות שבת ב,יח

If a building collapsed [on Shabbat] and there is a doubt whether or not a person is buried underneath, we must clear [the rubble and attempt a rescue, despite the prohibition of doing such work on the Shabbat]. If a person was discovered to be alive, even if crushed [by the fallen debris] to the extent of being fatally wounded, we still continue to clear [the rubble] to allow the victim to live a short while longer.

Maimonides, *Mishneh Torah*, Laws of Shabbat 2:18

Rabbi Moshe ben Maimon (1135–1204). Better known as Maimonides or by the acronym Rambam; born in Córdoba, Spain. After the conquest of Córdoba by the Almohads, he fled Spain and eventually settled in Cairo, Egypt. There, he became the leader of the Jewish community and served as court physician to the vizier of Egypt. His rulings on Jewish law are considered integral to the formation of halachic consensus. He is most noted for authoring the *Mishneh Torah*, an encyclopedic arrangement of Jewish law, and for his philosophical work, *Guide for the Perplexed*.

Text **1b**

אף על פי שנתברר שאי אפשר לו לחיות אפילו שעה אחת, שבאותה שעה ישוב בלבו ויתודה.

בית הבחירה, יומא פה,א

Even if it is clear that he will not survive for more than a short amount of time, for during that time, he will be able to mentally repent and confess his wrongdoings.

Rabbi Menachem Me'iri, *Beit Habechirah*, Yoma 85a

Rabbi Menachem Me'iri (1249–1310). Born in Provence, France. His monumental work, *Beit Habechirah*, is a digest summarizing the discussions of the Talmud as well as the comments of the major subsequent rabbis in a lucid style. Despite its stature, the work was largely unknown for many generations, and thus was excluded from general summaries of rabbinic law until recently.

Text **1c**

יפה שעה אחת בתשובה ומעשים טובים בעולם הזה מכל חיי העולם הבא.

משנה, אבות ד,יז

A single moment of repentance and good deeds in this world is better than all of the world to come.

Mishnah, Avot 4:17

Text **1d**

אמנם באמת נראה דכל זה הוא לטעמא בעלמא אבל לדינא לא תלוי כלל במצות

דאין הטעם דדחינן מצוה אחת בשביל הרבה מצות

אלא דחינן כל המצות בשביל חיים של ישראל . . . דאחיים של אדם קפיד רחמנא.

ביאור הלכה שכט

Rabbi Yisrael Meir Hakohen (1839–1933). Prolific author on topics of Halachah and head of the illustrious yeshivah in Radin. His first work was *Chafets Chayim*, a comprehensive digest of laws pertaining to prohibited speech; Rabbi Yisrael Meir is hence often called "the Chafets Chayim." His magnum opus, on which he worked for 28 years, is *Mishnah Berurah*, a concise commentary of the first section of the Shulchan Aruch. He also authored *Bi'ur Halachah* on the Shulchan Aruch.

However, it appears that the above reasoning is only an additional rationale. The actual law [regarding the obligation to violate the Shabbat in order to save another] does not depend on [the performance of] *mitzvot*. It is not that we suspend one mitzvah for the sake of many *mitzvot*; rather we suspend all the *mitzvot* for the sake of life . . . The Torah is particular about the life of a human [in and of itself].

Rabbi Yisrael Meir Hakohen, *Bi'ur Halachah* 329

Betting on Life

Text 2a

מרופא מומחה על חולה אחד שחלה את חליו שקרוב למות בו וכל הרופאים אומדין
שודאי ימות תוך יום או יומים אך שאומדין שיש עוד רפואה אחת שאפשר שיתרפא
מחוליו וגם אפשר להיפך שאם יקח רפואה זו אם אינו תצליח חס ושלום ימות מיד תוך
שעה או שתים אי מותר לעשות רפואה זו . . .
תשובה: הואיל שדין זה הוא דיני נפשות ממש וצריך להיות מתון מאוד בשאלה כזו
מש״ס ופוסקים בשבע חקירות ובדיקות כי כל המאבד נפש אחת מישראל וכו׳ וכן
להיפך המקיים נפש אחת כאלו קיים קיים עולם מלא.

שבות יעקב ג,עה

The question is from an expert doctor regarding a patient who is terminally ill. The prognosis of all the doctors is that he will die within the next couple of days. However, they suggest that there is a medicine that might cure him but might cause him to die within a couple of hours of taking it. Is it permitted to administer the medicine? . . .

Answer: since this is a matter of life and death, one needs to consider the question with great care, thoroughly reviewing the relevant passages in the Talmud and halachic works, for "if someone kills a single person it is as if [he has destroyed an entire world] and conversely, if someone saves a single person, it is as if [he has] upheld an entire world."

Rabbi Ya'akov Reischer, *Shevut Ya'akov* 3:75

Rabbi Ya'akov ben Yosef Reischer (ca. 1670–1733). Renowned rabbi, halachic authority, and author. He served on rabbinical courts in Prague, Ansbach, Worms, and Metz. He was accepted by contemporary rabbis as the ultimate authority on halachic issues, and problems were addressed to him from all over the Diaspora and Israel. His most famous works are *Chok Ya'akov*, an exposition on the section of the Shulchan Aruch pertaining to the laws of Passover, and his responsa *Shevut Ya'akov*.

Text 2b

ולכאורה היה נראה דשב ואל תעשה עדיף כי חיישינן לחיי שעה
אפילו מי שכבר הוא גוסס ממש.

שבות יעקב ג,עה

It would seem [that we should follow the principle] "it is preferable to sit and do nothing" because of the concern for *chayei sha'ah* even if the [ill person] is already a *goses* (in the final throes of life).

Rabbi Ya'akov Reischer, *Shevut Ya'akov* 3:75

Text 3a

אמר רבי יוחנן ספק חי ספק מת אין מתרפאין מהן ודאי מת מתרפאין מהן.
האיכא חיי שעה לחיי שעה לא חיישינן.

תלמוד בבלי, עבודה זרה כז,ב

Rabbi Yochanan said, "If [one is so sick that] it is doubtful whether he will live or die [and the only physician available is a heathen whose animosity to Jews leads us to suspect that he might deliberately kill the patient], he should not turn to him for treatment. But if [without medical help] the patient will surely die, then he may turn to him for treatment."

[The Talmud asks:] but what of the *chayei sha'ah* [that is being put in jeopardy]?

[The Talmud answers:] *chayei sha'ah* can be disregarded.

Talmud, Avodah Zarah 27b

Learning **Activity 1**

State of the Patient	Nature of the Doctor	May the Patient Visit the Doctor?
Perhaps patient will die if untreated	Perhaps doctor will kill the patient	
Patient will surely die if untreated	Perhaps doctor will kill the patient	

Text **3b**

ומנא תימרא דלחיי שעה לא חיישינן.

תלמוד בבלי, עבודה זרה כז,ב

n what basis do you say that one can disregard *chayei sha'ah?*

Talmud, Avodah Zarah 27b

Text 3c

וְאַרְבָּעָה אֲנָשִׁים הָיוּ מְצֹרָעִים פֶּתַח הַשָּׁעַר וַיֹּאמְרוּ אִישׁ אֶל רֵעֵהוּ מָה אֲנַחְנוּ יֹשְׁבִים פֹּה עַד מָתְנוּ.
אִם אָמַרְנוּ נָבוֹא הָעִיר וְהָרָעָב בָּעִיר וָמַתְנוּ שָׁם וְאִם יָשַׁבְנוּ פֹה וָמָתְנוּ.
וְעַתָּה לְכוּ וְנִפְּלָה אֶל מַחֲנֵה אֲרָם אִם יְחַיֻּנוּ נִחְיֶה וְאִם יְמִיתֻנוּ וָמָתְנוּ.
מלכים ב, ז,ג-ד

There were four men, stricken with *tsara'at* at the entrance of the gate. They said to one another, "Why are we sitting here until we die? If we decide to enter the city, we will die there due to the famine in the city, and if we stay here, we will [also] die. So now, let us go and let us defect to the Aramean camp. If they spare us we will live, and if they kill us we will die."

II Kings 7:3–4

Question for Discussion

In what way is this similar to the case of the dangerous physician?

Text 4

ברם אם אפשר שעל ידי רפואה זו שנותן לו יתרפא לגמרי מחליו ודאי לא חיישינן לחיי

שעה וראיה ברורה לחילוק זה מסוגיא דש״ס . . . אם כן גם כן בנדון זה כיון שודאי ימות

מניחין הודאי ותופסין הספק אולי יתרפא.

ומכל מקום אין לעשות הרופא כפשוטו כן רק צריך להיות מתון מאוד בדבר

לפקח עם רופאין מומחין שבעיר על פי רוב דיעות . . . והסכמת החכם שבעיר.

שבות יעקב ג,עה

I f it is possible that this treatment will completely cure him from his illness, then we certainly disregard *chayei sha'ah*. This is clearly proven by the aforementioned case in the Talmud. . . . In our case too, since he will certainly die [if the physician does not try the medication], we ignore the certainty [of a couple of days of life] and seize the chance that he will be fully healed.

However, the physician should not take this decision lightly; he must weigh the situation carefully in consultation with the other expert physicians in his town, accepting the majority opinion . . . and procure the agreement of the halachic authority of the town.

Rabbi Ya'akov Reischer, *Shevut Ya'akov* 3:75

Defining the Parameters
How Do We Define *Chayei Sha'ah*?

Text 5a

ואף על פי שאין בידינו ראיות לקצוב בבירור כמה יארך הזמן לצאת מכלל חיי שעה
לחיי עולם, ומסתברא מילתא שכל שאנו יודעים שעל ידי סבה זו, של הסכנה שהחלה
פעולתה, תבוא המיתה, בין אם תקדים ובין אם תאחר הכל בכלל חיי שעה.

משפט כהן קמד,ג

Rabbi Avraham Yitschak Hakohen Kook (1864–1935). Main ideologue of the Religious Zionist movement, and one of the renowned Torah scholars of the 20th century. Born in Griva, Latvia, he emigrated to Israel in 1904. In 1917, he was appointed rabbi of Jerusalem, and in 1921, he became the first Ashkenazic chief rabbi of pre-state Israel. His influence and outreach created greater respect for Torah and Jewish law in the secular Zionist agricultural settlements.

Despite the fact that the boundary marking the transition from *chayei sha'ah* to long-term life expectancy is not clearly delineated, it is logical to assume that as long as we know that the illness is already terminal, regardless of how much time will pass until death arrives, it is considered *chayei sha'ah*.

Rabbi Avraham Yitschak Hakohen Kook, *Mishpat Kohen* 144:3

Text 5b

לא נתפרש כמה הוא השיעור של חיי שעה ואין לומר דאם סופו למות תוך שנה או
שנתיים נמי יהא נחשב חיי שעה דאם כן איך משכחת לה חיי עולם הרי כל אדם
למות ומה לי שנה אחת או שתים או מאה סוף סוף לעולם לא יחיה,
ואם כן יהיה נחשב הכל חיי שעה.
ודוחק לומר דדוקא אם ימות מאותו חולי נחשב חיי שעה אבל אם ימות מחולי אחר
לא נחשב חיי שעה דזה אינו דמה לי מחולי זה או חולי אחר . . .
דמהא דקיימא לן דטריפה אינה חיה י״ב חודש מוכח דכל שאינו יכול לחיות מחמת
חולי זה י״ב חודש וסופו למות מחולי זה בתוך י״ב חודש לא נחשב חייו רק חיי שעה
אבל אם עומד למות רק לאחר י״ב חודש לא נחשב חיי שעה רק חיי עולם.

דרכי תשובה, יורה דעה קצה,ו

I t does not state clearly the definition of *chayei sha'ah*. It is clear that life expectancy of one to two years is not considered *chayei sha'ah* because if so, what is *chayei olam*? Ultimately everyone is mortal, and what difference is there between one year or two years or one hundred years, since no one can live forever? Are we to categorize all life as *chayei sha'ah*?

Nor does it appear correct to say that *chayei sha'ah* only refers to a situation in which the person will die from the specific illness [that he is seeking a cure from] and not from other ailments, for what difference should it make what illness will cause his death? . . .

[Rather it would appear that] just as a *tereifah* is defined as an ill person that will not live more than twelve months, so too anyone whose illness will not let him live for more than twelve months is considered to be in the category of *chayei sha'ah*. However, if the illness will cause death after twelve months, this is not *chayei sha'ah* but *chayei olam*.

Rabbi Shlomoh Kluger, cited by *Darchei Teshuvah, Yoreh De'ah* 195:6

Rabbi Shlomoh Kluger (1785–1869). Known as "the Preacher of Brody." He received his early education from his father who died during his boyhood, and soon became known as a prodigy. For a time he was a shopkeeper, but in 1820, he assumed the rabbinate of Brody, where he served for almost 50 years. A prolific writer, he wrote hundreds of responsa, some of which appear in *Ha'elef Lecha Shlomoh*, and is said to have written 375 books, the numerical equivalent of his name Shlomoh, though most of these were never published.

How Much Risk Is Acceptable?

Text 6a

Rabbi Eliezer Yehudah Waldenberg (1915–2006). Leading rabbi and judge on the Supreme Rabbinical Court in Jerusalem; considered an eminent authority on Jewish medical ethics and Jewish law. He published his halachic responsa, *Tsits Eliezer,* which is viewed as one of the great achievements of halachic scholarship of the 20th century. He served as rabbi for the Shaare Zedek Medical Center in Jerusalem.

אולם כל זה הוא כשעל כל פנים הסיכויים לחיים או למות על ידי ביצוע ניתוח כזה שוים הם, אבל לא בהיכא שהתוצאה מהניתוח הוא שימות על פי רוב.

ציץ אליעזר י, כה,ה

However, this [permission to operate] is only if the chances of life and death as a result of the surgery are equal, but not if in the majority of cases, the patient will die as a result of the operation.

Rabbi Eliezer Waldenburg, *Tsits Eliezer,* vol. 10, 25:5

Text 6b

Rabbi Chaim Ozer Grodzinski (1863–1940). Rabbi and leader of Lithuanian Jewry in the years prior to the Holocaust. In his youth, he studied at the famed yeshivah in Volozhin and was known for his superb memory. In 1887, at the young age of twenty-five, he was appointed judge of the famed rabbinical court of Vilna and was very active in the affairs of the community. He was one of the founders of the political party Agudat Yisrael and a pillar of the movement throughout his lifetime. His work *Achiezer* is a collection of his responsa.

דלחיי שעה לא חיישינן היכא דאפשר שיתרפא אף באופן רחוק כל שנתיאשו מרפואתו.

אחיעזר, יורה דעה טז,ו

In a situation when we have otherwise given up hope, we disregard *chayei sha'ah* even for a remote possibility that the patient will be healed.

Rabbi Chaim Ozer Grodzinski, *Achiezer, Yoreh De'ah* 16:6

How Do We Define a Successful Treatment?

Text 7

וחיים הרגילים הוא שיהיו חיים בלא החולי שמצד הטבע יכול לחיות כחיי סתם אדם,
לא מבעיא אם יתרפא לגמרי כבריא ממש . . . אלא אפילו כפי שיותר מצוי דאחר
ניתוח הוא נחלש וצריך לשמירת הרבה דברים באכילה ושתיה ולמעט בעבודה והרבה
פעמים גם ליקח מיני סמים לשמור מצבו שלא יחלה עוד הפעם, שגם כן פשוט שהוא
כחיי סתם אדם שאיכא בהם גם אנשים חלושים שצריכים לשמירה מדברים כאלו
ואפשר להם שיחיו הרבה שנים כאנשים הבריאים וגם עוד יותר . . . אך אם הניתוח
יועיל רק שאפשר שימשך במצב כזה זמן גדול תחת הזמן מועט ויש ספק שהניתוח ימיתהו
תיכף, מכיון שאף אם יעלה הניתוח יפה יהיה עלול בכל יום מצד המחלה למות אף שיעשה
אפשריות לימשך במצב סכנה כזה הרבה זמן מסתבר לעניות דעתי שאין להתיר.
אגרות משה, יורה דעה ג,לו

Regular life is life without the illness, that in the natural course of events, will allow one to live like a normal person. It goes without saying that [this includes] a case in which the patient is expected to be totally healed . . . but [even includes] the more common situation in which the patient is weak after surgery and needs to attend carefully to many things, such as a proper diet, avoiding excessive exertion, and often, taking medicine in order to avoid a relapse. This too is obviously like the life of a normal person, since there are many weak people who need to be careful regarding these things and it is possible for them to live for many years, just as long as healthy people and sometimes even longer . . .

Rabbi Moshe Feinstein (1895–1986). Rabbi and leading halachic authority of the 20th century. Born near Minsk, Belarus; became rabbi of Luban in 1921; immigrated to the U.S. in 1937 and became the dean of Metivta Tiferet Yerushalayim in New York. Rabbi Feinstein became the leading halachic authority of his time and his rulings are always considered. His halachic decisions have been published in a multi-volume collection titled *Igrot Moshe*. He also published works on the Talmud and was known for his fine character traits.

If, however, the surgery will only help in that the patient
will be able to continue in this ill state for a long period
of time instead of a short amount of time, and there is
also the possibility that the surgery can cause immediate death, then, since even if the surgery were to be successful, the patient would be prone to die from this illness at any time, even though the surgery will create the
possibility for him to go on in this dangerous state for
a long time, it is likely, in my humble opinion, that one
should not permit the surgery.

Rabbi Moshe Feinstein, *Igrot Moshe, Yoreh De'ah* 3:36

Resolution of Case Study I

Learning Activity 2

**Let us look at the case study again. The case is followed by some
questions. Which of them would be relevant to a rabbi trying to ren-
der a halachic decision in this case? Write "R" next to those that are
relevant and "I" next to those that are irrelevant. Check your answers with a friend, explaining your reasoning for cases about which
the two of you disagree.**

**Tom is a fifty-year-old heavy drinker and smoker. He is told
that he has serious heart disease that will lead to his death
in the near future. A quadruple bypass together with a dramatic change in lifestyle will alleviate his illness and allow
him many more years of life. Tom is aware that all such surgeries are risky, but his case is complex. Tom's underlying health
issues mean that the chances of success are not great. His
doctors sensitively inform him that his chances for surviving**

the surgery are not higher than the chances for failure. Tom wants the surgery. He wants a chance at living long enough to see his grandchildren grow up. His wife, however, prefers he let nature take its course. Her sister went in for surgery for heart problems just last year and died on the operating table.

1. How heavily does Tom drink?

2. Is his illness terminal?

3. How soon is he expected to die if no treatment is done?

4. Is there any hope that he can be cured without the need for making dietary changes?

5. If the surgery is successful, will his health condition stabilize so that his risk of dying of heart disease is substantially reduced?

6. Do the experts in the field concur with the opinion of his doctors?

7. What is the best estimate of the chances for success given his underlying condition?

8. Have the doctors been sufficiently sensitive in their manner of informing him of the risks of failure?

9. Does Tom's wife agree with his decision?

10. Is Tom willing to undertake the risk of the surgery?

Experimental Treatment

Case Study II

Baby Z had a one in a million chance of developing a rare metabolic disorder called molybdenum cofactor deficiency and zero chance of avoiding the inevitable death sentence that comes with it.

The Australian girl had a seemingly normal birth in May 2008 but, within hours, she began having multiple seizures—as many as ten an hour—as sulfite build-up began to poison her brain.

Molybdenum, like other organic metals, is essential for the human body. Its cofactor is a small, complicated molecule that acts as a carrier to help the metal interact with proteins and enzymes so they can function properly.

When the cofactor is missing, toxic sulfite builds and begins to cause degeneration of neurons in the brain and eventually death.

"This was the first time I ever saw this," said Dr. Alex Veldman, the Monash pediatrician and neonatologist who headed up Baby Z's treatment.

Veldman delivered the news that Baby Z had a fatal, untreatable disease but the parents refused to give up.

Baby Z's family enlisted the help of a friend who was a biochemist at Monash University, one of the most research-intensive institutions in Australia, and the search for a cure began.

On May 26, they found a 2005 research paper by Schwarz, a former plant biologist who is now a researcher-professor at the University of Cologne in Germany.

Molybdenum cofactor is found widely throughout nature, and Schwarz was able to discover the precurser molecule in E. coli bacteria, or "gut flora," that was chemically identical to that in humans. Using mice as human models, he injected the animals with the cofactor and, instead of dying of the disorder in eight days, they lived a hundred days.

Schwarz kept a large stock, thinking there might one day be a human application. That day came when Veldman called about Baby Z, whose sulfite levels were growing daily.

"We were all very skeptical of the animal model because it had never been tried in humans," he said. "But the baby would have certainly died."

Excited that his drug might save a child, Schwarz packed his glass tubes in dry ice and sent it on a plane to Australia.

Doctors had no idea of the proper dosages or side effects. "We had a million questions," Veldman said, but he didn't want to let the chance to cure Baby Z slip away.

Still, they knew they needed legal back up for what seemed a "free-style act."

With the clock ticking, doctors approached the hospital ethics board and a family court for approval to use the experimental treatment.

Adapted from Susan Donaldson James, *"Baby Z Cured of Rare Disease in Three Days,"* November 9, 2009, ABCnews.go.com

Learning Activity 3

You are a pediatric nurse in the neonatal unit where Baby Z is rapidly approaching death. Your supervisor passes you on her way to a meeting to review the ethics of the case. "Aren't you taking that Medicine and Morals course?" she asks. "Why don't you join us and present the board with a three minute presentation on what Jewish law would say about this case—Should the parent be allowed to use this treatment on her child or not?"

Based on what we have learned so far, decide whether you want to argue for or against this treatment. In preparing your presentation, consider how this case is the same or different from the other cases we have studied.

Discussion and Resolution of Case Study II

Text 8

מי שחולה במחלה קשה אשר אין הרופא רואה סיכוי להצילו בתרופות רגילות
הרי זה דומה לנתוח

דאף שיש ספק שאם לא יצליח ימות מיד אפילו הכי מותר והכא נמי גם כאן שפיר
רשאי להשתמש בתרופה מסופקת.

מנחת שלמה ב, פב,יב

I f one is seriously ill, and the physicians see no hope of saving the patient using standard drugs, the case is similar to a case of surgery which is permitted, although there is the possibility that if it does not succeed, the patient will die immediately. Similarly, it is permitted to use a doubtful drug in this case.

Rabbi Shlomoh Zalman Auerbach, *Minchat Shlomoh*, vol. 2, 82:12

Rabbi Shlomoh Zalman Auerbach (1910–1995). Born in Jerusalem, Israel; served as the dean of Yeshivah Kol Torah. He is recognized as one of the prominent halachic authorities of the 20th century. Many of Rabbi Auerbach's decisions and works are related to issues of medical ethics and the halachic problems that arose with the introduction of modern technology.

Text 9

ובאם החולה הוא תינוק או אף גדול שאינו יודע להחליט רשאין אביו ואמו וכל
המשפחה להחליט, והרשות שיש להם משום דרוב חולים סומכין על דעת האב והאם
ואף על המשפחה כאחים ואחיות ובניהם שרוצים מה שיותר טוב להחולה ולבני ביתו.

אגרות משה, חושן משפט ב, עג,ה

I f the patient is a young child or an adult that does not know how to decide, then the father and mother and the whole family can decide [on the patient's behalf]. They have this authority since most

patients rely on their father, mother, and also the rest
of the family like brothers, sisters, and children, as they
want what is best for the patient and the patient's family.

Rabbi Moshe Feinstein, *Igrot Moshe, Choshen Mishpat*, vol. 2, 74:5

Text 10

**Rabbi Dr. Abraham S. Abraham
MD, FRCP.** Born in Jerusalem and
received his medical training in
England. Since 1989, Dr. Abraham
has been chief of internal medicine
at the Shaare Zedek Medical Center
in Jerusalem, and since 1990, a professor of medicine at the Hebrew
University Hadassah Medical School.
His most notable work, *Nishmat
Avraham*, printed in both Hebrew
and English, is an essential text
addressing medical-halachic issues
in all branches of medicine and
surgery.

הקטן נמצא במצב של חולה שיש בו סכנה. מותר גם לבצע טיפול שהוא ניסיוני ומסוכן
אם ודאי ימות ללא הטיפול ובטיפול יש סיכוי—אפילו מועט—להבריאו,
כי לחיי שעה לא חיישינן.

נשמת אברהם, יורה דעה כח,ב

If a child is in a life threatening situation, one may
try a risky experimental treatment if without the
treatment the child will definitely die and the
treatment offers even a small chance of recovery. For we
disregard *chayei sha'ah*.

Rabbi Dr. Abraham S. Abraham, *Nishmat Avraham,
Yoreh De'ah 28:2*

Text 11

The bioethics panel scrutinized the treatment for three hours and agreed to support it. And the hospital's legal department also weighed in and agreed. They also got the legal back up they needed from Australia's family court at 3:30 p.m. on June 6, and at 5:00 p.m., they began treatment.

The team proceeded cautiously, injecting ten percent of the dosage they had calculated and waiting thirty minutes between dosages.

"The first half hour the baby was good, sleeping and looking better," Veldman said.

Within two days, sulfite levels dropped from three hundred to eighty. On the fourth day, when Schwarz arrived to see his experiment in action, Baby Z was nearly normal.

"She was comatose before on feeding tubes, and now she was looking around and drinking a bottle," he said.

The seizures that had been reoccurring ten times an hour decreased to two or three a day.

Today, at eighteen months old, Baby Z is active and social, communicating with her parents, although she has some brain damage from the six weeks of sulfite poisoning.

"It's difficult to tell what her prognosis is in terms of development but she's making progress," he said.

"It was the most challenging and most traumatic time of our lives," Baby Z's mother said. "We are looking at her now and she is just an absolute miracle. She has defied everybody."

Adapted from Susan Donaldson James, *"Baby Z Cured of Rare Disease in Three Days,"* November 9, 2009, ABCnews.go.com

Key Points

1. *Chayei sha'ah* is vital both because of what a person can accomplish in a mere moment and because of the inherent value of every second of human life.

2. A patient who has short life expectancy may take on serious risk in the hope of a cure, provided all other conventional methods have failed.

3. The exact definition of short life expectancy and the amount of risk one is allowed to undergo is a matter of debate.

4. There is no obligation for patients to agree to risky treatment if it is not successful in most cases. Patients may opt instead to allow the illness to take its course.

5. There are halachic grounds to say that the permission to take risks applies as well to experimental medicine.

6. Parents can make decisions on behalf of children who are unable to give their own consent to a risky procedure.

7. We must support patients through their tough decisions regarding risks.

8. Visiting the sick is an important mitzvah and serves multiple functions.

9. There are numerous laws pertaining to the dying, ensuring that their last moments are peaceful and meaningful.

Additional Readings

Should Terminally Ill Patients Have the Right to Take Drugs That Pass Phase I Testing?

Emil J Freireich

Professor Special Medical Education Programs, University of Texas MD Anderson Cancer Center, 1515 Holcombe Boulevard, Houston, TX 77030, USA **efreirei@mdanderson.org**

Yes

Around half a million people will die from cancer related causes in the United States this year. In the US, as in much of the Western world, patients know their diagnosis and are often given a hopeless prognosis. For most, the option of participating in phase I and phase II clinical trials of new drugs that offer some promise helps them remain optimistic. Clearly, they should have the right to take drugs that have passed phase I testing.

The problem is that most cancer patients cannot participate in phase II trials because they are either ineligible or they are unable to fulfil the financial and social requirements for participating in such trials, such as staying in the centres conducting these trials, sometimes for many weeks or months. The problem is clearly not one of safety because these drugs have completed phase I clinical trials and there is sufficient information about them to justify a phase II trial to determine efficacy.

Phase II trials are designed to give the highest probability of a positive outcome. Thus, they have patient eligibility requirements which assure that only the healthiest patients at the earliest point in their disease are entered. These decisions are not based on any reasonable evidence that patients who are ineligible would not benefit, but are strictly designed to fulfil the regulatory requirements established by bodies such as the Federal Drug Administration (FDA) and the regulatory components of industry and academia that govern these clinical trials.[1,2]

Compassionate prescribing

In the modern electronic era, most of the patients with hopeless cancer diagnoses have access through the media and the internet to information about promising new drugs that are in phase II clinical trials. These patients would like very much to receive these drugs to offer them some hope, but for the reasons mentioned above are unable to participate in those trials. So why not offer these drugs to these patients on a compassionate basis?

The first reason given is usually the safety concerns. Without knowledge about how renal function, cardiac function, age, etc affect the action of the phase I drug, side effects might occur that could be harmful to the patient or, perhaps more importantly, the continued development of the drug. I think this objection is relatively minor since it simply states the benefit: risk ratio problem—that is, these patients are prepared to volunteer to expose themselves to increased risk because of their hopeless prognosis and because of the promise of the new drug.

The second objection is that it will interfere with the development of the drug. However, in the past, the FDA and the National Cancer Institute have allowed compassionate use of drugs and have found that it actually accelerates development. This is because when patients are offered compassionate use of an experimental drug, their doctors have to collect information as systematically as in the research protocol and submit it to the sponsor. Information is therefore available about use of the drug outside trial conditions. For example, if patients with

---

[1] DeVita VT. Should the FDA be the doctor of last resort? *Nat Clin Pract Oncol* 2005;2:423.

[2] Seeber S, Braun AH. Phase III trials in oncology: setting standards of care? *Nat Clin Pract Oncol* 2005;2:426-7.

impaired renal function not only tolerate the drug but respond, it will assist in drug development to have that knowledge collected systematically.

Drug industry profits

Another objection is that the drug industry might use this device to profit from investigation of a phase I drug. I believe this is a trivial objection because the usual strategy for compassionate use is that the drug is provided at cost. The last, and perhaps the most serious, objection is that expanded access would interfere with the clinical trial process. This certainly should not be the case. The clinical trial process is governed by the regulatory bodies in government, in industry, and in academic institutions. The unfortunate consequence of this is that physician scientists, who have the most experience, the most training, the most knowledge, the most productivity, and the most creativity, are completely excluded from this process. Because of the relationship between the regulatory organisations of government, industry, and academia, the academic physician scientist can only implement protocols that have been developed by the drug developer with direction from the regulatory agencies. Expanded access would bring the doctors back into the drug development process and, rather than damage the clinical trial system, would greatly expand its effectiveness and value.

In summary, patients with advanced cancer and limited life expectancy should have the same privilege as all individuals in a free society—that is, to decide their own benefit: risk ratio. It is tragic that regulatory bodies have created a circumstance where people have to live in an aura of hopelessness even though they have the will, the resources, and the ability to expose themselves to the risk of participating in investigational studies and to enjoy the potential for benefit. The solution is legislation or judicial action to permit expanded access to experimental treatments for patients with limited life expectancy.[3][4]

Dean Gesme community medical oncologist, Minnesota Oncology Hematology Professional Association, 800 East 28th Street, Minneapolis, MN 55407-3799, USA
dean.gesme@usoncology.com

No

Partially tested therapies cannot be allowed to substitute for good medical care. Hippocrates stated that our role as doctors is always to help or, at least, to do no harm. Those precepts apply equally to patients with minor ailments and those with terminal conditions.

In the United States, the Food and Drug Administration has proposed expanded access to investigational drugs for patients with terminal illnesses after initial safety (phase I) trials but before final approval for marketing.[5] This would apply to selected drugs already in phase II and III testing. The legal action filed against the FDA by the Abigail Alliance also seeks to make available drugs for which phase I safety data are known.[6] The US Court of Appeal recently ruled against the alliance, but it is taking the case to the Supreme Court.

The use of drugs after phase I testing and outside clinical trials may still subject patients to toxicities while offering no reasonable expectation of benefit. Phase I trials are intended to evaluate dose safety, while effectiveness of drugs is assessed in phase II and III clinical trials. More than 90% of drugs entering phase I trials are found unacceptable,[7] and, of those approved, most provide incremental improvements rather than lifesaving treatments.

---

[3] Freireich EJ. The investigational new drug application—who benefits? *Nat Clin Pract Oncol* 2006;3:62-3.

[4] Abigail Alliance for Better Access to Developmental Drugs. www.Abigail-Alliance.org.

[5] Food and Drug Administration. Proposed rules for charging for investigational drugs and expanded access to investigational drugs for treatment use. 2006. www.fda.gov/cder/regulatory/applications/IND_PR.htm.

[6] Abigail Alliance for Better Access to Developmental Drugs v Von Eschenbach, 445 F3d 470(D 2006), vacated 2006 US App LEXIS 29874 (DC Cir November 21, 2006).

[7] Society for Clinical Trials Board of Directors. The Society for Clinical Trials opposes US legislation to permit marketing of unproven medical therapies for seriously ill patients. *Clin Trials* 2006;3:154.

The allure of promising new drugs continues to engender false hope, which has all too often diverted time, resources, and attention from more appropriate efforts to minimise symptoms and enhance the quality of life for terminally ill patients and their families. Inappropriate expectations for untested new drugs are commonly promulgated by investigators eager for grant funding, companies searching for capital, writers eager for a good storyline, and uncomfortable practitioners who would rather avoid dealing directly with the complexity of end of life issues.

Damage to clinical trials

Patients may prefer to take partially tested drugs outside trials to avoid the constraints of a larger protocol study. However, this would subvert accrual of patients to phase II and III trials and ultimately delay the approval of those new drugs. Thus the needs of the many may become subservient to the desperate desires of the few.

False hopes for unproved drugs can also erode the clinical trials system by substituting clinical enthusiasm and wishful thinking for evidence based medicine. The best analogy may come from the many years in which autologous bone marrow transplant was considered standard treatment for advanced breast cancer despite the lack of data concerning efficacy. Well designed clinical trials failed to find willing participants as both patients and many doctors were convinced that this procedure was life saving. We now know that thousands of women experienced unnecessary toxicities, prolonged hospital stays, and lost time with families for what has now been shown to be inappropriate care.[8] Rather than repeating this tragedy with each promising new drug, we should focus our clinical energies on the optimal use of existing treatments and the enhancement of the current clinical trials system.

Investigational drugs may not be accessible to patients even if government authorities grant patients the freedom to access them. Most doctors are likely to be unwilling or unable to assume the responsibility of obtaining adequate informed consent from patients who are desperate for treatment and often unable to assimilate the possible risks involved.

Similar issues of liability and oversight may stop institutions from allowing open access to partially tested drugs. The issue of defining who is, or is not, terminally ill[9] can be most difficult, let alone delineating when existing therapies might offer no possible benefit. Indeed, who will decide which of the many investigational drugs would be best for an individual patient? Do we allow the marketplace to substitute for best practices and evidence based medicine?

Many drug firms have opted not to join current expanded access programmes for drugs in later stages of development and are opposed to providing investigational products outside of approved phase II trials.[10] The costs of drug production can be high, with limited production early in a drug's life. More importantly, there is concern that anecdotal toxicities for drugs used outside structured trials might lead to delayed approval, additional expensive testing, or adverse publicity that could jeopardise a process on which costs and profits of millions of dollars are in the balance.

Who will bear the costs of open access to these partially tested drugs? Will government and other payers who are now seeking to minimise payments for marginally beneficial therapies be willing to pay for unproved drugs outside of formal clinical trials?

Finally, while all doctors dream of the miracle cure for each of their terminally ill patients, we must accept the duty and responsibility to conform to both the principles of evidence based medicine and the precepts of appropriate end of life care. This includes the identification of false hopes and the substitution of realistic goals, enlightened hopes, and attainable expectations.

---

[8] Rettig R, Jacobson P. False hope: bone marrow transplantation for breast cancer. New York: Oxford University Press, 2007.

[9] Christakis N, Lamont E. Extent and determinants of error in doctor's prognoses in terminally ill patients: prospective cohort study. *BMJ* 2000;320:471.

[10] Anand G. Saying no to Penelope. Wall Street Journal 2007 May 1:1.

This may be the greatest test for the truly caring and compassionate physician.

British Medical Journal 3358 (September 2007): 478–479. Reprinted with permission by publisher

Jewish Ethical Issues in Hazardous Medical Therapy

Fred Rosner

Dr. Rosner, a frequent contributor on medical subjects, is Director of Medicine at the Queens Hospital Center Affiliation of the Long Island Jewish Hillside Medical Center and Professor of Medicine at the State University of New York at Stony Brook.

In Jewish tradition a physician is given specific Divine license to practice medicine. According to Maimonides and other codifiers of Jewish law, it is in fact the physician's obligation to use his medical skills to heal the sick. Not only is the physician permitted and even obligated to minister to the sick but the patient is also obligated to care for his health and life. Man does not have title over his life or body. He is charged with preserving, dignifying and hallowing that life. He must eat and drink to sustain himself. And he must seek healing when he is ill.

A cardinal principle in Judaism is that human life is of infinite value. The preservation of human life takes precedence over all biblical commandments, with three exceptions: idolatry, murder and incest. Life's value is absolute and supreme. Thus, an old man or woman, a mentally retarded person, a monster baby, a dying cancer patient and their like, all have the same right to life as you or I. In order to preserve a human life, the Sabbath and even the Day of Atonement may be desecrated and all other rules and laws, save the above three, are suspended for the overriding consideration of saving a human life. The corollary of this principle is that one is prohibited from doing anything that might shorten a life even for a very short time since every moment of human life is of infinite value.

How are these basic principles applied when a physician is confronted with the following dilemma? His extremely ill patient will, under normal circumstances, die shortly, perhaps in a few days or weeks. His patient's only chance for survival is unique surgery or therapy. However, if the surgery or therapy fails to heal, the patient will die immediately. What should the physician do? Should he risk the definite short period of life remaining for the patient by administering the drastic remedy in the hope that the patient may be cured and live a prolonged period? In other words, should the physician abandon the *definite* short life span of the patient in favor of the *possible* significant prolongation of his life?

The difficult problem confronts not only the physician but also the patient and the family. They too must be able to decide this question which is not purely medical. Is the patient allowed to accept hazardous surgery or experimental therapy? These are basic decisions which include medical, moral and legal aspects. What is the view of Jewish law for the physician, the patient and the family to follow?

Let me use a case illustration to exemplify the problem:

A nine-year old girl with acute lymphoblastic leukemia was treated with the best chemotherapeutic regimens available yet failed to achieve remission of her disease after eight months of treatment. Further chemotherapy had less than 5 percent chance of success. She had a very low white blood cell count and was in constant danger of developing serious and even life-threatening infection. She also had a very low platelet count and was in constant danger of serious bleeding.

The pediatric hematologists suggested bone marrow transplantation as a final resort. Tissue typing was done and the father of the child was found to have the same tissue type as the child. The chances for a successful bone marrow transplant were thought to be about 60 percent but the procedure itself is associated with a 25 percent mortality and a high morbidity. Most patients suffer from a complication called graft-versus-host disease in which the donor bone marrow (in this case it is the father's) causes serious and sometimes fatal signs and symptoms in the recipient. Without the transplant, the child was thought to have no chance of remission or cure and life expectancy was weeks or months at best. On the other hand, long-term remissions following bone marrow transplants for acute leukemia, although unusual, do occur in perhaps 10 to 15 percent of patients.

Let us now examine the Jewish moral and ethical issues raised by this case. The child is nine years old. Does age play a role in deciding whether a bone marrow transplant is sanctioned in Jewish law? The disease afflicting the patient, acute leukemia, if untreated, is invariably fatal.

Does Judaism recognize the concept of risk-benefit ratio? Does Judaic law consider the statistical probability of prolonging life versus the mortality rate or the odds of shortening life? May a hazardous therapeutic procedure be instituted for a dying patient if there is a slim chance of a cure even though the chances of survival are much less than even? How does one define "slim"? Is a bone marrow transplant a recognized and accepted procedure as is a widely used modality of treatment like a kidney or eye transplant? Or is a marrow transplant still a highly experimental procedure? Does Jewish law differentiate between therapeutic approaches which are hazardous in nature and hazardous procedures which are entirely experimental?

The use of certain drugs such as daunorubicin to treat acute leukemia is certainly fraught with hazard since the toxicity is considerable. However, the efficacy of these and other drugs is also well known. They are able to produce long survival in about 50 percent of children with acute lymphoblastic leukemia. We as physicians administer these drugs in anticipation of a cure despite the known risks. Does Judaism sanction such risks in the use of a new experimental drug or procedure whose curative potential is unknown?

In the case at hand: may the child undergo bone marrow transplantation? Must she undergo this treatment? Is bone marrow transplantation therapeutic or experimental or both? May the doctor offer this form of hazardous treatment? Must he do so? Does Judaism have a discretionary or mandatory attitude toward procedures which involve significant risk? What is significant risk? Does Jewish law sanction bone marrow transplantation in this case because of the lie-threatening nature of the underlying illness, even though the procedure itself may lead to an early death of the patient?

Numerous other ethical questions are involved in this case. If the procedure is sanctioned, is consent required? From whom? May the father subject himself to the danger and risk, albeit small, of serving as a donor? If the child dies following the transplant, may an autopsy be performed?

Theological and philosophical questions can also be raised by this illustrative case. If God ordained that this child should die at age nine of acute leukemia, how dare we interfere with God's will and attempt a bone marrow transplant to cure the child? How can we as physicians add harm over and above the harm produced by the disease itself? If a physician cannot recommend a specific experimental treatment or procedure on the basis of sound scientific principles, may he offer it as "one chance in a million"? Would Judaism prefer an approach in which a patient is left to chance?

These are some of the Jewish ethical issues in hazardous medical therapy. They are being addressed by a variety of Jewish rabbinic and medical scholars. The dean of the American Orthodox rabbinate, Rabbi Moshe Feinstein, states that one is permitted to submit to dangerous surgery even though it may hasten death because of the potential, however small, of the operation being successful and effecting a cure.[1] Israel's Chief Rabbi, Shlomo Goren, writes that one should use hazardous experimental therapy in a case not only where the patient will certainly die without the medical or surgical therapy but also where the possibility exists of prolonging the patient's life by the therapy.[2] Britain's Chief Rabbi, Immanuel Jakobovits, also agrees that hazardous therapy may be given to patients if it may be potentially helpful to the patient, however remote the chances of success are.[3]

---

[1] Moshe Feinstein, "Responsa Iggrot Moshe" in Yoreh Deah, Part 2, No. 58 (New York: 1973).

[2] Shlomo Goren, Shanah BeShanah (Jerusalem: Hechal Shlomo, 1976), pp. 149-55.

[3] Immanuel Jakobovits, "Medical Experimentation on Humans in Jewish Law," in Jewish Bioethics, ed. F. Rosner & J.D. Bleich. (New York: Hebrew Publishing Co., 1979) pp. 377-383.

Two earlier rabbinic sources also clearly enunciate the Jewish legal view concerning human experimentation. Rabbi Hayim Ozer Grodzinski (1863-1940) was asked about the permissibility of performing a dangerous surgical procedure on a seriously ill patient. He answered that if all the attending physicians, without exception, recommend such an operation, it should be performed, even if the chances for success are smaller than those for failure.[4] A similar pronouncement is made by Rabbi Jacob Reischer (1670-1733) with regard to dangerous medical therapy for a seriously ill patient. Reischer permits such therapy since it may cure the patient although it may hasten the patient's death.[5] Reischer also requires a group of physicians to concur in the decision.

The basic tenet of Judaism is the supreme value of human life. This principle is based in part upon our belief that man was created in the image of God. Therefore, when a person's life is in danger, even when there is no hope for survival for a prolonged period but only for a very short time, all commandments of the Bible are set aside. Any act which can prolong life supercedes all the biblical commandments except the three cardinal ones.

Tradition 19, no. 1 (Spring 1981): 55–58.
Reprinted with permission by publisher

---

[4] Hayim Ozer Grodzinski, "Responsa Ahiezer." Yoreh Deah, Responsum, No. 16:6, (Jerusalem: 1946).

[5] Jacob Reischer, "Responsa Shevut Yaakov," Section 3, Responsum No. 75, (Lemberg, 1860).

A Lifesaving Checklist

Atul Gawande

In Bethesda, Md., in a squat building off a suburban parkway, sits a small federal agency called the Office for Human Research Protections. Its aim is to protect people. But lately you have to wonder. Consider this recent case.

A year ago, researchers at Johns Hopkins University published the results of a program that instituted in nearly every intensive care unit in Michigan a simple five-step checklist designed to prevent certain hospital infections. It reminds doctors to make sure, for example, that before putting large intravenous lines into patients, they actually wash their hands and don a sterile gown and gloves.

The results were stunning. Within three months, the rate of bloodstream infections from these I.V. lines fell by two-thirds. The average I.C.U. cut its infection rate from 4 percent to zero. Over 18 months, the program saved more than 1,500 lives and nearly $200 million.

Yet this past month, the Office for Human Research Protections shut the program down. The agency issued notice to the researchers and the Michigan Health and Hospital Association that, by introducing a checklist and tracking the results without written, informed consent from each patient and health-care provider, they had violated scientific ethics regulations. Johns Hopkins had to halt not only the program in Michigan but also its plans to extend it to hospitals in New Jersey and Rhode Island.

The government's decision was bizarre and dangerous. But there was a certain blinkered logic to it, which went like this: A checklist is an alteration in medical care no less than an experimental drug is. Studying an experimental drug in people without federal monitoring and explicit written permission from each patient is unethical and illegal. Therefore it is no less unethical and illegal to do the same with a checklist. Indeed, a checklist may require even more stringent oversight, the administration ruled, because the data gathered in testing it could put not only the patients but also the doctors at risk—by exposing how poorly some of them follow basic infection-prevention procedures.

The need for safeguards in medical experimentation has been evident since before the Nazi physician trials at Nuremberg. Testing a checklist for infection prevention, however, is not the same as testing an experimental drug—and neither are like-minded efforts now under way to reduce pneumonia in hospitals, improve the consistency of stroke and heart attack treatment and increase flu vaccination rates. Such organizational research work, new to medicine, aims to cement minimum standards and ensure they are followed, not to discover new therapies. This work is different from drug testing not merely because it poses lower risks, but because a failure to carry it out poses a vastly greater risk to people's lives.

A large body of evidence gathered in recent years has revealed a profound failure by health-care professionals to follow basic steps proven to stop infection and other major complications. We now know that hundreds of thousands of Americans suffer serious complications or die as a result. It's not for lack of effort. People in health care work long, hard hours. They are struggling, however, to provide increasingly complex care in the absence of effective systematization.

Excellent clinical care is no longer possible without doctors and nurses routinely using checklists and other organizational strategies and studying their results. There need to be as few barriers to such efforts as possible. Instead, the endeavor itself is treated as the danger.

If the government's ruling were applied more widely, whole swaths of critical work to ensure safe and effective care would either halt or shrink: efforts by the Centers for Disease Control and Prevention to examine responses to outbreaks of infectious disease; the military's program to track the care of wounded soldiers; the Five Million Lives campaign, by the nonprofit Institute for Healthcare Improvement, to reduce avoidable complications in 3,700 hospitals nationwide.

I work with the World Health Organization on a new effort to introduce surgical safety checklists worldwide.

It aims to ensure that a dozen basic safety steps are actually followed in operating rooms here and abroad—that the operating team gives an antibiotic before making an incision, for example, and reviews how much blood loss to prepare for. A critical component of the program involves tracking successes and failures and learning from them. If each of the hundreds of hospitals we're trying to draw into the program were required to obtain permissions for this, even just from research regulators, few could join.

Scientific research regulations had previously exempted efforts to improve medical quality and public health—because they hadn't been scientific. Now that the work is becoming more systematic (and effective), the authorities have stepped in. And they're in danger of putting ethics bureaucracy in the way of actual ethical medical care. The agency should allow this research to continue unencumbered. If it won't, then Congress will have to.

Atul Gawande, a surgeon at Brigham and Women's Hospital in Boston and a New Yorker staff writer, is the author of "Better."

Op-Ed, *New York Times*, December 30, 2007.
Reprinted with permission by publisher

Lesson 4

New Beginnings:
The Ethics of Reproductive Technologies

Introduction

G-d's blessing to Abraham was that his children would be as many as the stars of the sky and the sand of the sea. But for those who grapple with childlessness, the promise of even one child is miracle enough.

What guidance can Torah offer for those struggling with infertility? How open is Judaism to making use of the new reproductive technologies? What words of comfort and encouragement does our tradition offer to those traversing this difficult path?

The Desire for Children
The Struggle of Infertility

Text 1

שבע עקרות הן, שרה רבקה רחל ולאה ואשתו של מנוח וחנה וציון.

פסיקתא דרב כהנא כ,א

There are seven infertile women mentioned in the Bible: Sarah, Rebecca, Rachel, Leah, the wife of Manoah (the mother of Samson), Hannah, and Zion.

Midrash, Pesikta DeRav Kahana 20:1

Text 2a

אַחַר הַדְּבָרִים הָאֵלֶּה הָיָה דְבַר ה׳ אֶל אַבְרָם בַּמַּחֲזֶה לֵאמֹר

אַל תִּירָא אַבְרָם אָנֹכִי מָגֵן לָךְ שְׂכָרְךָ הַרְבֵּה מְאֹד.

וַיֹּאמֶר אַבְרָם ה׳ אֱלֹקִים מַה תִּתֶּן לִי וְאָנֹכִי הוֹלֵךְ עֲרִירִי . . . הֵן לִי לֹא נָתַתָּה זָרַע וְהִנֵּה בֶן בֵּיתִי יוֹרֵשׁ אֹתִי.

בראשית טו,א–ג

After these incidents, the word of the Lord came to Abram in a vision, saying, "Fear not, Abram; I am your shield; your reward is exceedingly great."

And Abram said, "O Lord G-d, what can You give me,
so long as I continue to be childless. . . . Behold, You
have given me no seed, and behold, one of my household will inherit me."

Genesis 15:1–3

Text 2b

וַתַּעַן חַנָּה וַתֹּאמֶר לֹא אֲדֹנִי אִשָּׁה קְשַׁת רוּחַ אָנֹכִי . . . וָאֶשְׁפֹּךְ אֶת נַפְשִׁי לִפְנֵי ה' . . . כִּי
מֵרֹב שִׂיחִי וְכַעְסִי דִּבַּרְתִּי עַד הֵנָּה.
שמואל א, א,טו–טז

And Hannah answered and said: "No, my lord,
I am a woman of sorrowful spirit . . . and I
poured out my soul before the Lord . . . Out
of the abundance of my complaint and my vexation have
I spoken until now."

I Samuel 1:15–16

Text 2c

וַתֵּרֶא רָחֵל כִּי לֹא יָלְדָה לְיַעֲקֹב וַתְּקַנֵּא רָחֵל בַּאֲחֹתָהּ וַתֹּאמֶר אֶל יַעֲקֹב הָבָה לִּי בָנִים וְאִם אַיִן מֵתָה אָנֹכִי.

בראשית לא,א

Rachel saw that she had not borne children to Jacob. Rachel became jealous of her sister; she said to Jacob, "Give me children! If not, let me die!"

Genesis 30:1

Procreation: Obligation and Significance

Text 3

Men and women of full age, without any limitation due to race, nationality or religion, have the right to marry and to found a family.

The Universal Declaration of Human Rights, Article 16:1

Question for Discussion

Do you think the right to found a family is a positive or negative right?

Text 4

וַיִּבְרָא אֱלֹקִים אֶת הָאָדָם בְּצַלְמוֹ בְּצֶלֶם אֱלֹקִים בָּרָא אֹתוֹ זָכָר וּנְקֵבָה בָּרָא אֹתָם.
וַיְבָרֶךְ אֹתָם אֱלֹקִים וַיֹּאמֶר לָהֶם אֱלֹקִים פְּרוּ וּרְבוּ וּמִלְאוּ אֶת הָאָרֶץ.

בראשית א,כז–כח

And G-d created man in His image; in the image of G-d He created him; male and female He created them.

And G-d blessed them, and G-d said to them, "Be fruitful and multiply and fill the earth."

Genesis 1:27–28

Question for Discussion

What does the above verse tell you about the Jewish attitude to reproduction?

Text 5a

והיא מצוה גדולה שבסיבתה מתקיימות כל המצות בעולם, כי לבני אדם ניתנו ולא למלאכי השרת.

ספר החינוך, מצוה א

It is a great mitzvah because as a result of it all the other *mitzvot* can be fulfilled. For the *mitzvot* were given to human beings, not to the ministering angels.

Sefer Hachinuch, Mitzvah 1

Text 5b

אף על פי שקיים אדם מצות פריה ורביה הרי הוא מצווה מדברי סופרים שלא יבטל מלפרות ולרבות כל זמן שיש בו כח שכל המוסיף נפש אחת בישראל כאילו בנה עולם. רמב״ם, הלכות אישות טו,טז

Although one has already fulfilled the obligation to be fruitful and multiply [by having a son and a daughter], the rabbis commanded that one should not cease from having children so long as one has the ability to do so, because adding another soul to the Jewish people is like building a world.

Maimonides, *Mishneh Torah*, Laws of Marriage 15:16

Text 5c

אין בן דוד בא עד שיכלו כל הנשמות שבגוף. תלמוד בבלי, נדה יג,ב

The [Mashiach], scion of [King] David, will not come until the Heavenly chamber is emptied of all of its souls.

Talmud, Nidah 13b

Artificial Reproduction
Artificial Insemination Donor

Text 6

וְאֶל אֵשֶׁת עֲמִיתְךָ לֹא תִתֵּן שְׁכָבְתְּךָ לְזָרַע.

ויקרא יח,כ

ou shall not lie carnally giving seed to your neighbor's wife.

Leviticus 18:20

Text 7

אמר רבי אליעזר בן יעקב: לא ישא אדם אשה במדינה זו וילך וישא אשה במדינה אחרת, שמא יזדווגו זה לזה, ונמצא אח נושא את אחותו.

תלמוד בבלי, יבמות לז,ב

Rabbi Eliezer ben Ya'akov said, "A man should not marry one woman in one province and another woman in another province lest [the children] be paired with each other, resulting in a brother marrying a sister."

Talmud, Yevamot 37b

Text 8

Twins who were separated at birth and raised by different families met later and married but were forced to break up when they discovered their true identities. . . .

"It's a tragedy for the couple who are involved, a terrible tragedy. Everyone's hearts will go out to people caught up quite unwittingly in a case of incest of this kind," David Alton, a member of the House of Lords, told BBC radio. . . .

"It involved the normal birth of twins who were separated at birth and adopted by separate parents," said Alton, who has no party affiliation. "They were never told that they were twins."

"They met later in life and felt an inevitable attraction and they got married," he said.

"When they did come to know their true identities, it led to their having to separate and also to a lot of heartbreak," Alton said on Friday. News reports said their marriage was annulled.

No further information was available about the twins or where they were from.

"This isn't a regular occurrence but it could become one with large numbers of people now being born by IVF and not knowing their true identities," Alton said. . . .

"The government . . . has not accepted the argument that you should have the right to know who your biological father is on the birth certificate," Alton said.

"It would be a terrible act of deception, with the state colluding in that deception, to remove the biological identity of your father from the birth certificate," he added.

Pam Hodgkins, head of a group that helps adults affected by adoption, said the story of the twins was very tragic.

"It is a lesson that we need to learn and apply to the situation of donor-conceived children," she told Sky News.

"Whilst . . . nowadays it would be most unusual for siblings to be separated . . . the risk of secrecy affecting the lives of people born as a result of egg and sperm donation is exactly the same as the risks that have affected adopted people in the past," she said.

"Separated Twins Married and Had to Break Up," Reuters, UK edition, Jan 11, 2008

Artificial Insemination Husband

Text 9a

A white woman from Staten Island who gave birth to a black couple's baby after an embryo mix-up at a fertility clinic was denied visiting rights to the boy yesterday by an appeals court.

A five-judge appellate panel of the State Supreme Court ruled unanimously that the case was similar to "a mix-up at the time of a hospital's discharge of two new-born infants, which should simply be corrected at once," rather than one in which the birth mother retained some rights.

The white woman, Donna Fasano, 38, was mistakenly implanted with the embryos of Deborah Perry-Rogers and Robert Rogers of Teaneck, N.J., as well as her own embryos, by a Manhattan clinic in 1998. In December 1998, she gave birth to two boys, one black, whom she named Joseph, and one white, named Vincent. Ms. Perry-Rogers, 34, was implanted with her own embryos, but none produced a fetus.

Andy Newman, "Visiting Rights Denied in Embryo Mix-Up Case," *The New York Times*, October 27, 2000

Text 9b

The mishandling of eggs and embryos that apparently took place at U.C. Irvine might have been avoided if the federal and state governments, in cooperation with medical societies, would agree on guidelines for licensing and regulating in vitro laboratories. As of the present, there is no central registry to which data from in vitro laboratories must be reported. And if physicians and scientists continue to fight the idea, there won't be one anytime soon.

Regulation problems exist on a state level as well as on a national one. Most states have kept their heads in the sand on the issue of standardizing and licensing in vitro laboratories. It is beyond comprehension to think that laboratories that do urine tests are required to have licenses, be inspected, and undergo annual reviews (in most states), while laboratories that generate embryos that grow into new human lives have no oversight or licensing requirements. . . . As things stand now, literally anyone can set up an IVF laboratory and run it without supervision. This lack of regulation leads to difficult problems, such as the recent case in The Netherlands in which a woman, after trying to become pregnant for five years, succeeded through in vitro fertilization to give birth to twins. One looked like its blond, blue-eyed parents. The other was black. The laboratory apologized for its "regrettable mistake."

We've pushed for standardized laboratory licensing for in vitro laboratories for over ten years. As consumers,

Dr. Richard Marrs. Published over 200 scientific articles and book chapters on human reproduction; authored the popular *"Dr. Marrs' Fertility Book."* A leading reproductive endocrinologist, Marrs played an essential role in establishing the second in vitro fertilization program in the U.S. in 1981, and made medical history in 1986 with the first pregnancy from a thawed frozen embryo. Dr. Marrs was founder and first president of the Society for Assisted Reproductive Technology.

you too should insist that federal and state government agencies work in concert with the medical and scientific communities in establishing guidelines that will protect both embryos and patients from unscrupulous activities.

Richard Marrs, Lisa Friedman Bloch, and Kathy Kirtland Silverman, *Dr. Richard Marrs' Fertility Book,* pp. 453–454

Text 10a

לזאת בנדון דידן נראה לפי עניות דעתי שאסור לעשות כן ואין כדאי להתחכם ביותר וישליכו יהבם על ה׳ אשר יזכה עוד אותם בזרע של קיימא . . . ונצטוינו לקיים פרו ורבו כדרך בני אדם ולא על ידי התחכמות כאלה אשר קרובים יותר לאיסור ולמכשול. דברי מלכיאל ד,קז

Therefore, in this case, it is my opinion that it is forbidden to do it. It is not worth trying to be too smart. They should place their trust in G-d who will yet bless them with healthy children . . . We have been commanded to fulfill the obligation of procreation in a natural manner, not through methods which can cause problems and are close to being forbidden.

Rabbi Malkiel Tsvi Tenenbaum, *Divrei Malkiel* 4:107

Text **10b**

במקרה של הוראת היתר להוציא זרע מהבעל להזריקו אחר כך לרחם אשתו, יש מאד

מאד להשגיח בשבע עינים שהרופא לא יקח ולא יערב חלילה וחלילה בזה זרע של איש

אחר. ופיקוח זה הוא תנאי קודם למעשה. אי אפשר לפרט על גבי הכתב דרכי הפיקוח

דהכל תלוי לפי נאמנות הרופא ובאופני דרכי הביצוע . . . אבל יש לדעת שכל חיסרון

פיקוח כל שהוא בזה עלול להפוך הקערה על פיה.

ציץ אליעזר ט, נא,ד

n a case where there is permission to perform AIH, the procedure must be very well supervised to ensure that the husband's sperm is not mixed with the sperm of another man. This supervision is a prerequisite for allowing the procedure. It is impossible to record in writing the method of supervision, for this all depends on the trustworthiness of the physician and on the particulars of the procedure. . . . It is important to be aware that any defect in the supervision can destroy the whole enterprise.

Rabbi Eliezer Waldenburg, *Tsits Eliezer,* vol. 9, 51:4

Rabbi Eliezer Yehudah Waldenberg (1915–2006). Leading rabbi and judge on the Supreme Rabbinical Court in Jerusalem; considered an eminent authority on Jewish medical ethics and Jewish law. His collected responsa, *Tsits Eliezer*, are viewed as one of the great achievements of halachic scholarship of the 20th century. He served as rabbi for the Shaare Zedek Medical Center in Jerusalem.

Text **10c**

ealth professionals who are not personally familiar with (or committed to) the limitations that are integral to their patients' religious commitments can be incredulous that such restrictions could be allowed to frustrate or complicate the fertility therapy if the couple had a real desire to conceive. Such value judgments have no place in the patient-doctor relationship. Fertility therapy, like all

Richard V. Grazi, MD. Director of the Division of Reproductive Endocrinology at Maimonides Medical Center and associate clinical professor of Obstetrics, Gynecology and Reproductive Sciences at Mount Sinai School of Medicine. Dr. Grazi has published and lectured extensively on clinical and ethical issues related to reproductive medicine. He is the author of *Overcoming Infertility: A Guide for Jewish Couples* and *Be Fruitful and Multiply*.

Joel B. Wolowelsky PhD.
Dean of faculty at Yeshivah of Flatbush High School where he teaches math and Jewish philosophy. He is associate Editor of *Tradition, The Journal of Jewish Thought* published by the Rabbinical Council of America, and *Sheurei Harav,* which brings to print the unpublished writings of Rabbi Joseph B. Soloveitchik. He authored *Woman, Jewish Law and Modernity*, as well as *Women at the Seder: A Passover Haggadah.*

legitimate medical therapy, must address the patient as a whole. The religious commitments of a patient may be at the core of his or her personal identity; understanding these commitments can help the physician construct a therapy protocol best suited for the patient at hand.

Richard V. Grazi and Joel B. Wolowelsky, "The Use of Cryopreserved Sperm and Pre-embryos in Contemporary Jewish Law and Ethics," Jlaw.com

Embryonic Stem Cell Research

Text 11

A judge today halted federally funded research of human embryonic stem cells, which had been approved under guidelines issued by President Obama shortly after his inauguration. . . .

The Justice Department said it is "reviewing the judge's ruling."

At the heart of the legal battle is a law known as the Dickey-Wicker Amendment, which prohibits federally funded research in which a human embryo is "destroyed, discarded, or knowingly subject to risk of injury or death greater than that allowed under applicable regulations."

The measure has been attached to every appropriations bill for the Department of Health and Human Services since 1996. The department oversees the federal government's primary health research arm, the National Institutes of Health.

The plaintiffs have argued working with embryonic stem cells by nature depends upon the destruction of an embryo, and that the new guidelines therefore violate the law. . . .

President George W. Bush banned federal funding of embryonic stem cell research in 2001, citing "moral concerns raised by the new frontier of human embryonic stem cell research. Even the most noble ends don't justify the means."

But President Obama reversed the policy by executive order in March 2009, saying federal agencies "may support and conduct responsible, scientifically worthy human stem cell research, including human embryonic stem cell research, to the extent permitted by law."

"In recent years, when it comes to stem cell research, rather than furthering discovery, our government has forced what I believe is a false choice between sound science and moral values," he said. "In this case, I believe the two are not inconsistent."

Devin Dwyer, "Court Suspends Federally Funded Embryonic Stem Cell Research," ABCnews.go.com, August 23, 2010

Learning **Activity**

Do you think Halachah supports or forbids stem cell research? Provide a reason in support of your view.

Text **12a**

Rabbi Dr. Avraham Steinberg, MD. Born in Hoff, Germany; studied in Yeshivat Merkaz Harav in Jerusalem, after which he studied medicine and completed his internship at the Hebrew University Hadassah Medical School. Dr. Steinberg lectures at numerous academic institutes and other forums and currently works as a physician in Pediatric Neurology, Shaare Zedek Medical Center, and is the director of the Center for Medical Ethics, Hebrew University Hadassah Medical School, Jerusalem. Dr. Steinberg has received a variety of prizes and awards, among them the Israel Prize in 1999 for his *Encyclopedia of Jewish Medical Ethics.*

From time immemorial, scientists and philosophers have argued about when life begins. From a pure scientific viewpoint it is impossible to answer this query. In fact, it is impossible to define scientifically the very term "life." Indeed, the definition of life and the beginning of life involves religious, ethical, legal and social considerations.

Similarly, from time immemorial scientists and philosophers have debated the status of the embryo/fetus. There has been, and continues to be, a great dispute as to whether or not the embryo has an independent claim for life and/or whether or not it possesses the status of an independent person.

Rabbi Dr. Avraham Steinberg, "Jewish Perspectives," in *Discovery and Medical Ethics*, Shraga Blazer and Etan Z. Zimmer eds., p. 32

Another moral issue pertains to the question whether or not there is a moral distinction between an embryo that is already implanted and developing in utero compared with a pre-embryo in a test tube after in vitro fertilization is performed.

Rabbi Dr. Avraham Steinberg, "Jewish Perspectives," in Discovery and Medical Ethics, Shraga Blazer and Etan Z. Zimmer eds., p. 33

Text **13**

ומהאי טעמא אפשרי גם כן לאבד הנשאר אחרי שרואים שהאשה נקלטה וההריון מתפתח לפי כל הסימנים באופן חיובי . . .

אבל לפי עניות דעתי אין בזה ספק כלל . . . היינו כשהוא כבר ברחם האם, והוא בגדר נפש וחי חיי עבור דעתיד להיות חי גמור, לא כן הרכבת זרע הבעל וזרע האשה מבחוץ דבלי רחם לא יתפתח לעולם, פשיטא דעדין אינו נקרא נפש, וגם לא חי של עבור . . . קודם העבור בגוף האשה לית דין ולית דיין דנדון רק כזרע ולא כלל כעבור.

שבט הלוי י,רלא

For this reason it is permitted to destroy the remaining [pre-embryos] if they are not needed once we see that [the mother] has conceived and gestation is developing positively. . . .

In my humble opinion there is not even doubt that we need be concerned [about the destruction of life or potential life] . . . for we need only be concerned once it is in utero and has some classification of life, for it will eventually develop into a full life. This is not so regarding in vitro fertilization where without implantation, these [pre-embryos] will never develop [into living humans]. Obviously, then, they cannot be referred to as life, not even the life of a fetus. . . .Before implantation into the womb, there is no law [protecting the pre-embryo]; it is considered to be like male seed, not at all like a fetus.

Rabbi Shmuel HaLevi Wosner, *Shevet HaLevi* 10:231

Text 14

We must also remember that embryonic stem cells come from human embryos that are destroyed for their cells. Each of these human embryos is a unique human life with inherent dignity and matchless value. We see that value in the children who are with us today. Each of these children began his or her life as a frozen embryo that was created for in vitro fertilization, but remained unused after the fertility treatments were complete. Each of these children was adopted while still an embryo, and has been blessed with the chance to grow up in a loving family. These boys and girls are not spare parts. They remind us of what is lost when embryos are destroyed in the name of research. They remind us that we all begin our lives as a small collection of cells. And they remind us that in our zeal for new treatments and cures, America must never abandon our fundamental morals.

President George W. Bush, July 19, 2006

כל זמן שלא הושתל ברחם אשה, אלא הוא רק תא מופרה מוקפא, אין עליו שום שם
עובר כלל, ואין כל איסור לאבדו . . .
ומכל מקום בכדי לצאת מכל ספק מן הראוי שלא להשמיד לגמרי את התאים המופרים
אלא במקום שאינם עומדים משום מה להשתלה ברחמה של בעלת הביצית (עקב
ריבוי הביציות המופרות ממנה או בשל סירוב אחד הצדדים, בעל הזרע או בעלת
הביצית, או מכל סיבה אחרת) הרי בודאי שאין להשתילם ברחמה של אשה אחרת . . .
והעצה היעוצה הנכונה והמתאימה ביותר היא להשתמש בהם לצורך הצלת נפשות,
וכגון לצורך מערכות עצבים שנפגעו וכדומה.

מעשה חושב ג, ב,ו

As long as it has not been implanted in the womb and it is still a frozen fertilized egg, it does not have the status of an embryo at all and there is no prohibition to destroy it . . .

However in order to remove all doubt [as to the permissibility of destroying it], it is preferable not to destroy the pre-embryo unless it will otherwise not be implanted in the woman who gave the eggs (either because there are many fertilized eggs, or because one of the parties refuses to go on with the procedure—the husband or wife—or for any other reason). Certainly it should not be implanted into another woman . . . The best and worthiest solution is to use it for life-saving purposes, such as for the treatment of people that suffered trauma to their nervous system, etc.

Rabbi Levi Yitschak Halperin, *Ma'aseh Choshev* vol. 3, 2:6

Rabbi Levi Yitschak Halperin (1934–). Founded and heads the Institute for Science and Jewish Law in Jerusalem, dedicated to the development of a sound halachic foundation for dealing with all matters connected with science and modern technology. Rabbi Halperin and his team of religious scholars, engineers, and scientists work to find answers to the challenges that the fast-paced, technology-dependent world creates for Jewish law. He has authored many articles on these issues, and has published a seven volume responsa, *Ma'aseh Choshev,* which includes discussion of Halachah and medicine.

Concluding Thoughts

Text 16a

אונס רחמנא פטריה.

תלמוד בבלי, עבודה זרה נד,א

The Torah exempts one who could not fulfill an obligation due to circumstances beyond his control.

Talmud, Avodah Zarah 54a

Text 16b

מחשבה טובה מצרפה למעשה . . . אמר רב אסי: אפילו חשב אדם לעשות מצוה, ונאנס ולא עשאה, מעלה עליו הכתוב כאילו עשאה.

תלמוד בבלי, קידושין מ,א

If one has a good intention, it is added to the [account of one's] good deeds. . . . Rabbi Asi said, "If a person thought of doing a mitzvah, and because of circumstances beyond his control, was not able to fulfill it, the Torah still considers it as if he had done the mitzvah."

Talmud, Kidushin 40a

Text **17a**

שכל המגדל יתום בתוך ביתו מעלה עליו הכתוב כאילו ילדו.

תלמוד בבלי, סנהדרין יט,ב

Whoever raises an orphan in his home is considered by the Torah as if he had given birth to him.

Talmud, Sanhedrin 19b

Text **17b**

אמר רבי שמואל בר נחמני אמר רבי יונתן: כל המלמד בן חבירו תורה מעלה
עליו הכתוב כאילו ילדו . . .
אהרן ילד ומשה לימד, לפיכך נקראו על שמו.

תלמוד בבלי, סנהדרין יט,ב

Rabbi Shmuel bar Nachmeni said in the name of Rabbi Yonatan, "Whoever teaches his colleague's child Torah is considered by the Torah as if he had given birth to him . . . Aaron bore children and Moses taught them; therefore they are called the children of Moses.

Talmud, Sanhedrin 19b

Text 18

כֹּה אָמַר ה' שִׁמְרוּ מִשְׁפָּט וַעֲשׂוּ צְדָקָה כִּי קְרוֹבָה יְשׁוּעָתִי לָבוֹא וְצִדְקָתִי לְהִגָּלוֹת. אַשְׁרֵי אֱנוֹשׁ יַעֲשֶׂה זֹּאת וּבֶן אָדָם יַחֲזִיק בָּהּ שֹׁמֵר שַׁבָּת מֵחַלְּלוֹ וְשֹׁמֵר יָדוֹ מֵעֲשׂוֹת כָּל רָע . . . וְאַל יֹאמַר הַסָּרִיס הֵן אֲנִי עֵץ יָבֵשׁ. כִּי כֹה אָמַר ה' לַסָּרִיסִים אֲשֶׁר יִשְׁמְרוּ אֶת שַׁבְּתוֹתַי וּבָחֲרוּ בַּאֲשֶׁר חָפָצְתִּי וּמַחֲזִיקִים בִּבְרִיתִי. וְנָתַתִּי לָהֶם בְּבֵיתִי וּבְחוֹמֹתַי יָד וָשֵׁם טוֹב מִבָּנִים וּמִבָּנוֹת שֵׁם עוֹלָם אֶתֶּן לוֹ אֲשֶׁר לֹא יִכָּרֵת.

ישעיהו נו,א–ה

So says the Lord, "Keep justice and practice righteousness, for the coming of My salvation is near, and My benevolence will soon be revealed."

Fortunate is the man who will do this and the person who will hold fast to it: he who keeps from profaning the Shabbat and guards his hand from doing any evil. . . .

Let not the infertile say, "Behold, I am a dry tree."

For so says the Lord to the infertile who will keep My Shabbat and will choose what I desire and hold fast to My covenant:

"I will give them in My house and in My walls a place and a name—better than sons and daughters—an everlasting name I will give him, which will never be discontinued."

Isaiah 56:1–5

Key Points

1. The Torah powerfully documents the deep inner pain of those suffering infertility and whose desire for a child is yet unfulfilled.

2. While society recognizes a right to have children, the Torah sees procreation as an obligation.

3. The use of donor sperm raises serious concerns regarding the structure of the family and the danger of not having accurate knowledge regarding one's parentage.

4. Artificial insemination from the husband is generally permitted by most authorities so long as there is oversight by a third party to prevent gametes from being mixed up.

5. Despite the current debate raging about embryonic stem cell research, Jewish law has no objection to the destruction of unused pre-implanted embryos.

6. Using unused pre-embryos for research is preferable to giving them to other couples for adoption.

7. Those who are unable to fulfill a mitzvah despite reasonable attempts have fulfilled their obligation and G-d considers it as if the mitzvah had been fulfilled.

8. There is no obligation to pursue ART in the quest to have children.

9. There is great merit in raising orphans or in mentoring others in their spiritual development.

10. Every person can forge an eternal legacy.

Additional Readings

Pre-Implantation Genetic Diagnosis, Stem Cells and Jewish Law

Michael J. Broyde

Rabbi Broyde is Professor of Law at Emory University, Rabbi of the Young Israel of Toco Hills, Atlanta, GA, and a member of the Beth Din of America.

Reproductive genetic technology continues to advance. The ability to examine sperm, eggs, and embryos for genetic indications of illness represents one of the great horizons that is rapidly approaching as a normative activity in our society. Within the past five years Pre-implantation Genetic Diagnosis (PGD) has become a technique used to examine fertilized eggs (embryos) to determine the presence or absence of particular genetic code in a specific embryo. This article will examine PGD to determine how Jewish law ought to view this new technological development, both as a matter of technical legality and as a matter of societal values and public policy.

This article is divided into four main parts. The first section explains how PGD works as a matter of science, and why people seek such tests. The second section explores the general Jewish view toward genetic engineering and germ-line treatments. The third section explains why a person might use PGD and what its advantages over competing technologies are, both as a matter of Jewish law and as a matter of public policy. The fourth section explores the technical issues in Jewish law raised by such technology and presents a number of examples and hypothetical cases. A brief postscript following the conclusion discusses what other possibilities are on the horizon and attempts a Jewish-law analysis of them as well.

I. PRE-IMPLANTATION GENETIC DIAGNOSIS

The frontier of PGD lies at the intersection of the worlds of in vitro fertilization (IVF) and genetic screening. The development of the IVF process has enabled the creation of embryos outside the uterus for subsequent implantation. Enhanced scientific understanding of the human genome and improvements in gene-mapping technology have vastly improved the medical community's ability to test for genetic indications of disease. PGD combines the two: it applies genetic screening to IVF embryos. With PGD, these laboratory embryos can now be tested for genetic abnormalities or the presence of genetic material linked to disease development. PGD thus provides an earlier alternative to prenatal (or even post-birth) diagnosis as it allows testing even before implantation of the embryo in the womb. It also revolutionizes the formerly random selection of IVF embryos by now offering the ability to screen for specific traits. Following PGD, an embryo or embryos with the desired characteristics is then implanted in the uterus to initiate pregnancy. Embryos screened out for undesirable characteristics are set aside (and perhaps discarded).[1]

---

1 This material is taken from the Genetics and Public Policy Center manual entitled "Reproductive Genetic Testing: The Science and Regulatory Environment," distributed at the conference of January 6-7, 2003, Washington, DC, and their preliminary report, *Preimplantation Genetic Diagnosis: A Discussion of Challenges, Concerns, and Preliminary Policy Options Related to the Genetic Testing of Human Embryos,* dated January 2004, available at their website, www.dnapolicy.org.

In the real world, PGD serves as an alternative to prenatal testing in which one diagnoses a genetic disease or condition in a developing fetus. Two broad categories of prenatal testing are available. Invasive procedures, such as amniocentesis or chorionic villus sampling, are those in which a sample of fetal cells or tissue is obtained. The non-invasive procedures are ultrasound or taking a sample of the mother's blood. All of these prenatal testing techniques lead to abortion as a way of avoiding the birth of a child with a defect, although CVS testing is at a much earlier stage in pregnancy than amniocenteses.

PGD is a somewhat broad term that encompasses a number of related techniques. Doctors can analyze the polar body cells cast off from eggs following maturation and fertilization to infer the genetic makeup of the embryo. More commonly, they directly test one or two cells from an eight-cell embryo. The types of analysis also vary. The chromosomes can be evaluated to assess their number and structure; alternatively, the DNA is analyzed to detect specific gene mutations or problematic genetic sequences. These various forms of analysis inform the selection of embryos for implantation.[2]

Over 1000 babies have been born worldwide after having undergone this procedure and the number is growing rapidly. PGD can now be applied to detect chromosomal rearrangements such as translocation, as well as inherited chromosomal abnormalities and single-gene disorders such as Tay Sachs, cystic fibrosis, and sickle cell anemia. PGD can also be used to screen for genetic mutations linked to many ordinary diseases whose onset is only much later in life, like Alzheimer's disease, or even illnesses for which genetic makeup is only one of many risk factors predicting occurrence, such as breast cancer. Indeed, more than 100 different singlegene disorders have been diagnosed in pre-implantation embryos, and the number is increasing each year. In addition, PGD techniques have been used to detect chromosomal abnormalities in the eggs or embryos produced by women of advanced maternal age who are undergoing fertility treatment. These patients usually do not have a known inheritable disease or chromosomal abnormality; rather, PGD serves to detect chromosomal abnormalities arising in mitosis or early phase mitoses that are more common in older women—for example, Down's syndrome.[3]

Another application of PGD screening arises when parents seek to have a child whose HLA type (human leukocyte-associated antigens—a specific set of proteins) will closely match those of another person (typically, another sibling) who needs a bone marrow transplant. PGD allows these embryos to be examined for the match prior to implantation, and selected to insure that they are a perfect HLA match.

The ground-breaking and challenging aspect of PGD is that it "allows parents to identify and select the genetic characteristics of their children."[4] On the horizon is the possibility that PGD will be used by individuals to create children with specific positive characteristics. We have at this point very little genetic information about such complex characteristics as height or intelligence or physical ability, but it is quite possible that over time we will develop a firm enough understanding of the human genome that we will be capable of performing PGD testing, not just to screen out certain illnesses, but to screen *in* certain enhancing characteristics. PGD can already be used to screen for gender. In later sections we will return to examine in greater detail this and other related, difficult questions posed by PGD.[5]

II. JEWISH LAW AND MODERN TECHNOLOGY

The relationship between modern technology, biomedical ethics, and Jewish law has been well developed over the last fifty years. As has been noted in a variety of sources and in diverse contexts, Jewish law insists that new technologies—and particularly new reproductive technologies—are neither categorically prohibited nor categorically permissible. Rather, they are subject to a case-by-case, method-by-method analysis of the consequences of the new technology as well as the methodology employed, and both need to be permissible for a new technology to be proper in the eyes of Jewish law. The central theme and thrust of this section is that Jewish law is comfortable with humans as caretakers of nature, and that within those parameters genetic engineering is to be treated like any other

---

[4] Kathy Hudson, Director of the Genetics and Public Policy Center, in preface to the preliminary PGD options report, *ibid.*

[5] This analysis raises a set of very complicated conversations about what is a disease and what is a trait and what are the limits of human variability. Illnesses such as sickle cell anemia can confer immunity to malaria, which has advantages in certain—likely tropical—societies. It is commonly believed that cystic fibrosis for example produces heightened immunity against the bubonic plague and this accounts for its wide presence in eastern European and western European communities. It is a result of the heightened survivability of cystic fibrosis sufferers had in the Black Death of the Middle Ages. So too, undoubtedly even Tay Sachs provides a form of heightened immunity to some illness or another.

---

[2] *Ibid.*

[3] *Ibid.*

form of medical treatment, which is proper when used to benefit humanity.

Rabbi Judah Loew (Maharal of Prague) speaks eloquently about the power of human creativity to reshape the universe, and how that power was given to humanity at the time of creation. He states:

"The creativity of people is greater than nature. When God created in the six days of creation the laws of nature, the simple and complex, and finished creating the world, there remained additional power to create anew, just like people can create new animal species through interspecies breeding. . . . People bring to fruition things that are not found in nature; nonetheless, since these are activities that occur through nature, it is as if it entered the world to be created. . . ."[6]

Rabbi Loew's point is that human creativity is part of the creation of the world, and this creativity changes the world, which is proper. The fulfillment of the biblical mandate to conquer the earth[7] is understood in the Jewish tradition as permitting people to modify—conquer, dominate and control—nature to make it more amenable to humans. PGD and all other forms of genetic engineering are but one example of that conquest, which, when used to advance humanity, is without theological problem in the Jewish tradition.

Rabbi Loew continues, noting that even when Jewish law prohibits a certain activity (such as inter-species crossbreeding, an explicit biblical violation and the oldest form of genetic engineering), one should not assume that such conduct is immoral or unethical, but merely something Jewish law prohibits *to Jews.*

"There are those who are aghast at the interbreeding of two species. Certainly, this is contrary to Torah which God gave the Jews, which prohibits inter-species mixing. Nonetheless, Adam (the First Person) did this. Indeed, the world was created with many species that are prohibited to be eaten. Inter-species breeding was not prohibited because of prohibited sexuality or immorality. . . . Rather it is because [Jews] should not combine the various species together, as this is the way of Torah. As we already noted, the ways of the Torah, and the [permissible] ways of the world are distinct. . . . Just like the donkey has within it to be created [but was not created by God] . . . but was left to people to create it. Even those forms of creativity which Jewish law prohibits for Jews are not, by definition, bad. Some are simply prohibited to Jews."[8]

What flows most clearly from this is that there is nothing *intrinsically* wrong with crossbreeding, even if it violates Jewish law; indeed, Rabbi Loew nearly states that such conduct by general society is good—and after all, there is nothing wrong with using a donkey to plow or eating a nectarine.[9]

What then about the possibility of humans "playing God," so to speak? As the late Lord Immanuel Jakobovits stated, speaking for the Jewish tradition:

"We can dismiss the common argument of 'playing God' or 'interfering with divine providence.' Every medical intervention represents such interference. In the Jewish tradition this is expressly sanctioned in the biblical words: 'And he [an attacker] shall surely cause him [his victim] to be healed.'[10] The Talmud states: 'From here we see that the physician is given permission to heal.'"[11]

This articulation of the Jewish view is deeply rooted in Jewish law and ethics. The world was not created

---

[6] Judah Loew of Prague (Maharal), *Bi'ur ha-Gola*, pp. 38-39 (Jerusalem, 5731).

[7] *Genesis* 1:26.

[8] *Bi'ur ha-Gola*, pp. 38-39.

[9] Jewish law permits this enjoyment. Such conduct was prohibited by Jewish law because it was not part of the Divine mission for the Jewish people. Jewish law is not a general ethical category governing the conduct of all, but its scope and application is limited to Jews, not merely jurisdictionally, but even theologically. This point of view would seem apparent from the general attitude that the Jewish tradition takes to a number of proselytizing issues; for more on this, see Michael Broyde, "Proselytizing and Jewish Law," in John Witte, Jr. and Richard C. Martin, eds., *Sharing the Book: Religious Perspectives on the Rights and Wrongs of Proselytism*, pp. 45-60 (Maryknoll, NY, 1999).

[10] *Exodus* 21:19.

[11] "Will Cloning Beget Disaster?" *Wall Street Journal,* Friday, May 2, 1997.

a perfect place—people are responsible for their own conduct and condition and need not be accepting of the conditions of nature around them. Indeed, people are charged with improving on the handiwork of the Creator. The classic code of Jewish law states simply:

"Jewish law gives the doctor the license to heal, and it is a good deed, and within the category of life saving activity. One who withholds medical treatment is a spiller of blood [a murderer]."[12]

In the Jewish tradition, people were put on this earth to "improve the world in the image of the Divine,"[13] and not to accept the perilous condition of the world, whatever it might be. Tampering with nature is part of the human mission in the Jewish tradition; curing illness is one facet of that mission. Genetic engineering—the making of better people—is no less a fulfillment of this religious mandate than healing the sick.

The Jewish approach is in direct tension with both of the predominant trends in American law and ethics. One trend found in American law—consistently advanced by the Catholic Church in the name of canon law—is to seek to limit the ability of science to change fundamentals of nature, whether it be in the area of assisted reproduction, cloning, or genetic engineering. In this view, playing Creator with a capital 'C' is the problem. As a group of Catholic physicians noted:

"The cloning of human beings would be a violation of the natural moral law. Research in cloning as it applies to man is degrading. It destroys the dignity of human nature by treating the human person as a material commodity to be manipulated according to whim and fancy."[14]

Reproduction, according to this argument, is solely God's domain. When we take it upon ourselves to create humans through reproductive cloning, we are infringing on the divine domain, "playing God," as it were. In this view, finite and fallible beings should not make decisions properly limited to the infinite and infallible.[15]

The second trend in American law is to defer to individual choices and abhor governmental regulation.[16] A recent *New York Times* article accurately captures the spirit of modern medical ethics in America in the reproductive area by noting:

"In the hubbub that ensued (after Dolly was cloned), scientist after scientist and ethicist after ethicist declared that Dolly should not conjure up fears of a Brave New World. There would be no interest in using the technology to clone people, they said. They are already being proved wrong. There has been an enormous change in attitudes in just a few months; scientists have become sanguine about the notion of cloning and, in particular, cloning a human being. 'The fact is that, in America, cloning may be bad but telling people how they should reproduce is worse. . . .'"[17]

In secular America, freedom to choose one's own reproductive method, and market forces that make such choices profitable, will determine who the parent is, and what the law should permit. "America is not ruled by ethics. It is ruled by law."[18]

Such is, simply put, not the methodology of Jewish law—Jewish law focuses as much on use and purpose as on process and procedure. Thus, understanding why a person might undergo PGD affects very much how we view a technology. Of course, one might decide that this technology can be used for good or bad and permit it as a matter of public policy, while telling adherents of Jewish law that this technology may only be used in particular cases; on the other hand, one might decide that the amount of bad from the technology so overwhelms

---

[12] *Shulhan Arukh, Yoreh De'a* 336:1.

[13] The Hebrew phrase *le-takken olam be-malkhut Shaddai* is taken from the *Alenu* prayer, which is recited three times daily in the traditional liturgy.

[14] Catholic Medical Association, *Human Cloning: Position Paper of the Catholic Medical Association*, reprinted in *Issues of Law & Medicine* 15:323, pp. 323-324 (2000).

[15] See *Hastings Law Journal* 53:1143, 1182.

[16] See Laurence Tribe, "Second Thoughts on Cloning," *New York Times*, Dec. 5, 1997 (advocating the free market approach to cloning).

[17] Gina Kolata, "Human Cloning: Yesterday's Never Is Today's Why Not?" *New York Times*, Dec. 2, 1997.

[18] *Ibid.*

the good that one should simply prohibit it in all cases, notwithstanding the potential good that is present from a smaller number of cases. Consider the comments of Rabbi Gedalya Dov Schwartz, Av Beth Din of the Beth Din of America, in the context of stem cell research:

"Halakha does not consider any embryonic development within forty days of conception as having the sacred protected status of a human being. Therefore, the use of embryos for stem cell research is not considered an act of destruction of life. This use of the embryo does not come under any category of abortion after forty days of conception, which is forbidden by Halakha, unless the mother's life is in danger. Consequently, in view of the possible, very positive results of stem cell research for the cure of various diseases, it is not only permitted but it is an imperative to support and proceed with this field of science.

"At this time, this decision is limited to the removal of stem cells from embryos resulting from in-vitro fertilization developed for reproductive purposes. The decision is based on the current assumption that such embryos provide sufficient quantities and variety of types to proceed with stem cell research, to the end of scientific knowledge for the relief of serious illness and the saving of lives. Should this category of embryos prove to be insufficient in quantity; or should it consist of too narrow a profile of humanity, and not reflective of the variety of genetic and histological types, thus limiting the potential for healing and for saving lives, then it will be necessary to reconsider the scope of this decision."[19]

A Jewish law analysis of PGD presents a series of conversations similar to those raised by stem cell research.

III. GENETIC ENGINEERING: PERMITTED OR PROHIBITED?

The previous section's analysis was limited and theoretical. How to respond to attempts at genetic engineering abstractly, and PGD testing directly, is more complex, and requires a certain amount of categorization and analysis. Enhancement of the human gene pool has not

less than three different permutations, each with its own set of issues and complexities.

1. Gene enhancement can take place in the somatic (non-reproductive) cells of people (or fetuses). This form of therapy would introduce genetic material into a person with the goal of changing this person's cell line to provide some missing chemical or enzyme, needed by this person.[20]

2. Gene enhancement can take place in the germ (reproductive) cells of people (or fetuses). This form of therapy would introduce genetic material into a person with the goal of changing the reproductive cells of the person, such that their progeny have characteristics that they lack, or lack characteristics that they have.[21]

3. Gene enhancement can take place through genetic testing for specific genes with the results from the testing being used to prevent reproduction by the bearers of specific (bad) genes. This can be done though PGD, selective abortion, voluntary or mandatory restrictions on whom one may marry, and even forced sterilizations.[22]

Of these three cases, somatic-cell enhancement seems to be the easiest to address from a Jewish point of view. These genetic enhancements, grounded in healthcare tools derived from genetic engineering, would appear to be a form of medical therapy aimed at treat-

---

[20] See Leroy Walters and Julie Gage Palmer, *The Ethics of Human Gene Therapy* (1997) and *President's Commission for the Study of Ethical Problems in Medicine and Biomedical and Behavioral Research: Splicing Life*, pp. 25-30 (1982).

[21] *Ibid.*

[22] *Ibid.* See also "Note, Regulating Human Gene Therapy: Legislative Overreaction to Human Subject Protection Failures," *Administrative Law Review* 53:315, pp. 320-321 (2001).

It may not be readily apparent to all readers that this third category—testing—belongs in a discussion of genetic engineering. Examination and analysis, after all, is a far cry from actually altering the structure of genetic material within living beings. Nonetheless, testing here should be viewed in the broader context of sorting and selecting for the purpose of passing genetic material on to future generations. In a world of limited resources, the process of sorting is a form of genetic engineering.

---

[19] Press release dated August 21, 2001, which can be found online at www.jlaw.com/PressReleases/01-08-21.html

ing the sickly, and thus a proper activity in the eyes of the Jewish tradition.[23] The options of treating a Type I diabetic by daily injection of insulin or by monthly injection of insulin-producing cells (a remedy not yet available) or by a once-in-a-lifetime treatment of gene therapy of insulin- producing genes seem to be, from a Jewish ethical perspective, identical. Medical treatment, once it is proven to treat illness effectively, is mandatory in the Jewish tradition.[24] Until the point where it is well-accepted medically, such treatments (so long as they are designed to be medically palliative for each particular patient) are permitted to be used according to Jewish law or ethics, although they are not mandatory.[25] While undoubtedly some will object to gene therapy by pointing to the unknown or the possibility of abuse, these objections are no more persuasive in this form of medical treatment than in any other—that is not to say that significant abuse is impossible, but absent clear definitive evidence of harm, improving the human lot by providing effective medical care is part of the human mission, and should be done.[26] One should not stop medical treatments and scientific advances merely because of the unknown and not-quantifiable possibility of abuse.

So too, developing genetic tests as an application of genetic engineering in its broadest sense is not inherently problematic in Jewish law. That, of course, forces one to ask what the tests will be used for, and that remains the crucial question that can only be answered with a great deal of uncertainty. As others have noted, amniocentesis is a genetic test, which, independent of the value of the test itself, must be evaluated in the context of the possibility of abortion. Presumably, the correctness of a fetal genetic test very much depends on what one does with the data after the test is done. Genetic tests designed to induce abortion when the 'wrong' genotype is found as a result of the test, would presumably violate Jewish law except in one of the few situations where abortion is permitted.[27] On the other hand, the exact same test, when its results are used for treatment or therapy of the fetus or child, or merely to address pastoral concerns of the parents, is without any intrinsic Jewish law controversy.

Indeed, many have argued that the moral problems with genetic engineering have nothing to do with the technical issues relating to it; rather, it is the fear that the individuals produced through genetic engineering will give rise to two closely related problems.

The first is the problem of social inequality. Enhanced individuals will achieve social success more easily than those who remain un-enhanced. For example, studies

---

[23] See J. David Bleich, "The Obligation to Heal in the Judaic Tradition," in J. David Bleich and Fred Rosner eds., *Jewish Bioethics* (Hebrew Publishing Company, NY, 1979).

[24] See for example *Shulhan Arukh, Orah Hayyim*, 328 and comments of *Magen Avraham*, 328:6. The observation of R. Yaakov Emden, *Mor u-Ketsi'a* 328, is worth noting: "A person is obligated to be treated . . . only when the doctor is using a well established medically effective cure which has been proven reliable. When it has, a person in danger may be treated against his will."

[25] The exact point at which no one can claim that a specific medical treatment is mandatory is a matter in dispute, and the same is true with regard to how risky a medical treatment has to be before it is prohibited. Consider the case of a dying person who has a course of treatment which can restore long term health, unless the treatment kills the patient more quickly, which is the more likely result. May the patient use the treatment? Must the patient use the treatment? Is the treatment prohibited? R. Hayim Ozer Grodzinsky in *Ahi'ezer, Yoreh De'a* 16 rules that a patient may (but need not) undertake such a treatment. R. Moses Feinstein in *Iggerot Moshe, Yoreh De'a* 3:36, quotes *Mishnat Hakhamim* as prohibiting such treatment. Indeed, R. Feinstein's view is itself unclear, as in *Iggerot Moshe, Yoreh De'a* 2:58 he formulates a rule different from the one he formulates in *Yoreh De'a* 3:36.

[26] Consider for example human growth hormone. While undoubtedly there will be abuses of such a substance, few would claim that we ought not ever allow such a substance to be developed and used to address the consequences of children lacking in enough growth hormone. This example is particularly important, as one is hard-pressed to call being short a "health hazard" but yet, human growth hormone is a drug that is given to children to assist them in becoming more "normal" and thus permitted according to Jewish law.

[27] See "The Foetus and Foeticide," from David M. Feldman, *Birth Control In Jewish Law* (Third edition, New York, 1995), and "Abortion in Halakhic Literature," in J. David Bleich, *Contemporary Halakhic Problems*, vol. 1, pp. 325-371.

show that people who are tall and physically attractive are more likely to be hired and promoted than people who are short or unattractive. Although Western democratic societies can accommodate a certain degree of inequality, the difference in prospects between the enhanced and the un-enhanced could become so pronounced that serious social instability would ensue. Taken to the extreme, enhancements could be installed by manipulating germ lines, resulting in social advantages that are inherited by succeeding generations. This could eventually create a political system dominated by a genetic aristocracy, or "genobility," that possesses a lock on wealth, privilege, and power.

The second, and related, problem created by wealth-based access to genetic enhancement is the individual unfairness that would arise at the micro level if genetically enhanced individuals competed for scarce resources, or found themselves in conflicts of interest, with persons who were un-enhanced. Genetic enhancement could confer a decisive advantage in social interactions.[28]

In essence, this moral argument posits that the advances genetic engineering will provide may lead to a number of gross violations of normative laws and ethics—both Jewish and secular.

The correctness or incorrectness of this assertion of prospective ethical violation in human social conduct is difficult to evaluate in the Jewish tradition, but in the end, it simply cannot be accepted as grounds for halting all scientific progress and advancement—as a public policy, it is unacceptable. Many medical advantages initially accrue to the benefit of the wealthy or privileged, and allow certain advantages to go to those who have better access to health care. While one can express some social sadness over the inequitable division of resources, and even seek increased social justice to insure the proper allocation of the right to medical care, solving this problem by preventing the development of genetic engineering and related tests or procedures (as some explicitly advocate[29]) seems to deny the fundamental Jewish obligation to cure people of illness, something which genetic engineering can (we hope) do. Retrospectively insisting that the development of insulin to treat diabetics was unethical because the initial beneficiaries of the development for insulin were the wealthy, who could pay for insulin,[30] seems incorrect—we instead hope that treatments that were once expensive become available to all, and that is a better alternative than halting medical advancement, and preventing cure.[31]

Yet others fear that society will mislabel such genetic-engineered individuals as something other than human, and engage in activities tantamount to murder or enslavement, by treating these individuals as organ sources, or as individuals to be experimented upon, or as forced labor. One could imagine a rabbinic authority, aware of the possibility of ethical lapses in our society, arguing that as a temporary measure based on the exigencies of the times, genetic engineering should not be engaged in until such time as the appropriate educational activity can be embarked on to teach people

---

[29] See George J. Annals, "The Man on the Moon, Immortality and Other Millennial Myths:

> The Prospects and Perils of Human Genetic Engineering," *Emory Law Journal* 49:753 (2000) who states: On the national level, I (and others) called for a moratorium on human gene transfer experiments, what are more commonly (and incorrectly) referred to as "gene therapy" in early 2000. Many experiments were halted, but others continued, as does the debate about whether we know enough at this time to use them on humans. Formal moratorium or not, we must have a national (and international) debate on the goals of the research, and whether the lines between somatic cell and germ line research, or between treatment and enhancement research are meaningful. My own view is that the boundary line that really matters is set by the nature of the species itself, and that species-altering experiments should be outlawed.

[30] See Seale Harris, *Bunting's Miracle: The Story of the Discovery of Insulin* (Lippincott, 1946).

[31] For a fine volume on this topic, see *The Orthodox Forum Proceedings VI: Jewish Responsibilities to Society*, (D. Shatz & C. Waxman eds., 1997).

---

[28] Maxwell J. Mailman, "The Law of Above Averages: Leveling the New Genetic Enhancement Playing Field," *Iowa Law Review* 85:517 (2000).

that genetic engineering is a form of medical treatment and products of genetic engineering are human beings entitled to be treated with full and complete human dignity.[32] However, this type of prophylactic rule, which argues that permitted activity should be prohibited in light of the ethical failures of the times, is not the same as asserting as a normative rule of Jewish law that such conduct is prohibited. Rather, it is a temporary measure to prohibit that which is intrinsically permissible.[33]

The same is true about arguments against genetic engineering grounded in efficiency. Some have argued that Jewish law should prohibit genetic engineering because so much human reproductive material has to be expended to produce a single successful genetic

---

[32] It has been reported to this writer that such is the position of Meir Lau, the former chief rabbi of Israel, although I have been unable to verify these reports. News reports state that "Israeli Chief Rabbi Meir Lau said . . . the use of genetic engineering to create life is totally prohibited,' the rabbi said during a conference at Tel Aviv's Bar-Ilan University." See *AFP–Extel News Limited, AFX News* March 5, 1997. However, subsequent reports indicate that the "Chief Rabbinate doesn't reject genetic engineering in principle, but limits must be set, Chief Rabbis Eliyahu Bakshi-Doron and Yisrael Lau told the Knesset Science and Technology Committee at Hechal Shlomo on Monday;" *Jerusalem Post*, April 2, 1997, p. 3, "News in Brief."

[33] A recent article reported ("Cloning," *Pittsburgh Post Gazette*, March 1, 1997 at A):

> Rabbi Moshe Tendler, professor of medical ethics, Talmudic law and biology at Yeshiva University in New York, sees other potential good use for human cloning. In theory, the Orthodox scholar might permit cloned children when a husband cannot produce sperm. But he believes that the danger of abusing the science is too great to allow its use. As a Jew, he lives in the historical shadow of the Nazi eugenics program, in which people with "undesirable" traits were weeded out of society, forbidden to have children and ultimately killed. . . . "The Talmud says that man has to learn to sometimes say to the bee, 'Neither your honey nor your sting.' Are we good enough to handle this good technology? Of course we are, if we can set limits on it. And when we can train a generation of children not to murder or steal, we can prepare them not to use this technology to the detriment of mankind."

engineering cure.[34] Whatever the merits of this argument, it is likely that the march of scientific progress will vastly reduce the inefficiency of this process.

It could be argued that genetic engineering should be prohibited based on the various Talmudic dicta that seem to praise the importance of genetic diversity.[35] This, however, paints with too broad a brush. Eliminating the Tay Sachs gene or the sickle cell anemia gene seems to reduce genetic diversity in a positive way, in that it is part of the divine license to heal people—indeed, genetic cures can be more permanent and thus more effective. It is clear that the Jewish tradition views the natural process of genetic diversity as some sort of ideal, for a variety of reasons, including that it allows for the expression of a vast multiplicity in God's world—and thus intense genetic engineering, for a variety of reasons, falls far short of the ideal and should not be used absent illness or significant need. However, to claim that a single case or single category of genetic

---

[34] Robert Langreth, "Cloning Has Fascinating, Disturbing Potential" (*Wall Street Journal*, Monday, February 24, 1997), states that:

> In producing the first clone of an adult mammal, researchers plied a seemingly simple technique to achieve what many thought to be impossible. Here's how it worked:
>
> —Researchers took mammary-gland cells culled from an adult sheep, put them into a test tube and forced the cells into an inactive state by limiting their intake of nutrients.
>
> —Next, they took unfertilized eggs from female sheep and mechanically removed the DNA-containing nucleus from each egg.
>
> —They then used standard lab techniques to insert 277 of the adult DNA cells into 277 eggs.
>
> —Of these fused egg cells, only 29 survived for a few days and were surgically implanted into the wombs of 13 ewes.
>
> —One of the 13 sheep became pregnant and gave birth to a lamb that was an exact genetic replica of the adult donor, carrying none of the mother's genes.

[35] See *Sanhedrin* 38a and *Berukhot* 58a. R. Loew also indicates that genetic diversity is part of the divine plan; see his *Derekh Hayyim* 4, p. 204, and sources cited in note 6.

engineering, as an alternative to children being born with significant health problems, should be prohibited based on this analysis is no more persuasive than to claim that Jewish law should forbid artificial insemination or in vitro fertilization since it is less than ideal. The correct response should be that these less-than-ideal methods should only be used in circumstances where the ideal method does not or cannot work. The Talmudic dicta about genetic diversity stand for the proposition that wholesale genetic engineering should be discouraged, and nothing more.

More generally, Jewish law denies the authority of the post-Talmudic rabbis to make prophylactic decrees permanently prohibiting that which is permissible on these types of grounds.[36] This is even more so true when such a decree (*takkana*) would permanently prohibit an activity which is, in some circumstances, the only way a person can fulfill the obligation to cure themselves (or others) of a life threatening illness and could, in a variety of circumstances, have incredibly positive results.

So too, the Jewish tradition would not look askance at the use of genetic engineering to produce individuals when they are created primarily to be of specific assistance to others in need of help. Consider the case of an individual dying of leukemia, in need of a bone marrow transplant, who agrees to participate in a cloning experiment with the hopes of producing another like him or her who, in suitable time, can be used to donate bone marrow and save the life of a person (and even more so, the donor). The simple fact is that Jewish law and tradition view the donation of bone marrow as a morally commendable activity, and perhaps even morally obligatory such that one could compel it even from a child.[37] Jewish law and ethics see nothing wrong with

having children for a multiplicity of motives other than one's desire to "be fruitful and multiply." Indeed, the Jewish tradition recognizes that people have children to help take care of them in their old age, and accepts that as a valid motive.[38] There is no reason to assert that one who has a child because this child will save the life of another is doing anything other than two good deeds—having a child and saving the life of another.[39] The same is true for a couple who conceive a child with the hopes that the child will be a bone marrow match for their daughter who is dying of leukemia, and is in need of bone marrow from a relative. While the popular press condemns this conduct as improper, the Jewish tradition would be quite resolute in labeling this activity as completely morally appropriate. Having a child is a wonderful, blessed activity; having a child to save the life of another child is an even more blessed activity. Such conduct should be encouraged rather than discouraged. Motives for genetic engineering ought not to be seen as so important.

IV. PRE-IMPLANTATION GENETIC DIAGNOSIS AND JEWISH LAW

PGD might lay claim to a near uniqueness as a matter of public policy in the Jewish tradition, given its relationship to abortion. However, it is quite clear that normative Jewish law does not view pre-embryos as human life, no matter what one's general views are on the status of an implanted fetus in Jewish law. As Rabbi Gedalya Dov Schwartz stated in his letter in the name of the Beth Din of America concerning stem cell research:

"Halakha does not consider any embryonic development within forty days of conception as having the sacred protected status of a human being."[40]

---

36 Menachem Elon, *Jewish Law: History, Sources Principles* (Philadelphia, 1996), pp. 1103-1204.

37 See "Compelling Tissue Donations," J. David Bleich, *Tradition* 27:4, pp. 59-89 (1993). The rationale for this being that such donations (which are not really donations according to Jewish law, as they can be compelled) are neither statistically harmful nor particularly painful, and thus one who engages in this activity fulfills the biblical obligation not to stand by while their neighbor's blood is shed. This activity is compulsory activity in the same way one must jump into the water to save one who is drowning,

if one knows how to swim and such activity poses no danger.

38 See *Yevamot* 64a; *Shulhan Arukh, Even ha-Ezer* 154:6-7; and Yehiel Michel Epstein, *Arukh ha-Shulhan, Even ha-Ezer* 154:52-53.

39 The birth of the child itself is a fulfillment of the *mitsva* to be fruitful and multiply, and the donation by the child of bone marrow or blood or other replenishable body serums that can save the life of another—particularly of a parent—is a second good deed.

40 See note 19.

A similar such view is endorsed in a recent article by Rabbi Yitzchok Breitowitz on this topic.[41] Indeed, it is the common practice within the halakhic community to accept this view, and not require that all pre-embryos be implanted.

PGD is simply another variation of the process of in vitro fertilization, albeit one that, by incorporating genetic testing, allows for a higher degree of analysis of the embryo prior to implantation.

(On a parenthetical level, even if one were to disagree with this halakhic analysis, a strong public policy case could be made that, in fact, in our society the common alternative to PGD would be abortion; the destruction of the fetus after its implantation, as such, is permitted in American law. Given that reality, PGD might be the acceptable, and indeed preferred, technique given the wide presence of legal abortion. This is even more so true given the common, but rarely discussed, practice of declining to provide even life sustaining treatment for a child who is born with a serious genetic illness. Given that the alternative to PGD is typically either a post-implantation abortion or an even worse alternative, Jewish public policy ought to support the ready availability of PGD. Public policy is sometimes a matter of seeking the best alternative in the real world.)

The question of what form of PGD ought to be permitted according to Jewish law, and who should decide these questions, remains a difficult question. However, Jewish law generally assigns to adults, as the lawful guardians of children—and certainly to parents as guardians of their own children—the right to make decisions that are reasonably in the best interests of children. Using PGD to create a child without a specific illness would seem to be permitted according to Jewish law at the discretion of the child's parents. The same can be said for PGD that is designed to enhance any given characteristic in a child that increases the child's ability or functionality, in the discretion of the parents. However, were PGD to be used in a manner that were designed to harm children, even if the parents sincerely

believed that the conduct they were embarking on was not harmful, such activity would seem to violate Jewish law and in this circumstance would empower a Jewish court (as well a secular court) to intervene to prevent such conduct from occurring.[42] When it comes to the rights of parents, Jewish law only gives parents the right to conduct themselves in the best interests of their children, bounded by the range of activities found in the best interest of the child.[43]

This, of course, returns us to the conversation about whether PGD is a *mitsva* according to Jewish law. It would seem to this writer that PGD, once it becomes established as a non-experimental form of medical treatment and a form of standard medical care that is used in a certain set of cases, becomes mandatory in those (medically appropriate) cases. While assisted reproduction is not mandatory in Jewish law, PGD is different, precisely because it is a treatment not for fertility but of the child's underlying illness. Of course, determining whether a particular form of treatment is an established cure (*refu'a beduka*) or experimental treatment is a complex matter.[44] However, it is well established in Jewish law that just as treating illness is mandatory, avoiding illness is mandatory. People who have the ability to take a vaccine that will immunize them from a particular medical problem would seem, in this author's opinion, to be mandated by Jewish law to do so. PGD is an inoculation of some sort, in certain cases.[45]

---

[41] "Halakhic Approaches to the Resolution of Disputes Concerning the Disposition of Preembryos," Yitzchok A. Breitowitz, *Tradition* 31:1, 64-91 (1996).

[42] Consider the classic hypothetical discussed in the PGD literature about whether deaf parents can intentionally create deaf children through PGD, when they think that such is best for their child (as such is what they are).

Such is undoubtedly true even about such mundane matters as the balance between schizophrenia and artistic tendencies or the intentional creation of an idiot savant with a particular strong set of skills but also dramatically diseased.

[43] See Michael Broyde, "Child Custody and Jewish Law: A Review," *Journal of Halacha and Contemporary Society* 36, pp. 21-46 (1999).

[44] For further discussion on this topic see "Experimental Procedures and Pikuach Nefesh: The Concept of Refu'ah Bedukah," J. David Bleich, *Tradition* 25:1, pp. 50-58 (1989).

[45] That the notion of cost plays a role in the Jewish tradition's understanding of public policy is worthy of note. Treatment

Consider three different cases where PGD might be used. The first, and perhaps most troubling, is sex selection. PGD is a biologically simple, readily available technique for sex selection without engaging in the prohibited activity of abortion.[46] As a general matter, Jewish law treats sex selection as a trivial decision in its typical circumstances, and thus not a valuable or proper use of PGD (according to Jewish law). One could imagine situations where sex selection might be proper according to halakha—perhaps in the (rare) instances of personal status where such Jewish law status applies disadvantageously to members of one gender[47] or in situations where for a particular medical reason one gender poses a greater risk of a specific illness, although PGD ought to prevent that from happening in almost all cases. Simple selection in order to have a boy or a girl, would seem to be a violation of a sense of Jewish law

can be phenomenally expensive; such treatments do not become a *refuah beduka*, simply due to their functional unavailability as a matter of cost. Thus so long as PGD remains beyond the economic range of normal people (i.e., is not covered by health insurance), it cannot be an established cure in Jewish law.

In addition, PGD is in no way shape or form a *mitsva* when it is used merely to enhance one's genotype whether it be as a matter of height or intelligence or beauty as opposed to curing an illness. The enhancement of one's physical attributes is not always mandatory in Jewish law and indeed in this writer's opinion perhaps does not even rise to the level of permitting the discharge even of pre-embryos other than in severe cases. Thus, this writer thinks that pre-implantation genetics diagnosis as a form of enhancement of one's ability is much more complicated as a matter of Jewish law than as a treatment for an illness or a disease or to save the life of one's sibling in need of a blood or bone marrow transplant.

[46] It is more effective than sperm sorting, a common technique used in these circumstances medically, but yet a less effective technique.

[47] Consider the cases of *Moavi* and *halal* where, for status reasons, parents might choose to specify the gender of a future child. The prohibition in Deuteronomy 23:4 for a *Moavi* (Moabite) to enter (i.e., marry into) the congregation is limited to men. Thus a *Moavi* couple who converts to Judaism might choose to have a daughter to facilitate her marriage to a Jew. Similarly, a *Kohen halal* who has desecrated his kohen status with a prohibited relationship might sex-select a son, as a daughter's status would preclude her from marrying a *kohen*.

in that pre-embryos ought not be discarded for trivial reasons.[48]

Another case where PGD testing can play a vital role is in illnesses like Huntington's disease (which is an adult-onset dominant genetic characteristic that typically kills its carrier when the carrier is in his or her mid-30s). PGD would be a way of preventing Huntington's disease from being transmitted to the next generation. It would seem to this writer that the use of PGD to avoid the transmission of Huntington's disease (or Tay Sach's) unquestionably would be proper according to Jewish law. The goal would be to produce children who are more viable—this is a form of inoculation against such a disease.

A further situation that might be just over the horizon is the use of PGD in combination with gene transfer technology. This poses the question of genetic engineering and designing one's children. PGD and genetic engineering together appear ready to allow one to have robust gene therapy in order to provide certain genetic characteristics to be implanted in embryos, heightening genetic resistance or immunity to certain characteristics. Consider for example, the P53 gene, which is commonly referred as a cancer vaccine, in that the presence of this gene seems to vastly reduce the likelihood of suffering from certain cancers (by more closely monitoring DNA replication), and it is quite possible that this gene can simply be encoded in individuals in embryo through gene therapy and PGD. As explained above, the introduction of genetic sequences into the human genome as a way of increasing human health would not be controversial according to Jewish law—that is not to say it is medically wise or scientifically possible. It is, however, merely to note that Jewish law does not perceive a ready difference between a genetic cure and a non-genetic cure for an illness. If P53 is in fact a cancer vaccine, we ought to use it. If it has other consequences, then we ought not to use it. But the fact that it is genetic rather than non-genetic seems to pose no significant variant in Jewish law.

[48] A related question is whether sex selection may be permitted in cases where PGD is already being done for another reason—parents have sought to examine for another illness and only afterward is sex selection brought up. This would seem easier to justify.

Another application of PGD screening which is not undertaken to detect the child's own illness, arises when parents seek to have a child whose HLA type (human leukocyte-associated antigens—a specific set of antigens) will closely match to another person (typically, another sibling) who needs a bone marrow transplant. PGD allows these embryos to be examined for the match prior to implantation, and selected to insure that they are a perfect HLA match. Without PGD testing, the odds of naturally producing an HLA match is less than 15%, whereas with PGD, the odds can be raised to nearly 100%. This child will be born to save the life of the sibling. Although contemporary American culture seems to find this "designer children" issue to be problematic, we have already seen that the Jewish tradition would not look askance at the application of PGD technology to produce individuals who can be of specific assistance to others. It is worth repeating that one who has a child because this child will save the life of another is doing nothing other than two good deeds—having a child and saving the life of another.[49] Having a child is a wonderful, blessed activity; having a child to save the life of another child, even more so. Such conduct should be encouraged rather than discouraged.

CONCLUSION

The combination of in vitro fertilization with PGD is a less than an ideal way to have children, as all assisted reproduction removes fertilization from loving sexuality, which is the Biblical ideal. Nonetheless, the Jewish tradition favors healing people from their illnesses even in situations where to effectuate a cure, deviation from the ideal is needed. Human life is sacred, and the eradication of illness a *mitsva*. It is a brave and very new world in the medical sciences, and we await our opportunity to fix the world—by curing illness, inventing vaccines, and otherwise changing nature to make it more amenable to human life. PGD could be such.

POSTSCRIPT

Advancements in human reproductive genetic technology move forward at an astonishingly rapid pace. (As this paper was being finalized, a report came from the South Korean scientific community announcing the creation of human embryos through cloning and the extraction of embryonic stem cells.[50]) These developments may be hard to ponder, but they nonetheless deserve careful consideration from the perspective of Jewish law. This section will briefly present five of them to contemplate what the future could look like in certain circumstances and speculate as to how Jewish law might approach them.

The first is the human artificial chromosome (HAC). Rather than using a virus to add genes to cells, researchers are working to create entire chromosome structures in a laboratory from synthetic material. This technology is a long way off, and at first would be used alongside natural chromosomes for gene therapy purposes. But the HAC scenario raises the possibility that one day the root source genetic material implanted into a particular sperm or egg will not come from humans at all but will be an artificially created string of genetic code that serves the function of either sperm or egg and resembles neither parent in any genetic way. Rather, it is simply a programmed sequence of DNA taken out of a data-bank code and then synthesized to have certain characteristics. It would seem to this author that there is no father according to Jewish law in that situation, although this author remains convinced of the correctness of the view that the mother is the person who carries the child to term independent of any other genetic contribution; but this matter is quite disputed.[51]

A second development, much closer to actual implementation, is "ooplasm transfer," in which a woman of advanced reproductive years who suffers from mitochondrial disabilities is given mitochondria (cytoplasm) from another woman. (This was done briefly already in the United States, but was subsequently prohibited through a directive of the Food and Drug Administration.) In this model, a child would be born with the sperm from one person, the genetic material in the nucleus of the egg is from another person, and the mitochondrial DNA from yet another person. This creates complex models of motherhood, in that one has

---

[49] See note 39.

[50] Gina Kolata, "Human Embryos Created Through Cloning," *New York Times*, February 12, 2004.

[51] See Michael Broyde, "Cloning People: A Jewish View," *Connecticut Law Review* 30:2, pp. 503-535 (1997).

to evaluate the various contributions of the possible mothers. However, as noted above, the author's view is that the mother is the person who carries the child to term independent of any other genetic contribution.

Yet a third genetic technology to consider is intentional human chimerism, in which the embryonic material of two fetuses is intentionally mixed at the two, eight, sixteen, or thirty-two cell level, creating a human being who is a mixture of two different fetuses. (This sometimes, albeit very rarely, occurs in nature when fraternal twins are created but then one is subsumed in utero into the other, giving rise to a human being who has two distinctly different genetic sequences and codes.) The creation of a human chimerism is a distinctly real possibility in modern technology.[52] In essence, two blastospheres are combined producing only a single fetus but with diverse characteristics. This might be done medically in order to give the child enhanced immunities that can't be provided through a single direct genetic manipulation. (It also might be designed for social-cultural reasons in order to create a child with more than one mother or more than one father.) This child would appear to have more than one father and/or maybe more than one mother, depending on the genetic contributors in each case, and depending further on one's view of the birth mother as the mother according to Jewish law, at least as a matter of doubt, and maybe even as a matter of certainty. There is some precedent in halakha for the possibility of more than one mother or father, and doubt about these matters is clearly a possibility in halakha. On the other hand, one could well see halakha simply following the rule of majority to determine who is a parent, and the other potential parent is just a '*safek*' (uncertain).

A fourth case is a different form of chimerism, in which cells of a human are mixed with cells of another mammal,[53] so as to provide heightened immunity or other characteristics that cannot be found in the human genetic sequence. This case raises basic questions of human identity. It is the author's view that basic questions of humanness are resolved by asking whether the living creature in question had either a human mother, in which case it is human independent of its mental abilities, or by looking at its mental function. High level mental function, like that found in a small child, makes one 'human' according to halakha. Indeed, support for the proposition that "humanness" is determined by human function in cases where apparent definition of humanness—birth from a human mother—does not apply, can be found in an explicit discussion of humanness along these lines in the Jerusalem Talmud.[54]

A fifth (but by no means final) issue to consider is reproductive xenotransplant—the placing of a fertilized embryo of one species into the uterus of another species. I think this case is easier, and not harder, than the case discussed above and it has some Talmudic precedent in the discussion about mermaids, and whether they are human or kosher,[55] where Rashi seems to claim that these mermaids can be impregnated by humans. So too, there seems to be a discussion in the Mishna of the humanness of orangutans (in Hebrew, *adnei ha-sadeh*).[56] Both Tiferet Yisrael and Rambam appear to grant these creatures human status with regard to certain issues. This might relate to the substantive discussion in the previous paragraph.

Tradition 38, no. 1 (Spring 2004): 54-75.
Reprinted with permission by publisher

---

[52] This technology has proponents in the homosexual community and is growing in popularity among same-sex couples who wish to have offspring that resembles both of them genetically, but who recognize the need for the contribution of genetic material from a member of the opposite sex. Indeed, this author has already faced a query from a lesbian couple, one of whom was Jewish, who used the sperm of a gay man for in vitro fertilization, then proceeded to combine the genetic material from two IVF eggs before implanting the resulting fetus in the womb. This situation is referred in the lesbian community's colloquial slang as an "omelet," as one needs to break two eggs to create this fetus.

[53] Human-mouse hybrid experiments have been considered—see Nicholas Wade, "Stem Cell Mixing May Form a Human-Mouse Hybrid," *New York Times*, November 27, 2002; as have human-cow hybrids—see Nicholas Wade, "Human-Cow Hybrid Cells Are Topic of Ethics Panel," *New York Times*, November 18, 1988.

[54] *Niddah* 3:2.

[55] Rashi *Bekhorot* 8a, s.v. *benai yama*.

[56] *Kil'ayyim* 8:5.

My Father Was an Anonymous Sperm Donor

Katrina Clark

I really wasn't expecting anything the day, earlier this year, when I sent an e-mail to a man whose name I had found on the Internet. I was looking for my father, and in some ways this man fit the bill. But I never thought I'd hit pay dirt on my first try. Then I got a reply—with a picture attached.

From my computer screen, my own face seemed to stare back at me. And just like that, after 17 years, the missing piece of the puzzle snapped into place.

The puzzle of who I am.

I'm 18, and for most of my life, I haven't known half my origins. I didn't know where my nose or jaw came from, or my interest in foreign cultures. I obviously got my teeth and my penchant for corny jokes from my mother, along with my feminist perspective. But a whole other part of me was a mystery.

That part came from my father. The only thing was, I had never met him, never heard any stories about him, never seen a picture of him. I didn't know his name. My mother never talked about him—because she didn't have a clue who he was.

When she was 32, my mother—single, and worried that she might never marry and have a family—allowed a doctor wearing rubber gloves to inject a syringe of sperm from an unknown man into her uterus so that she could have a baby. I am the result: a donor-conceived child.

And for a while, I was pretty angry about it.

I was angry at the idea that where donor conception is concerned, everyone focuses on the "parents"—the adults who can make choices about their own lives. The recipient gets sympathy for wanting to have a child. The donor gets a guarantee of anonymity and absolution from any responsibility for the offspring of his "donation." As long as these adults are happy, then donor conception is a success, right?

Not so. The children born of these transactions are people, too. Those of us in the first documented generation of donor babies—conceived in the late 1980s and early '90s, when sperm banks became more common and donor insemination began to flourish—are coming of age, and we have something to say.

I'm here to tell you that emotionally, many of us are not keeping up. We didn't ask to be born into this situation, with its limitations and confusion. It's hypocritical of parents and medical professionals to assume that biological roots won't matter to the "products" of the cryobanks' service, when the longing for a biological relationship is what brings customers to the banks in the first place.

We offspring are recognizing the right that was stripped from us at birth—the right to know who both our parents are.

And we're ready to reclaim it.

Growing up, it didn't matter that I don't have a dad—or at least that is what I told myself. Just sometimes, when I was small, I would daydream about a tall, lean man picking me up and swinging me around in the front yard, a manly man melting at a touch from his little girl. I wouldn't have minded if he weren't around all the time, as long as I could have the sweet moments of reuniting with his strong arms and hearty laugh. My daydreams always ended abruptly; I knew I would never have a dad. As a coping mechanism, I used to think that he was dead. That made it easier.

I've never been angry at my mother—all my life she has been my hero, my everything. She sacrificed so much as a single mother, living on food stamps, trying to make ends meet. I know that many people considered her a pioneer, a trailblazer for a new offshoot of the women's movement. She explained to me when I was quite young why it was that I didn't have a "dad," just a "biological father." I used to love to repeat that word—biological—because it made me feel smart, even though I didn't understand its implications.

Then when I was 9, the mother of one of my classmates ran for political office. I remember seeing a television ad for her, and her family appeared at the end—the complete nuclear household in the back yard, the kids playing on a swing suspended from a tree and eating their father's barbeque. I looked back at my lonely, tired mother, who sat there with a weak smile on her face.

In the middle of the fifth grade, I met a new friend, and we had a lot in common: We both had single mothers. Her mother had suffered through two divorces. My friend didn't have much to say about her dad, mainly because she knew so little about him. But at least she got to visit him and his new family. And I was jealous. Later, in the eighth grade, another friend's father had an affair and her parents divorced. She was in so much pain, and I tried to empathize for the loss of her dad. But I was jealous of her, too, for all the attention she was getting. No one had ever offered me support or sympathy like that.

Around this time, my mother and I moved in with a friend and—along with several other teenagers, one infant and some other adults—lived with her for nearly a year. I went through a teenage anger stage; I would stay in my room, listening to Avril Lavigne and to Eminem's lyrics of broken homes and broken people. I felt broken, too. All the other teenagers in the house had problems with their dads. I would sit with them through tears during various rough times, and then I'd go back to my room and listen to some more Eminem. I was angry, too, and angry that I had nowhere to direct my anger.

When my mother eventually got married, I didn't get along with her husband. For so long, it had been just the two of us, my mom and I, and now I felt like the odd girl out. When she and I quarreled, this new man in our lives took to interjecting his opinion, and I didn't like that. One day, I lost my composure and screamed that he had no authority over me, that he wasn't my father—because I didn't have one.

That was when the emptiness came over me. I realized that I am, in a sense, a freak. I really, truly would never have a dad. I finally understood what it meant to be donor-conceived, and I hated it.

It might have gone on this way indefinitely, but about a year ago I happened to see a television show about a woman who had died of a heart attack. A genetic disease had caused her heart to deteriorate, but she didn't know about her predisposition because she had been adopted as a baby and didn't know her biological families' medical histories. It hit me that I didn't know mine, either. Or half of it, at least.

So I began to research Fairfax Cryobank, the Northern Virginia sperm bank where my mother had been inseminated. I knew that sperm donors are screened and tested thoroughly, but I was still concerned. The bank had been established in 1986, a mere two years before my conception. Many maladies have come to light since then.

I e-mailed the bank five times over the course of a year, requesting medical information about my donor, but no one responded. Then one Friday last spring, I started surfing the Web. Eventually I came upon an archive of "Oprah" shows. One was a show about artificial insemination using anonymous donors. A girl perched on Oprah's couch. Next to her sat her "donor," the man who was her biological father.

I froze. Why hadn't I thought of that? If I wanted medical information and a sense of roots, who better to seek out than the man responsible for them?

I set out to find my own donor. From the limited information my mother had been given—his blood type, race, ethnicity, eye and hair color and hair texture; his height, weight and body build; his years of college and course of study—I concluded that he had probably graduated from a four-year university in Northern Virginia or the District within a span of three years. Now all I had to do was search through the records and yearbooks of all the possible universities and make some awkward phone calls. I figured if I worked intensely enough, my search would take a minimum of 10 years. But I was ready and willing.

A few days later, searching for an online message board for donor-conceived people, I came across a donor and offspring registry. Scanning past some entries for more recent donors, I spotted a donation date closer to what

I was looking for. I e-mailed the man who had posted the entry. A few days later he sent a warm response and attached a picture of himself. I read through his pleasant words and scrolled down to look at the photo. My breath stopped. I called for my mother, who rushed in, thinking something was terribly wrong. "I think I've found my biological father," I gasped between sobs. "Look at the picture. . . . That's my face."

After a few weeks of e-mailing, this stranger and I took DNA tests. When the results arrived, I tore open the envelope, feeling like a character in a soap opera. Most of the scientific language went over my head, but I understood one fact more clearly than I have ever understood anything in my life: There was, the letter said, a 99.9902 percent chance that this man was my father. After 17 years, I let out a long sigh.

I had found the man who had given me blue eyes and blond hair. And it had taken me only a month.

My life has changed since then. Once the initial disbelief that I had found my father wore off, my thoughts turned to all the other donor-conceived kids out there who have been or will be holding their breath much longer than I. My search for my father had been unusually successful; most offspring will look for many, many years before they succeed, if they ever do.

My heart went out to those others, especially after I participated in a couple of online groups. When I read some of the mothers' thoughts about their choice for conception, it made me feel degraded to nothing more than a vial of frozen sperm. It seemed to me that most of the mothers and donors give little thought to the feelings of the children who would result from their actions. It's not so much that they're coldhearted as that they don't consider what the children might think once they grow up.

Those of us created with donated sperm won't stay bubbly babies forever. We're all going to grow into adults and form opinions about the decision to bring us into the world in a way that deprives us of the basic right to know where we came from, what our history is and who both our parents are.

Some countries, such as Australia and the United Kingdom, are beginning to move away from the practice of paying donors and granting them anonymity, and making it somewhat easier for offspring to find their biological fathers. I understand anonymity's appeal for so many donors: Even if their offspring were to find them one day—which is becoming more and more probable—they have no legal, social, financial or moral obligation to their children.

But perhaps if donors were not paid and anonymity were no longer guaranteed, those still willing to participate would seriously consider the repercussions of their actions. They would have to be prepared to someday meet the people whom they helped create, to answer questions and to deal with a range of erratic emotions from their offspring. I believe I've let go of any resentment about the way I was conceived. I'm playing the cards I've been dealt and trying to make the best of things. But not all donor-conceived people share this mindset.

As relief about my own situation has come to me, I've talked freely and regularly about being donor-conceived, in public and in private. In the beginning, I also talked about it a lot with my biological father. After a bit, though, I noticed that his enthusiasm for our developing relationship seemed to be waning. When I told him of my suspicion, he confirmed that he was tired of "this whole sperm-donor thing." The irony stings me more each time I think of him saying that. The very thing that brought us together was pushing us in opposite directions.

Even though I've only recently come into contact with him, I wouldn't be able to just suck it up if he stopped communicating with me. There's still so much I want to know. I want to know him. I want to know his family. I'm certain he has no idea how big a role he has played in my life despite his absence—or because of his absence. If I can't be too attached to him as my father, I'll still always be attached to the feeling I now have of *having* a father.

I feel more whole now than I ever have. I love our conversations, even the most trivial ones. I don't love him, and I don't know if I ever will, but I care about him a lot.

Now that he knows I exist, I'm okay if he doesn't care
for me in the same way. But I hope he at least thinks
of me sometimes.

Katrina Clark is a student in the undergraduate hearing program at Gallaudet University.
clarkatrina@gmail.com

The Washington Post, Sunday, December 17, 2006.
Reprinted with permission by publisher

Lesson 5

With You In Mind:
Ethical Treatment of the Mentally Disabled

Introduction

In the seventeenth century, the mentally ill were often chained to walls, whipped, and housed in dungeons with vagrants and criminals. Nineteenth-century reformer Dorothy Dix was at the vanguard of creating humane asylums for the insane, where patients were provided sunny rooms and opportunity to exercise outdoors. A century later, many asylums were overcrowded and filthy, and the chains of the Middle Ages had been replaced with surgery, electro-convulsive therapy, and stupor-inducing drugs.

With the development of new psychiatric drug treatments in the seventies and eighties, it was felt that the asylums were no longer needed, and most of them were shut down. Today, a third of the homeless are mentally ill, yet they are unable to procure adequate housing or follow-up care. More than 100,000 people in American jails today are mentally ill, and some are held without charges while they await a bed in a psychiatric hospital.

If excessive interference into the lives of people who are mentally ill has often resulted in travesty, benign neglect has not yielded more humane results. In this lesson, we explore some Jewish ethical guidelines for the development of compassionate treatment for people suffering from mental illness.

Stewardship

Text 1

אַתָּה חוֹנֵן לְאָדָם דַּעַת, וּמְלַמֵּד לֶאֱנוֹשׁ בִּינָה. חָנֵּנוּ מֵאִתְּךָ חָכְמָה בִּינָה וָדָעַת.
בָּרוּךְ אַתָּה ה׳ חוֹנֵן הַדָּעַת.
תפלת העמידה, סידור תהלת ה׳

You graciously bestow knowledge upon humans and teach mortals understanding. Graciously bestow upon us from Your wisdom, understanding, and knowledge. Blessed are You, G-d, who graciously bestows knowledge.

Amidah prayer, Sidur Tehilat Hashem

Text 2

רבונו של עולם כל מה שעשית בעולמך יפה, חכמה יפה מן הכל, חוץ מן השטות, מה הנאה בשוטה הזה, אדם מהלך בשוק וקורע בגדיו והתינוקות משחקין בו ורצין אחריו והעם משחקין עליו, זה נאה לפניך.
ילקוט שמעוני, שמואל א, קלא

G-d, everything that You have made in Your universe is beautiful—and wisdom the most beautiful of all—except for madness. What benefit can there be in a person being mad? A mad person walks in the marketplace and tears his clothes while children mock him and chase him and people jeer at him; is this beautiful before You?

Midrash, Yalkut Shimoni, I Samuel 131

Text 3a

לֹא תְקַלֵּל חֵרֵשׁ וְלִפְנֵי עִוֵּר לֹא תִתֵּן מִכְשֹׁל וְיָרֵאתָ מֵאֱלֹקֶיךָ אֲנִי ה'.

ויקרא יט,יד

ou shall not curse a deaf person. You shall not place a stumbling block before a blind person, and you shall fear your G-d. I am the Lord.

Leviticus 19:14

Text 3b

הזכיר גם כן שהשומע לא יקלל חרש והרואה לא ישגה עור בדרך והוא דבור המשליי לכל בעל כח שלא יענה את חלושי הכח כי יבא מפחיתות המדות.

אברבנאל, שם

The verse tells us that the hearing person should not curse the deaf person, and the seeing person should not cause the blind person to trip on his path. This is a metaphor instructing any powerful person not to oppress those who are weaker, for this is an indication of poor character.

Rabbi Don Yitschak Abarbanel, ibid.

Rabbi Don Yitschak Abarbanel (1437–1508). Born in Lisbon, Portugal; rabbi, scholar, and statesman. Abarbanel served as minister to King Alfonso V of Portugal. After intrigues at court led to accusations against him, he fled to Spain, where he once again served as a counselor to royalty. It is claimed that Abarbanel offered Ferdinand and Isabella 600,000 crowns for the revocation of their Edict of Expulsion of 1492, but to no avail. After the expulsion, he eventually settled in Italy where he wrote commentaries on the scriptures, as well as other esteemed works. He is buried in Padua.

Text 4

ובית דין מעמידין אפוטרופוס לשוטים כדרך שמעמידין לקטנים
כדי שלא יבזבזו את שלהם.
לבוש, חושן משפט רלה,כ

The *beit din* should appoint a guardian for the mentally ill just as they do for [orphaned] minors, so that others do not loot their belongings.

Rabbi Mordechai Jaffe, *Levush, Choshen Mishpat* 235:20

Text 5

. . . החובל בחברו חייב עליו משום חמשה דברים בנזק בצער ברפוי בשבת ובבשת
החובל בהן חייב והם שחבלו באחרים פטורין.
משנה, בבא קמא ח,א–ד

One who wounds another person is obligated [to pay monetary compensation] on five counts: damage, pain, medical expenses, loss of income (due to being unable to work), and embarrassment. . . .

[Regarding people suffering from insanity:] One who harms them is obligated to pay compensation, whereas they are exempt for the damage they cause to others.

Mishnah, Bava Kama 8:1–4

Question for Discussion

Might these laws seeking to protect the mentally ill also create some disadvantages for them?

Two Case Studies

Text 6a

זכין לאדם שלא בפניו ואין חבין לאדם שלא בפניו.

משנה, עירובין ז,יא

We may act to bring benefit to a person who is absent; we are not permitted to make decisions that are disadvantageous to a person who is absent.

Mishnah, Eiruvin 7:11

Case Study I

Tommy Strunk was twenty-eight years old in 1969, and dying of a fatal kidney disease. Only a transplant could save his life. Doctors considered the possibility of using a kidney from a cadaver if and when one became available, or one from a live donor if a donor could be found. His mother, father, and a number of other relatives were tested. Because of incompatibility of blood type or tissue, none were medically acceptable as live donors. His brother Jerry Strunk was the only member of his extended family who was found to be an acceptable organ match.

But Jerry, though he idolized Tommy, was confined to a state mental hospital. His mental age had been assessed at approximately six years. Even if he had fully understood the crisis, Jerry was mentally incompetent to authorize surgery on himself.

Jerry's mother went to court to get permission, and the surgery was approved. But then Jerry's guardian attempted to overturn the decision, arguing that the surgery was not in Jerry's best interests.

The question before the court of appeals was whether the court could grant the request of Jerry's mother to permit a kidney to be removed from an incompetent ward of the state in order to save his brother.

The majority opinion made the following arguments in support of allowing the transplant:

1. Tom's best chance for survival was receiving a kidney from his brother.

2. The risks to Jerry as a donor were relatively slight.

3. Jerry would be harmed by Tom's death because despite his disability, Jerry showed emotional reactions, and he frequently asked about Tom's visits.

4. While Jerry might not understand the details of Tom's kidney failure, Jerry was aware that he played a role in the relief of the current tension about Tom's health. Were Tom to die, Jerry would be burdened with guilt.

The dissenting judge made the following arguments:

1. While parents may become martyrs themselves, it does not follow that they are free, in identical circumstances, to make martyrs of their children before they reach the age of legal discretion and can make that choice for themselves. The ability to understand and consent is a prerequisite to the donation of part of the human body.

2. There was no guarantee that the transplant would save Tom's life; the body frequently rejects transplanted organs.

3. While the surgery would not greatly endanger Jerry's life, it did contain some risks.

4. The permission of the court was based on the fact that there would be psychological benefits to the ward. However, the ward had the mentality of a six-year-old child. It is common knowledge beyond dispute that the loss of a close relative of a six-year-old child is not of major impact. Opinions concerning psychological trauma are, at best, nebulous.

Adapted from Strunk vs. Strunk, 445 S W 2d 145 (K.Y.App, 1969)

Questions for Discussion

Do you agree with the majority opinion or the minority opinion? Which argument was most compelling in shaping your view?

בהשתלת מוח עצם התורם סובל מכאבים חזקים עד כדי כך שצריכים להרדימו בהרדמה
כללית בזמן לקיחת מוח העצם. ואמר לי הגרש״ז אויערבאך זצ״ל שמותר לקחת ילד
כתורם, אם הוא בר דעת ומסכים לזה, כדי להציל את בן משפחתו הנמצא בסכנת נפשות.
ואם הוא עדיין לא הגיע לגיל להיות בר דעת, והוא התורם היחיד האפשרי, צריך עיון
גדול אם להוריו יש רשות להסכים עבורו כדי להציל בן משפחתו, מכוח הכלל שזכין
את האדם שלא בפניו וזכות גדול הוא לו שמציל נפש מישראל.

נשמת אברהם, חושן משפט רמג,א

Abone marrow transplant is extremely painful to the donor, to the extent that the donor must be put under general anesthesia while the bone marrow is harvested. Rabbi S. Z. Auerbach told me that it is permitted to use a child as a donor to save the life of a terminally ill family member, so long as the child is mature in understanding and agrees.

If the child is the only available donor but has not reached the age of mature understanding, it is very questionable if the parents have the right to consent on behalf of the child to save a family member by applying the principle, "We benefit a person in their absence" [to assert] that it is a great benefit for the donor to save another's life.

Rabbi Dr. Abraham S. Abraham, *Nishmat Avraham, Chosen Mishpat* 243:1

Rabbi Dr. Abraham S. Abraham MD, FRCP. Born in Jerusalem and received his medical training in England. Since 1989, Dr. Abraham has been chief of internal medicine at the Shaare Zedek Medical Center in Jerusalem, and since 1990, a professor of medicine at the Hebrew University Hadassah Medical School. His most notable work, *Nishmat Avraham*, printed in both Hebrew and English, is an essential text addressing medical-halachic issues in all branches of medicine and surgery.

Question for Discussion

In light of Text 7, what is the key piece of information a rabbinic court would have to weigh in order to determine whether it could authorize Jerry to donate a kidney?

Case **Study II**

The Willowbrook State School in Staten Island, New York housed and cared for children who suffered from severe mental disabilities. At the time, public facilities were considered the best care option for children suffering from a mental disability. Because there were very few state institutions that served this population, the facility was forced to accept more children than were recommended for its size.

Hepatitis was a major problem at Willowbrook for patients and staff because of the overcrowding and unsanitary conditions. It was known at the time that the response to infection was milder in the younger children and that once infected with hepatitis, children were protected from getting hepatitis again.

Dr. Saul Krugman from the New York University School of Medicine and his coworkers began conducting hepatitis studies at Willowbrook in 1955 and continued for more than fifteen years. Krugman was interested in using gamma globulin antibodies taken from the blood of hepatitis patients as a way to create immunity in others. Krugman thought that if a child was infected with hepatitis after he or she had been injected with these protective antibodies, only a mild case of hepatitis would result, and the child would have long-lasting protection against future, potentially more serious, infections. His goal was to find the best ways to protect children from hepatitis.

More than seven hundred children at Willowbrook were involved in the studies, which fell into two categories. The first used children who were already at Willowbrook. Researchers injected some with the protective antibodies (the experimental group) and did not inject others (the control group). Then, they observed the children's degree of immunity to hepatitis.

In another series of studies, intended to further examine the effectiveness of gamma globulin, researchers gave newly admitted children the protective antibodies. Then a subset of these children was deliberately infected with a hepatitis virus (obtained from sick children). Those who had received protective antibodies but were not deliberately infected served as the controls. The children in this experiment were housed in a well-equipped and well-staffed facility, where they could be given special care and kept away from the other types of infections at the institution. Only children under ten years of age were used in the study, since they seemed to recover more easily from these infections.

As the studies progressed, the researchers noticed differing symptoms caused by different virus samples. They concluded that there were two strains of hepatitis, A and B. Those children who were deliberately infected with hepatitis A had a mild reaction (a swollen liver, yellowing of the skin and eyes, and a few days of vomiting and not eating). They found that hepatitis B is more difficult to transmit to others because it is normally spread through the exchange of body fluids, but can lead to long-term (chronic) infection.

Adapted from National Institutes of Health Curriculum

Learning Activity 1

Working with a partner, list all the ethical arguments in favor of enrolling the children in this study.

Then list all the ethical arguments against enrolling the children in this study.

דאם הרופאים קובעין שאין כל סכנה בניסוים כאלה שמציעים, שאז מותר לו לאדם
למסור את עצמו לעריכת ניסוים שכאלה בגופו לטובת חולה אחר . . . וגם מקיים מצוה
בכך, אבל לחייב אותו עבור כן על פי דין תורה, זה אי אפשר בשום פנים.
ציץ אליעזר יג,קא

Rabbi Eliezer Yehudah Waldenberg (1915–2006). Leading rabbi and judge on the Supreme Rabbinical Court in Jerusalem; considered an eminent authority on Jewish medical ethics and Jewish law. His collected responsa, *Tsits Eliezer*, are viewed as one of the great achievements of halachic scholarship of the 20th century. He served as rabbi for the Shaare Zedek Medical Center in Jerusalem.

If the doctors are confident that there is no danger involved in the experiment that is being proposed, then it is permitted to volunteer one's body to participate in a clinical trial that will benefit other patients . . . and indeed one is considered to have performed a mitzvah. However, there are certainly no grounds to suggest that the Torah would consider this an obligation at all.

Rabbi Eliezer Waldenberg, *Tsits Eliezer* 13:101

מחקר בקטנים או שוטים: אין כל כאב או צער לקטן. אין איסור לבדוק הפרשותיו, כגון שתן או צואה, בבדיקות מעבדה. וכן אם צריכים לקחת ממנו דם לשם בדיקה כחלק מטיפולו, מותר גם לקחת קצת יותר באותו זמן כדי לבצע בו בדיקות לשם המחקר . . . יש צער לקטן החולה בעצם ביצוע המחקר. אם המחקר הוא לטובתו כך שהוא בעצמו ייהנה מתוצאותיו, נראה שמותר לעשות זאת כל זמן שהצער או הכאב קטן, מדין זכין לאדם שלא בפניו. אך אם המחקר יגרום לו כאב או צער והוא בעצמו לא ייהנה מתוצאותיו אלא רק חולים אחרים, אין לבצע אותו על גופו. יש קצת סכנה בביצוע המחקר. אם הסכנה קטנה לעומת התועלת שהוא עצמו עשוי להפיק מהניסוי, מותר לעשות זאת, כי גם בכל טיפול יש סכנה ומותר לטפל בקטן כשהסיכון שבטיפול הוא קטן לעומת התועלת הצפוייה מאותו טיפול. אך אם הסכנה גדולה וכל שכן אם התועלת הוא רק לחולה אחר —אסור, ולא מועילה הסכמת הוריו.

נשמת אברהם, יורה דעה כח,ב

egarding experimentation on a child or mentally incompetent person:

If there is no discomfort or pain to the child: There is no problem with examining his natural bodily secretions (such as urine, or stool samples) . . . Likewise, if doctors are in any case taking blood for medical purposes, it is permissible to take a little extra for the use of a study.

If the experiment itself will cause pain to the child: If the experiment is for the child's benefit in a way that the child will gain directly from the study's results, it would seem that the study may be done, so long as the pain or discomfort involved is minor—[relying on the rule that] we benefit someone in their absence. However, if the study will cause pain or discomfort, and only others will benefit from the results of the study, but not the child, then the child's body may not be used.

If there is danger in the actual experiment: If the danger is small compared to the benefits that the subject will gain from the experiment, it is permitted to do it, for in every treatment there is some risk which is permitted when the expected benefit from the procedure is greater than the risks. However, if the risks are great, or if the benefit will be only for other patients, it is forbidden to conduct the study on the child, regardless of whether there is parental consent.

Rabbi Dr. Abraham S. Abraham, *Nishmat Avraham, Yoreh De'ah 28:2*

Question for Discussion

Based on this text, do you think the Willowbrook study would be considered ethical by a rabbinic court?

Text **10a**

ואהבת לרעך כמוך (ויקרא יט,יח), רבי עקיבא אומר זה כלל גדול בתורה. בן עזאי
אומר זה ספר תולדות אדם (בראשית ה,א), זה כלל גדול מזה.

ספרא, קדושים, פרשה ב, ד,יב

"And you shall love your fellow like yourself" (Leviticus 19:18). Rabbi Akiva said, "This is a great principle in the Torah." Ben Azzai said, "'This is the narrative of the generations of man; [on the day that G-d created man, in the likeness of G-d He created him]' (Genesis 5:1)—this is a greater principle."

Sifra, Kedoshim, Parshah 2, 4:12

Text **10b**

שאלו מן הפסוק הראשון לא שמענו אלא כמוך, הרי שנתבזה הוא או נתקלל הוא ונגזל
ונחבל יתבזה חברו עמו ויתקלל עמו ויחבל עמו. לכך נאמר בדמות אלהים עשה אותו,
את מי אתה מבזה ואת מי אתה מקלל, דמות דיוקנו של מקום.
זה הכלל גדול מן הראשון.

ראב״ה, שם

Because from the first verse we only learn [to love another] "like yourself." Thus, a person who has been shamed or cursed, or was a victim of theft, or had been beaten, [might think that it was permissible to] let his friend be shamed or cursed or beaten in the same way. Therefore, the Torah says "In the likeness of G-d he created him"— [as if to say:] Who are you shaming? Who are you cursing? One created in the image of G-d! [That is why] this verse is a greater principle than the first.

Rabbi Avraham ben David, ibid.

Rabbi Avraham ben David (ca. 1125–1198). Also known as Ra'avad III, mystic, author, and rabbi of Posquieres (today Vauvert) in Provence. He is most famous for his critical notes on Maimonides' *Mishneh Torah*; he wrote commentaries on the Talmud, *Sifra*, and *Rif*. He also authored *Ba'alei Hanefesh*, a compilation of laws relating to family purity, along with a treatise teaching the proper perspectives on intimacy. Ra'avad was wealthy and served as a patron for the charity institutions in Posquieres.

The Value of Inclusion

Text **11a**

בשעה שאמר לו הקב״ה ועשו לי מקדש ושכנתי בתוכם (שמות כה,ח) אמר משה מי יוכל לעשות לו מקדש שישרה בתוכו . . .

אמר הקב״ה איני מבקש לפי כחי אלא לפי כחן.

במדבר רבה יב,ג

At the time that G-d told [Moses], "Let them make for Me a sanctuary so I may dwell among them" (Exodus 25:8), Moses said, "Who is capable of building a [fitting] sanctuary for G-d within which His divine presence may rest?" . . .

G-d said, "I do not request of them to build a sanctuary according to My ability to do so but to build one according to *their* ability."

Midrash, Bamidbar Rabah 12:3

Text 11b

בא וראה היאך היה הקול יוצא אצל ישראל כל אחד ואחד לפי כחו, הזקנים היו שומעין
את הקול לפי כחן והבחורים לפי כחן והנערים לפי כחן והקטנים לפי כחן והיונקים לפי
כחן . . . וכן הוא אומר קול ה׳ בכח (תהלים כט,ד) בכחו לא נאמר
אלא בכח שכל אחד ואחד מהן יכול לסבול.

מדרש תנחומא, שמות כה

ome and see how the voice [of G-d came] forth to the Jewish people—to all according to their ability. The elderly heard the voice according to their ability, the young adults according to their ability, the adolescents according to their ability, the children according to their ability, and the infants according to their ability. . . . Likewise it says, "The voice of G-d with strength" (Psalms 29:4). The verse does not say "with G-d's strength," rather [the voice was heard] in accordance with the strength that each person was able to handle.

Midrash Tanchuma, Shemot 25

Text 12

פתי הוא מי שדעתו קלישתא, שאינו מבין הדברים כמו שהן, ואינו יודע לחלק בין
הדברים שרואה ולהבין צורכם. והוא בגדלו כדעת קטן, יש שהוא כדעת בן שש ויש
גם כפחות . . .
והנה שודאי חייבים במצות כשהביאו שערות והם בני י״ג ובנות י״ב ויש חיוב על האבות
ללמדם מה שאפשר להם מקטנותם בזמן ששייך שיבינו לפי כוחם . . . קריאת שמע
בעל פה עד שידע פרשה ראשונה, ותמונת האותיות וקריאתן, וללמדו שיש בורא עולם
ובורא כל הדברים שאוכל ושותה וכדומה . . . וכמובן שלא ביום אחד שייך שילמדהו,
אלא לאט לאט . . .

ולעניין כשבאים בבית הכנסת, ודאי צריכים הציבור לקבלם בסבר פנים יפות . . . וגם
לראות שיענו אמן וקדושה לומר עמהם . . . שיקיימו מה שאפשר . . .
וישקו את ספר התורה.

אגרות משה, יורה דעה ד,כט

A *pesi* is someone who is weak of mind and cannot correctly understand things as they are nor accurately categorize what is observed. In adulthood the mind of a *pesi* is similar to that of a child; sometime like a six-year-old, and sometimes less. . . .

They are certainly obligated in *mitzvot* when they reach maturity—boys at the age of thirteen and girls at twelve. And there is an obligation for their parents to educate them in their youth, once they are able to understand, according to their ability. . . . [They should be taught] the recital of the first chapter of the *Shema* prayer until they know it by heart, the alphabet and how to read, and they should be taught about the Creator of the world who creates everything that they eat and drink, etc. Obviously it not possible to teach it all in one day, rather it should be taught slowly. . . .

When they attend a synagogue, the community should certainly welcome them pleasantly . . . They should be helped to recite *Amen* and *Kedushah* . . . they should observe what they are able to . . . and they should kiss the Torah.

Rabbi Moshe Feinstein, *Igrot Moshe, Yoreh De'ah* 4:29

Rabbi Moshe Feinstein (1895–1986). Rabbi and leading halachic authority of the 20th century. Born near Minsk, Belarus; became rabbi of Luban in 1921; immigrated to the U.S. in 1937 and became the dean of Metivta Tiferet Yerushalayim in New York. Rabbi Feinstein became the leading halachic authority of his time and his rulings are always considered. His halachic decisions have been published in a multi-volume collection titled *Igrot Moshe.* He also published works on the Talmud and was known for his fine character traits.

Text 13

There is surely no need to emphasize at length that, as in all cases involving Jews, their specific Jewish needs must be taken into account. This is particularly true in the case of retarded Jewish children, yet all too often disregarded. There is unfortunately a prevalent misconception that since you are dealing with retarded children, having more limited capabilities, they should not be "burdened" with Jewish education on top of their general education, so as not to overtax them. In my opinion this is a fallacious and detrimental attitude, especially in light of what has been said above about the need to avoid impressing the child with his handicap. Be it remembered that a child coming from a Jewish home probably has brothers and sisters, or cousins and friends, who receive a Jewish education and are exposed to Jewish observances. Even in the American society, where observant Jews are not yet in the majority, there is always some measure of Jewish experience, or Jewish angle, in the child's background. Now therefore, if the retarded child sees or feels that he has been singled out and removed from that experience, or when he will eventually find out that he is Jewish, yet deprived of his Jewish identity and heritage, it is very likely to cause irreparable damage to him.

On the other hand, if the child is involved in Jewish education and activities and not in some general and peripheral way, but in a regular and tangible way, such as in the actual performance of mitzvos, customs, and traditions, it would give him a sense of belonging and

Rabbi Menachem Mendel Schneerson (1902–1994). Known as "the Lubavitcher Rebbe," or simply as "the Rebbe." Born in southern Ukraine. Rabbi Schneerson escaped from the Nazis, arriving in the U.S. in June 1941. The towering Jewish leader of the 20th century, the Rebbe inspired and guided the revival of traditional Judaism after the European devastation, and often emphasized that the performance of just one additional good deed could usher in the era of Mashiach.

attachment, and a firm anchorage to hold on to, whether consciously or subconsciously. Eventually even a sub-conscious feeling of inner security would pass into the conscious state, especially if the teacher will endeavor to cultivate and fortify this feeling.

Rabbi Menachem Mendel Schneerson, Correspondence from August 15, 1979

Text 14

מעשה ברבי שמעון בן אלעזר שבא ממגדל עדר מבית רבו והיה רוכב על החמור ומטייל על שפת הים. ראה אדם אחד שהיה מכוער ביותר אמר לו: ריקה כמה מכוער אתה, שמא כל בני עירך מכוערין כמותך. אמר לו: ומה אעשה. לך לאומן שעשאני ואמור לו כמה מכוער כלי זה שעשית. כיון שידע רבי שמעון שחטא ירד מן החמור והיה משתטח לפניו. אמר לו נעניתי לך מחול לי.

מסכת אבות דרבי נתן מא,א

A story is told of Rabbi Shimon ben Elazar who traveled from the house of his teacher in Migdal Eder, riding on a donkey by the sea shore. He saw a very ugly man. He said to him, "Empty one! Look how ugly you are! Are all the people of your city as ugly as you?"

He replied, "What can I do? Go to the craftsman who made me and say to him, 'How ugly is this vessel which you have made.'"

Once Rabbi Shimon realized that he had sinned, he dismounted from the donkey, prostrated himself in front of him, and said, "I have misspoken to you; forgive me."

Tractate Avot DeRebbi Natan 41:1

Key Points

1. Judaism accords psychiatrists the same level of respect and trust as other medical professionals.

2. Jewish law requires the courts to appoint a guardian for those who are unable to represent their own interests and enacts laws to protect the mentally incompetent person.

3. It is highly questionable whether it is permitted to take bone marrow from a mentally incompetent person, even to save a life.

4. One may only allow mentally incapacitated people to undergo experimental treatment if the treatment is for their own direct benefit.

5. G-d only expects people to do what is within their capacity. People are responsible for religious obligations only according to their own pace and ability, and are exempt from those that are beyond their ability to fulfill.

6. Engaging in spiritual activities can have positive effects on the well-being of people who are mentally impaired. In addition, partaking in communal religious programs creates a feeling of attachment and belonging.

7. One Craftsman has made us all; we are all created in the divine image.

Additional Readings

On People with Special Needs

Correspondence of the Rebbe, Rabbi Menachem Mendel Schneerson, of righteous memory, and Dr. Robert Wilkes, at the time director of the Child Development Center at the Coney Island Hospital, on the subject of assisting people with special needs.

Coney Island Hospital
2601 Ocean Parkway • Brooklyn, New York 11235
212-743-4100
Child Development Center
August 9, 1979

Rabbi Menachem Mendel Schneerson
Lubavitcher Rebbe
770 Eastern Parkway
Brooklyn, N.Y. 11213

Dear Rabbi Schneerson:

As a Jewish social worker and the chairman of Region II Council For Mental Retardation in Brooklyn, I would be most interested in learning what your views are regarding "the care and education of Jewish retarded individuals"—those persons who, from birth, are slow in thinking, speaking and learning.

For many years, the retarded individual, especially the severely retarded, was placed in a large, state-operated institution, often quite a distance from the individual's home and community. During the past few years, efforts have been made to create "group homes" in all our neighborhoods throughout the city so that parents who cannot continue to care for their retarded sons or daughters have the choice of placing their child in a small, home-like setting: situated either within or nearby the individual's community.

This policy of creating "group homes" for the retarded—Jewish as well as non-Jewish—has been a source of controversy and often bitter opposition pitting parent against parent, neighbor against neighbor, and political leaders against one another. The basis for these heated discussions include predictions about lowering the economic value of homes in a community; fear that retarded individuals will commit vandalism or, even worse, commit crimes; and that the retarded themselves will feel uncomfortable surrounded by normal people. On the other hand, parents of the retarded want their children to live in a safe and healthy environment.

How may we view this issue—that is, caring for individuals who have a disability which requires life-long care and supervision—from a Jewish perspective? As a concerned Jew, I care very much about our Jewish community: how we treat one another and how we conduct ourselves as human beings. I am particularly interested in your comments and opinions, because the Lubavitcher movement, with its deep concern for every Jewish individual's welfare, has added a spiritual dimension—a spark—to all our lives!

As a married man with—thank G-d—two beautiful, healthy children (ages 2 and 5), I am also aware that there has to be an equal concern for both the individual as well as for one's total community. The question is: how do we protect and safeguard all of our Jewish children—the retarded and the non-retarded—so that they can have the opportunity to grow, to develop, and to live "Jewishly"?

I would also welcome the opportunity to discuss any of the above with you or your representatives. Thank you for your cooperation.

Respectfully yours,

Robert Wilkes,
Assistant Program Director/
Chairman, Region II Council For Mental Retardation

Rabbi Menachem M. Schneerson
Lubavitch
770 Eastern Parkway
Brooklyn, N.Y. 11213
By the Grace of G-d
22 Av, 5739 [August 15, 1979]
Brooklyn, N.Y.

Mr. R. Wilkes, Asst. Program Director/
Chairman, Region II Council For Mental Retardation
Coney Island Hospital
260l Ocean Parkway, Brooklyn, N.Y. 11235

Greeting and Blessing:

This is in reply to your letter of Aug. 9, in which you ask for my views on "the care and education of Jewish retarded children," outlining some of the problems connected therewith and prevailing policies, etc.

I must, first of all, make one essential observation, namely, that while the above heading places all the retarded in one group, it would be a gross fallacy to come up with any rules to be applied to all of them as a group. For if any child requires an individual evaluation and approach in order to achieve the utmost in his, or her, development, how much more so in the case of the handicapped.

Since the above is so obvious, I assume that you have in mind the most general guidelines, with a wide range of flexibility allowing for the necessary individual approach in each case. All the more so, since, sad to say, our present society is poorly equipped in terms of manpower and financial resources to afford an adequate personal approach to each handicapped boy and girl. Even more regrettable is the fact that little attention (at any rate little in relation to the importance of the problem) is given to this situation, and consequently little is done to mobilize more adequate resources to deal with the problem.

Now, with regard to general guidelines, I would suggest the following:

(l) The social worker, or teacher, and anyone dealing with retarded individuals should start from the basic premise that the retardation is in each case only a temporary handicap, and that in due course it could **certainly** be improved, and even improved substantially. This approach should be taken regardless of the pronouncements or prognosis of specialists in the field. The reason for this approach is, first of all, that it is a **pre**condition for greater success in dealing with the retarded. Besides, considering the enormous strides that have been made in medical science, human knowledge, methodology, and know how, there is **no** doubt that in this area, too, there will be far-reaching developments. Thus, the very confidence that such progress is in the realm of possibility will inspire greater enthusiasm in this work, and hopefully will also stimulate more intensive research.

(2) Just as the said approach is important from the viewpoint of and for the worker and educator, so it is important that the trainees themselves should be encouraged both by word and the manner of their training to feel confident that they are not, G-d forbid, "cases," much less unfortunate or hopeless cases, but that their difficulty is considered, as above, only temporary, and that with a concerted effort of instructor and trainee the desired improvement could be speeded and enhanced.

(3) Needless to say, care should be taken not to exaggerate expectations through far-fetched promises, for false hopes inevitably result in deep disenchantment, loss of credibility and other undesirable effects. However, a way can surely be found to avoid raising false hopes, yet giving guarded encouragement.

(4) As part of the above approach which, as far as I know has not been used before, is to involve (some of) the trainees in some form of leadership, such as captains of teams, group leaders, and the like, without arousing the jealousy of the others. The latter could be avoided by making such selections on the basis of seniority, special achievement, exemplary conduct, etc.

(5) With regard to the efforts which have been made in recent years to create "group homes" for retarded individuals, which, as you say, has been a source of controversy it is to be expected that, as in most things in our imperfect world, there are pros and cons. However, I believe that the approach should be the same as in the

case of all pupils or students who spend part of their time in group environments school, dormitory, summer camp, etc., and part of their time in the midst of their families, whether every day, or at weekends, etc. Only by individual approach and evaluation can it be determined which individual fits into which category.

(6) There is surely no need to emphasize at length that, as in all cases involving Jews, their specific Jewish needs must betaken into account. This is particularly true in the case of retarded Jewish children, yet all too often disregarded. There is unfortunately a prevalent misconception that since you are dealing with retarded children, having more limited capabilities, they should not be "burdened" with Jewish education on top of their general education, so as not to overtax them. In my opinion this is a fallacious and **detrimental** attitude, especially in light of what has been said above about the need to avoid impressing the child with his handicap. Be it remembered that a child coming from a Jewish home probably has brothers and sisters, or cousins and friends, who receive a Jewish education and are exposed to Jewish observances.

Even in the American society, where observant Jews are not yet in the majority, there is always some measure of Jewish experience, or Jewish angle, in the child's background. Now therefore, if the retarded child sees or feels that he has been singled out and removed from that experience, or when he will eventually find out that he is Jewish, yet deprived of his Jewish identity and heritage it is very likely to cause irreparable damage to him.

On the other hand, if the child is involved in Jewish education and activities and not in some general and peripheral way, but in a regular and **tangible** way, such as in the actual performance of Mitzvos, customs and traditions it would give him a sense of belonging and attachment, and a firm anchorage to hold on to, whether consciously or subconsciously. Eventually even a subconscious feeling of inner security would pass into the conscious state, especially if the teacher will endeavor to cultivate and fortify this feeling.

I am, of course, aware of the arguments that may be put forth in regard to this idea, namely, that it would require additional funding, qualified personnel, etc., not readily available at present. To be sure, these are arguments that have a basis in fact as things now stand. However, the real problem is not so much the lack of resources as the prevailing attitude that considers the Jewish angle as of secondary importance, or less; consequently the effort to remedy the situation is commensurate, resulting in a self-fulfilling prophecy. The truth of the matter is that if the importance of it would be seen in its true light that it is an essential factor in the development of the retarded Jewish child, in addition to our elementary obligation to all Jewish children without exception, the results would be quite different.

Perhaps all the aforesaid is not what you had in mind in soliciting my views on "group homes."

Nevertheless, I was impelled to dwell on the subject at some length, not only because it had to be said, but also because it may serve as a basis for solving the controversy surrounding the creation of "group homes" for those children who are presently place in an environment often quite distant from the individual's home and community to paraphrase your statement.

Finally a concluding remark relating to your laudatory reference to the Lubavitch movement, "with its deep concern for **every** Jewish individual's welfare," etc.

Needless to say, such appreciation is very gratifying, but I must confess and emphasize that thisis not an original Lubavitch idea, for it is basic to Torah Judaism. Thus, our Sages of old declared that *ve'ohavto lre'acho ko'mocho* ("Love your fellow as yourself") is the Great Principle of our Torah, with the accent on "as yourself," since every person surely has a very special, personal approach to himself. To the credit of the Lubavitch emissaries it may be said, however, that they are doing all they can to implement and live by this Golden Rule of the Torah, and doing it untiringly and enthusiastically.

May the *Zechus Horabbim*, the merit of the many who benefit from your sincere efforts to help them in their need, especially in your capacity as Regional Chairman of the Council For Mental Retardation, stand you in good stead to succeed in the fullest measure and stimulate your dedication for even greater achievements.

With esteem and blessing, [sig.]

August 12,1980
Rabbi Menachem M. Schneerson Lubavitch
770 Eastern Parkway,
Brooklyn, New York 11213

Dear Rabbi Schneerson:

Rabbi Dr. Benjamin Sharfman, chairman of Federation's prospective conference on issues and needs of the Jewish retarded, has given me the honor and privilege to invite you (and/or your representatives) to address this conference. . . .

What should be remarkable about this conference is that not only will the participants be discussing how to make all aspects of Jewish living (e.g., education, community living, recreation, woreship) available to the developmentally disabled individual and his/her family but also the participants, perhaps for the first-time for a "Jewish" conference. . . .

It is no secret that the Lubavitch movement—perhaps more than any other Jewish group – has emphasized the critical significance of Jewish education for all Jewish boys and girls as well as the overall need of Yiddishkeit for all Jews. We would.welcome a statement from you prepared for this occasion: to be read at the conference by either yourself or::by a representative. You may also consider the possibility of sending a specially prepared taped message. Please feel free to consider any form of communication which you think would be most meaningful. . . .

May I take this opportunity to once again thank you for your continued interest and support. . . .

Wishing you and your entire family a very happy and healthy New Year.

Respectfully yours,
Robert Wilkes, DSW
Chairman, Brooklyn
Region 11 Council For The Retarded

Rabbi Menachem M. Schneerson
Lubavitch
770 Eastern Parkway
Brooklyn, N.Y. 11213

By the Grace of G-d
9th of Kislev, 5741 [November 17, 1980]
Brooklyn, N. Y.

Dr. R. Wilkes, DSW
Chairman, Brooklyn
Region 11 Council for The Retarded
c/o Coney Island Hospital
2601 Ocean Parkway
Brooklyn, N. Y. 11235

Greeting and Blessing:

This is to acknowledge receipt of your letter of Nov. 13th, with the enclosures in connection with the forthcoming Conference.

Since the matter is of the greatest importance, I have taken time out, despite the pressure of duties, to respond with the enclosed message. You can also supplement it with my past correspondence with you on this subject.

May G-d grant that every one of us should do the utmost along the lines suggested in my message, especially since we have the promise of Divine aid in all such good efforts.

With esteem and blessing [sig.]

Rabbi Menachem M. Schneerson
Lubavitch
770 Eastern Parkway
Brooklyn, N.Y. 11213
By the Grace of G-d
9 Kislev, 5741
Brooklyn, N.Y.

To All Participants in the
Major Conference for the Jewish Community
On Issues and Needs of Jewish Retarded
New York City

Greeting and Blessing:

I was pleased to be informed of the forthcoming Conference. I trust it will mark a turning point in the attitude of community leaders to Jewish education in general, and to so-called Special Education in particular.

In any discussion relating to the wellbeing of the Jewish community, the primary, indeed pivotal, issue should surely be Jewish Identity—that which truly unites our Jewish people and gives us the strength to survive and thrive in a most unnatural, alien, and all too often hostile environment.

Historically—from the birth of our nation to this day—Jewish identity, in the fullest sense of this term, has been synonymous with traditional Torah-Judaism as our way of life in everyday living.

Other factors commonly associated with a national identity, such as language, territory, dress, etc., could not have played a decisive role in Jewish survival, since these changed from time to time and from place to place. The only factor that has not changed throughout our long history has been the Torah and Mitzvos which are "our life and the length of our days." The same Tefillin, Tzitzis, Shabbos and Yom-Tov have been observed by Jews everywhere in all generations. Clearly there is no substitute for the Torah-way as the source and essence of our Jewish people.

Recognizing this prima facie fact, means recognizing that Jewish survival depends on the kind of Education that develops and nourishes Jewish identity in the fullest measure. And this must surely be the highest priority of all communal services.

With regard to Jewish retarded—parenthetically, I prefer some such term as "special" people, not simply as a euphemism, but because it would more accurately reflect their situation, especially in view of the fact that in many cases the retardation is limited to the capacity to absorb and assimilate knowledge, while in other areas they may be quite normal or even above average—the Jewish identity factor is even more important, not only per se but also for its therapeutic value. The actual practice of Mitzvos in the everyday life provides a tangible way by which these special people of all ages can, despite their handicap, identify with their families and with other fellow Jews in their surroundings, and generally keep in touch with reality. Even if mentally they may not fully grasp the meaning of these rituals, subconsciously they are bound to feel at home in such an environment, and in many cases could participate in such activities also on the conscious level.

To cite one striking example from actual experience during the Festival of Succos this year. As is well known, Lubavitch activists on this occasion reach out to many Jews with Lulov and Esrog, bringing to them the spirit of the Season of Our Rejoicing. This year being a year of Hakhel, I urged my followers to extend this activity as much as possible, to include also Nursing Homes and Senior Citizens' Hotels, as well as other institutions. I was asked, what should be the attitude and approach to persons who are senile or confused, etc. I replied—all the more reason to reach out to them in this tangible way. Well, the reports were profoundly gratifying. Doctors and nurses were astonished to see such a transformation: Persons who had spent countless days in silent immobility, deeply depressed and oblivious to everything around them, the moment they saw a young man walk in with a Lulav and Esrog in his hand suddenly displayed a lively interest, eagerly, grasped the proffered Mitzvah-objects, some of them reciting the blessings from memory, without prompting. The joy in their hearts shone through their faces, which had not known a smile all too long.

One need not look for a mystical explanation of this reaction. Understandably, the sight of something so tangible and clearly associated with the joy of Succos evidently touched and unlocked vivid recollections of experiences that had permeated them in earlier years.

If there is much that can be done along these lines for adult and senior Jews in special situations, how much more so in regard to special children, when every additional benefit, however seemingly small, in their formative years will be compounded many times over as they grow older. In their case it is even more important to bear in mind that while they may be handicapped in their mental and intellectual capacity, and indeed because of it, every possible emphasis should be placed on the tangible and audio-visual aspects of Jewish education in terms of the actual practice of Mitzvos and religious observances—as I have discussed this and related aspects at greater length in my correspondence with Dr. R. Wilkes of the Coney Island Hospital.

There is surely no need to elaborate on all above to the participants in the Conference, whose Rabbinic, academic, and professional qualifications in the field of Jewish Education and social services makes them highly sensitive to the problems at hand. I hope and pray that the basic points herein made will serve as guidelines to focus attention on the cardinal issues, and that this Conference will, as mentioned earlier, mark a turning point in attitude, and even more importantly in action vis-a-vis Jewish Education, long overdue.

With prayerful wishes for Hatzlocho, and with esteem and blessing, [sig.]

Is OCD A Jewish Disease?

Avigdor Bonchek

Dr. Bonchek, a musmach *of Ner Israel Rabbinical College, is a practicing clinical psychologist in Jerusalem. He has taught psychology at The Hebrew University of Jerusalem for thirty years and directs an anxiety disorders clinic. He is the author of* Studying the Torah *(New Jersey, 1996) and the* What's Bothering Rashi? *series (Jerusalem,1997-2002). He is presently preparing a treatment manual for professionals on treating OCD. He lives with his family in Jerusalem.*

Obsessive-compulsive disorder (OCD) has come out of the closet and joined the growing ranks of psychiatric acronyms that have become household words, such as ADHD, PTSD and BPD.[1] (Remember the good old days when the only abbreviations we knew were IBM and NBA?)

It is estimated that about 2 percent of the population suffer from OCD at some point in their lives. To be sure, there are no epidemiological studies showing that Orthodox Jews are more inclined to suffer from OCD than the general population. However, because of the complex relationship between religion and OCD (Orthodox compulsives tend to be obsessed with halachic matters), OCD is no longer known only to those in the mental health profession. Indeed, a fourteen-year-old client of mine, a yeshivah boy, recently turned to his mother during a session and exclaimed, "I think I have OCD!" (Which, in fact, he does.) During last year's Torah Umesorah convention, my wife and I were stunned to discover a young Chassidic man delivering a lecture (in Yiddish!) to educators on treating OCD in school. (While not a professional, he was quite knowledgeable about this psychological enigma.)

What is OCD? How did it become a household word in the Orthodox community? Referred to in Yiddish as

---

[1] ADHD (attention deficit hyperactivity disorder), PTSD (post-traumatic stress disorder) and BPD (borderline personality disorder).

nervin, OCD manifests itself in repetitive, compulsive behaviors. Sufferers from OCD are in extreme stress since their uncontrollable thoughts and behaviors rule, and often ruin, their lives. They are continuously plagued with doubts. There is the woman who worries about her halachic readiness for immersion and spends four hours preparing to go to the mikvah. There is the man, who, uncertain if his *kavanot* were correct, takes up to three hours to say morning prayers that should take twenty-five minutes. And there is the boy who washes his hands upwards of twenty times a day because of his fears that his hands are not clean enough to learn Torah or say a blessing. Other manifestations of OCD include obsessive, intrusive thoughts of forbidden things, such as *avodah zarah* (idolatry); plaguing doubts about whether a fleeting thought is halachically considered a *neder* (vow); long hours spent in washroom activities and extreme vigilance about meat and milk "contamination."

Regarding Orthodox sufferers, a number of questions can be raised. Wouldn't these people's lives be more peaceful without the restrictions of the *Shulchan Aruch* weighing down on them? In other words, would they suffer from compulsivity were they not Torah observant? Does observing *halachah* make them compulsive, or would they be compulsive regardless? Furthermore, how is a parent, spouse or *rosh yeshivah* to differentiate between a sincere striving for *kedushah* and a psychiatric condition that feeds on *halachah*? How can a person himself know whether he's crossed the line between healthy religiosity and unhealthy compulsivity? Indeed, many sufferers have no idea that their condition is a *condition*.

Sigmund Freud, the father of twentieth-century psychotherapy, took the unsympathetic position that all religion is a form of obsessional neurosis. Accordingly, anyone who engages in ritualistic religious behaviors is, by his definition, acting obsessively. Is such an assumption correct? Is OCD a "Jewish disease," or is there a difference between the religious rituals we are all accustomed to performing (for example, *netillat yadayim*) and obsessive rituals (for example, excessive handwashing)?

There are two easily spotted signatures of OCD. Firstly, there is the stress the sufferer experiences. One can see that the compulsive person is shouldering a heavy emotional burden.

He walks around somber, semidepressed, in a constant state of pressure. Secondly, there is the compulsive's inflexibility. The truly religious person will even eat on Yom Kippur if, because of an illness, his rabbi determines that he must. The compulsive, on the other hand, will find it nearly impossible to violate even a less-serious commandment, despite being advised to do so by a rabbinic authority.

Flexibility is a key to true religious observance. Avraham is our model. Commanded to bring his only beloved son as an offering, he had three days to internalize an act that was diametrically opposed to every fiber of his being. He reached the conclusion that he must do as he was commanded. Yet once he was told not to kill Yitzchak, he obeyed immediately, making an emotional about-face in a moment. His flexibility enabled him to follow God's will, irrespective of the difficulties involved.

The compulsive's inflexibility, however, reveals that he is acting in response to internal pressure rather than Godly demands. Indeed, many rabbis are familiar with individuals who bombard them relentlessly with questions that are only distantly related to *halachah*. But if religious behavior is not, in and of itself, compulsive, why are so many compulsives obsessed, almost exclusively, with religious themes?

This is because obsessions and compulsions fester in areas that the individual considers to be weighty matters of life and death. Washing is a common compulsion (though certainly not the only one) among religious and non-religious people alike. For the religious person, washing has cosmic significance because of religious reasons; for the non-religious, washing is equally significant due to health concerns.

Fortunately, treatment for this debilitating illness has progressed rapidly in the past twenty years. It is important that a parent or spouse not ignore the symptoms of OCD, believing it will go away with time. On the other hand, one should not jump to conclusions and immediately offer a "diagnosis." The problem may be just a phase, as is often the case with teenagers. Check for the signs mentioned above: stress and inflexibility. Speak with the individual; ask him how he sees his behaviors. In this way, you can test his flexibility. Does he listen to reason, or does he agree to let up on his "religious" behaviors while actually continuing to perform them compulsively and possibly surreptitiously?

If you think there is a real problem, seek professional help. Psychiatrists will almost invariably recommend medications, of which there are some good ones (from the Prozac family) that are not addictive. However, in order to be effective, these medications must be taken daily for months, if not years. Moreover, in over 50 percent of cases, once one ceases to take the medication, the affliction returns.

Currently, the prevailing opinion among professionals is that all serious treatment should include medication. I beg to differ. All treatment, in my opinion, must strive to get the sufferer to a state where he is both symptom and medication free.

An effective psychological, as opposed to a psychiatric, treatment for OCD is behavior therapy. This approach involves exposing the patient to situations that make him feel uncomfortable and then preventing him from engaging in a compulsive response. For example, the patient is asked to touch something that he considers "dirty," and then he is not to wash his hands. Or, in the case of a woman who has doubts regarding mikvah issues and repeatedly questions her rabbi, the correct (but difficult) course is for the rabbi to refuse to answer her questions. The rabbi can, of course, act so only after he has determined that her questions stem from an unhealthy obsession and not from a healthy concern for *halachah*. This may seem harsh, but the woman herself realizes that receiving answers only leads to more questions, an endless chain. She should be encouraged to complete her mikvah preparations as quickly as possible.

When compulsions involve halachic issues, it is also advisable to have the cooperation of a *rav* whom the patient respects. There must be close coordination between the therapist and the *rav* so that both are aware of the advice the patient is receiving.

Religious devotion is certainly a good thing. But serving Hashem sincerely and authentically is not always easy. It must be done with joy and sensitivity. Rabbi Ralph Pelcovitz, rabbi emeritus of Congregation Kneseth Israel, in Far Rockaway, New York, once said that performing *mitzvot* is similar to holding a bird in your hand. If you hold the bird too tightly, you smother it; if you hold it too loosely, it will fly away. This fine balance is what we must all achieve. It is the ultimate therapeutic aim of treating the religious individual with OCD.

Jewish Action 65, no.2 (Winter 5765/2004).
Reprinted with permission by publisher

Treatment of Depression by Maimonides (1138–1204): Rabbi, Physician, and Philosopher

Benjamin Gesundheit, M.D., Ph.D., Reuven Or, M.D., Chanoch Gamliel, Ph.D., Fred Rosner, M.D., and Avraham Steinberg, M.D.

Moses Maimonides, an illustrious figure in Jewish history, medicine, and philosophy[1], dedicated much of the last 10 years of his life to medical writings[2], in the course of which he also studied mental illnesses and provided what may be the first description of psychosomatic medicine[3]. In his medical letter to the ill-fated nephew of Saladin the Great in Cairo, who suffered from manic-depressive disorder, Maimonides discusses the possible intake of alcohol by his Muslim patient—the only available treatment for depression at the time. Maimonides analyzes the conflict between his patient's religious prohibition of drinking alcohol and

[1] Gesundheit B, Hadad E: Maimonides (1138–1204): Rabbi, Physician, and Philosopher. Isr Med Assoc J 2005; 7:547–553.

[2] Rosner F, Kottek S (eds): Moses Maimonides: Physician, Scientist, and Philosopher. Northvale, NJ, Aronson, 1993.

[3] Rosner F: The Medical Legacy of Moses Maimonides. Hoboken, NJ, KTAV Publishing, 1998

his own professional responsibility. This letter illustrates Maimonides' attitude regarding the patient-physician relationship, forges a synthesis of religion and medicine, and demonstrates intercultural respect and psychological sensitivity to his Muslim patient. Maimonides artfully incorporates sources from Jewish and Islamic culture and leaves the final decision to his patient.

We offer here this new English translation of his medical letter[4] to let Maimonides speak for himself. In our brief comments afterward, we elaborate on Maimonides' ethical messages for modern readers.

Maimonides' Medical Letter

"His servant is well aware that our Master, with his broad intelligence and profound understanding, will be able to conduct himself in the proper manner, in accordance with the previous treatise and these chapters. All the more so, when there stands before him [a physician] from whom he may request professional guidance or seek out practical instruction.

"G-d, may He be exalted, is a witness, and His testimony suffices (Koran 4:79–81), that his humble servant's great desire is to serve our Master with his own person and conversation, and not with paper and pen.

"However, his poor constitution and the weakness of his natural faculties—already in his youth, and how much more so in his old age—constitute a barrier between him and many pleasures. I do not mean pleasures, rather good deeds, the most important and elevated of which is to serve our Master in actual practice. G-d be thanked for all the circumstances that befall us, the general and the particular, in the totality of existence and its particulars, in each and every individual, in accordance with His will, which accords with what is dictated by His wisdom, the depths of which no man can fathom. And G-d be thanked for every circumstance, whatever direction events may take.

"Our Master should not criticize his humble servant for having mentioned in this treatise the use of wine and

songs, both of which are abhorred by the religion. For this servant did not command acting in this manner; he merely stated that which is dictated by his profession. Indeed, the religious legislators know, as do the physicians, that wine has benefits for man.

"A physician is bound, inasmuch as he is a physician, to present with a beneficial regimen, whether it is forbidden or permitted; the patient is endowed with the freedom to choose whether to follow or not. If [the physician] fails to mention everything that may be helpful, be it forbidden or permitted, he is guilty of acting dishonestly, for he did not offer trustworthy advice.

"It is well known that religious law commands what is beneficial and prohibits what is harmful with respect to the world-to-come. The physician, on the other hand, instructs what will benefit the body and warns about what will harm it in this world.

"The difference between religious commandments and medical counsel is that religion commands and coerces a person to do what will benefit him in the future, and prohibits what will harm him in the future, and punishes for it. The physician, on the other hand, counsels [a person] about what will benefit him, and warns him about what will cause him harm. He does not use coercion, nor does he punish; he merely presents the information to the patient in the manner of advice. And it is [the patient's] choice [whether to follow that advice].

"The reason for this is obvious. The harm and benefit from a medical perspective are immediate and clearly evident. Thus, there is no need for coercion or punishment. As for religious commandments, however, the harm and benefit that they bring are not evident in this world. The fool might, therefore, imagine to himself that everything that is said to be harmful is not harmful, and everything that is said to be beneficial is not beneficial, because these things are not clearly evident to him. For this reason religious law compels one to practice good and punishes for doing evil, for the good and evil will only become apparent in the world-to-come. All this is benevolence toward us, a favor to us in light of our foolishness, mercy upon us owing to the weakness of our understanding. This is the measure of what the servant saw fit to set before his Master and Ruler,

---

[4] Kroner H: Der Mediciner Maimonides im Kampfe mit dem Theologen. Oberdorf-Bopfingen, 1924.

may G-d grant him long years. I remain readily available to serve our Master. Thanksgiving and praise to G-d."

Discussion

Introduction

Maimonides emphasizes at the beginning his patient's insight as the key for the patient-physician relationship and the success of the treatment; Maimonides is the "servant" for the patient, his "master" (the Sultan's nephew). By quoting the Koran, Maimonides presents the religious foundation of his medical mission according to his patient's belief system. For the patient's confidence, the physician must also be familiar with his spiritual and religious world.

Maimonides' Medical Condition

For Maimonides, preventing suffering and providing medical and spiritual support to those who need it is also a religious duty. By partially sharing with his patient his own medical condition, which does not hinder him from his manifold activities, he encourages his patient to cope in the same way with his medical issues. Maimonides and his Muslim patient share a deep belief in the Creator, rooted in their respective religions.

The Physician's Medical Obligation Versus Religious Commandments

Drinking wine might be justified medically to treat depression, but Maimonides is fully aware of his patient's religious prohibition of drinking alcohol (Koran 2:219; 5:90–91). Following his overriding obligation as a physician, Maimonides frankly discusses the benefits of alcohol with his patient, who is the religious leader of an Islamic kingdom.

The Physician's Medical Obligation and the Patient's Autonomy

Based on the physician's professional obligation, anchored also in Maimonides' religious writings, the physician is bound to advise his patient according to his medical knowledge, even if it contradicts the patient's religious tradition. Withholding medical information from his patient would violate the physician's obligation to inform his patients. Maimonides elaborates on the ethical complexity of a religiously questionable treatment for his Muslim patient but leaves the final decision to his patient. This key role of the patient's autonomy is in accordance with Maimonides' religious philosophy.

Religious Commandments Versus Medical Instructions

Maimonides distinguishes between medicine and religion: The goal of medicine is well-being in this material world. Religion focuses on the spiritual future in the world-to-come, where the benefits are "not evident in this world." Saving lives and promoting human well-being in this world are not to be neglected in favor of religious commandments. According to Jewish tradition, saving life must be given preference over religious commandments. Therefore, Maimonides permits the enjoyment of wine within certain limits and encourages his sick Muslim patient to consider the benefit of alcohol in treating his illness.

Conclusions

Important ethical values are presented in Maimonides' medical letter: The *physician's personal qualities* include modesty, honesty, and obligation to his profession. The *patient's autonomy* to decide about his treatment must be fully respected, including with psychiatric patients, reflecting a remarkably modern attitude in a medieval physician, at a time when paternalism was the prevailing attitude. In his *patient-physician relationship*[5], Maimonides demonstrates familiarity with his patient's religious world by quoting the Koran. By frankly addressing both the religious issues of his Islamic ruler and the physician's professional duties, Maimonides deals with his medical and philosophical values together with his patient. He analyzes the *conflict between medicine and religion* by defining their different features and goals. For Maimonides, saving life is itself a religious duty that supersedes virtually all other religious obligations. Since Maimonides respects many common values of

---

[5] Emanuel EJ, Emanuel LL: Four models of the physician-patient relationship. JAMA 1992; 267:2221–2226.

various religions, these concepts of Jewish law are consequently also relevant for his Muslim fellow man. The *intercultural bridges* between this outstanding Jewish scholar and his Muslim patient are remarkable for the 12th century, a period when religious persecution defined the political and social atmosphere in Christian and Muslim countries. In his clinical work, Maimonides successfully combined medical, religious, philosophical, and psychological talents, creating a respectful intercultural discussion for the benefit and well-being of his patients. For these special achievements, Maimonides, an outstanding medieval rabbinical authority, philosopher, and physician, remains a bioethical role model for contemporary clinicians.

The authors thank Eli Hadad, Ph.D., Shimon Glick, M.D., Samuel Kottek, M.D., David Strauss, and Einat Budowski.

American Journal of Psychiatry 165 (April 2008):425-428. Reprinted with permission by publisher

Lesson 6

Secret Code:
Genetics and the Ethics of Patient Confidentiality
Introduction

New genetic testing procedures give doctors access to many medical secrets they would rather not know. How should this information be handled? Do people have a right to knowledge that will destroy their peace of mind? Can patients keep their doctors from sharing important genetic information with other relatives? See how the traditional values of discretion and confidentiality play out in a brave new world.

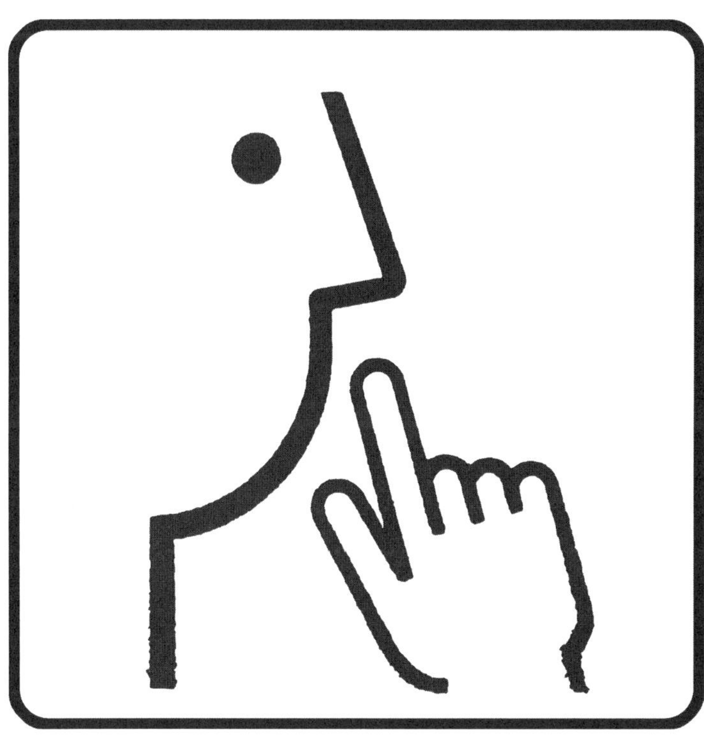

The Ethics of Medical Confidentiality
Lesson Overview and Case Study

Case Study

Jim (60) has recently been diagnosed with Huntington's disease (HD). There is no reported family history of HD, but in retrospect, several of his deceased relatives may also have had the condition. He has expressed a view, strongly shared with his wife Mary, that he does not want any of their four children (aged 27–37 years) to be informed of the diagnosis nor of the risk to them. Jim and Mary can only see negative consequences arising out of the sharing of such information and anticipate that they will be blamed. Mary says, "They either have it or they don't."

The couple has been advised by genetic staff that their children might in fact want to know so they can make their own choices. They have been offered help in communicating with their children, but have declined.

At a staff case discussion, most health professionals on the team feel that Jim and Mary's confidentiality should be respected. Justification for this decision is based on the lack of effective treatment for HD. Nevertheless, concern is also expressed that the children have a right to know what they are actually at risk of.

Adapted from, Anneke Lucassen and Michael Parker, "Confidentiality and Serious Harm in Genetics—Preserving the Confidentiality of One Patient and Preventing Harm to Relatives," *European Journal of Human Genetics* vol. 12:2 (Feb. 2004): 95

Learning **Activity 1**

**Should the health care professionals respect Jim and Mary's wishes?
Why or why not? Be prepared to defend your view.**

Reasons to Listen to Jim and Mary	Reasons Not to Listen to Jim and Mary
Children are happier not knowing.	Children have right to know in the future can make life Decision.

Foundations of Medical Confidentiality

Text 1

What I may see or hear in the course of the treatment, or even outside of the treatment, in regard to the life of men, which on no account one must spread abroad, I will keep to myself, holding such things shameful to be spoken about.

Hippocratic Oath

Text 2a

Perhaps the most fundamental reason why medical confidentiality is deemed central to the relationship between health care professional and patient is a pragmatic reason that focuses on optimizing this therapeutic relationship. As Margot Brazier explains: "Doctors, like priests and lawyers, must be able to keep secrets. For medical care to be effective, for patients to be able to trust their doctor, they must be confident that they can talk frankly to him." There is evidence that breaches in confidentiality will affect the level of information imparted by patients. Thus, the consequences of breaching confidentiality are likely to result in patients being less candid about the information they divulge to health care professionals, which is likely to have a further consequence of impeding the level of treatment, support, or counselling they will receive. . . . Confidentiality is fundamental for pragmatic, therapeutic reasons.

Rebecca Bennett, "Confidentiality," in Richard Ashcroft et al., eds., *Principles of Health Care Ethics*, p. 325

Dr. Rebecca Bennett. Senior lecturer in bioethics, and fellow of the Institute of Medicine, Law and Bioethics at University of Manchester. Dr. Bennet's specific research interests include assisted reproductive technologies, pre-implantation genetic diagnosis, genetic testing in pregnancy, responsibility in pregnancy, HIV/AIDS, cloning, stem cell research, and men's reproductive rights.

Text 2b

It is generally accepted that respecting individual autonomy is a fundamental moral principle, enabling individuals to have control over their own lives. . . . Respect for individual autonomy dictates that patients should be in control of their medical treatment, emphasizing the importance of informed consent and confidentiality. Medical Research Council expresses this link with the notion of respect for autonomy well saying: "Keeping control over facts about one's self can have an important role in a person's sense of security, freedom of action, and self-respect." Just as an insistence on informed consent to medical treatment allows patients to make authentic choices about their lives, so medical confidentiality allows patients to remain in control of information about their lives, the disclosure of which may be detrimental.

Rebecca Bennett, "Confidentiality," in Richard Ashcroft et al., eds., *Principles of Health Care Ethics*, p. 326

Jewish Sources for Confidentiality

Text 3a

לֹא תֵלֵךְ רָכִיל בְּעַמֶּיךָ לֹא תַעֲמֹד עַל דַּם רֵעֶךָ אֲנִי ה'. לֹא תִשְׂנָא אֶת אָחִיךָ בִּלְבָבֶךָ.
ויקרא יט,טז–יז

You shall not go around as a *rachil* (gossipmonger) amongst your people. You shall not stand by the shedding of your fellow's blood. I am the Lord. You shall not hate your brother in your heart.

Leviticus 19:16–17

Text 3b

אי זהו רכיל זה שטוען דברים והולך מזה לזה ואומר כך אמר פלוני, כך וכך שמעתי על פלוני אף על פי שהוא אמת הרי זה מחריב את העולם. יש עון גדול מזה עד מאד והוא בכלל לאו זה והוא לשון הרע, והוא המספר בגנות חבירו אף על פי שאומר אמת.
רמב"ם, הלכות דעות ז,ב

Who is a *rachil?* One who peddles tidbits from one person to another, saying "Mr. A said so and so; I heard so and so about Mrs. B." Even if it is true, it destroys the world. There is a more serious wrongdoing included in this prohibition: *lashon hara*—speaking disparagingly about others, even if speaking the truth.

Maimonides, *Mishneh Torah*, Laws of Temperaments 7:2

Question for Discussion

What is the reason for the prohibition against *rechilut*? Why does Maimonides see this as something that destroys the world?

Text 4

ונזק הרכילות חדל לספור כי אין מספר כי הוא מרבה שנאה בעולם ומכשיל את בני אדם לעבור על מה שכתוב בתורה לא תשנא את אחיך בלבבך. והנה העולם קיים על השלום. ומפני השנאה נמוגים ארץ וכל יושביה . . . ופעמים רבות יתן הרכיל חרב ביד חברו להרוג את רעהו.

שערי תשובה ג,רכב

The damage caused by *rechilut* is incalculable. It multiplies hate in the world and causes people to violate the commandment, "You shall not hate your brother in your heart." The world rests on [a foundation of] peace. As a result of hate, the earth and all its inhabitants tremble . . . Many times, the gossiper puts a sword in the hand of a person to kill a peer.

Rabbi Yonah of Gerona, *Sha'arei Teshuvah* 3:222

Rabbi Yonah ben Avraham of Gerona (d. 1263). Rabbi, talmudist, and teacher of ethics. Born in the late 12th century in Gerona, Spain; dean of the yeshivah in Barcelona. He was a cousin and friend of Nachmanides, and a teacher of the Rashba and Re'ah. Authored works on Tanach, Mishnah, and Talmud, but is most famous for his *Sha'arei Teshuvah*, a work on ethics and repentance

Text 5a

מניין לאומר דבר לחבירו שהוא בבל יאמר עד שיאמר לו לך אמור
שנאמר (ויקרא א,א) וידבר ה' אליו מאהל מועד לאמר.

תלמוד בבלי, יומא ז,ב

From whence do we know that when a person tells something to a friend, that it should not be repeated until he is told "go and tell"? For it says, "And G-d spoke to him from the tent of meeting to say" (Leviticus 1:1).

Text 5b

הוֹלֵךְ רָכִיל מְגַלֶּה סּוֹד וְנֶאֱמַן רוּחַ מְכַסֶּה דָבָר.

משלי יא,יג

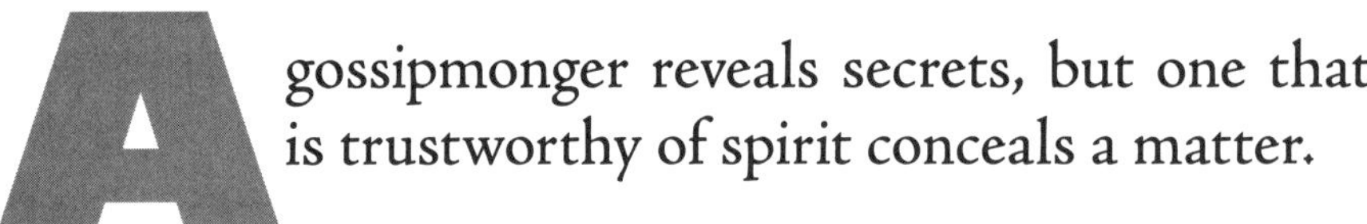

A gossipmonger reveals secrets, but one that is trustworthy of spirit conceals a matter.

Proverbs 11:13

Text 5c

שהרכיל ממדותיו ומפעלותיו לגלות סוד, רצונו לומר אף מה שהוזהר עליו להסתירו
ולכסותו, אבל נאמן רוח לא דיו לכסות סוד, רצונו לומר מה שהוזהר ממנו, אבל אפילו
הדברים ששמע במקרה מבלי שיוזהר על הסתרם אחר שידע ויכיר שיש צורך בהסתרם
יכסה אותם ויסתירם.

חיבור התשובה א,ד

Rabbi Menachem Me'iri (1249–
1310). Born in Provence,
France; famous rabbi, talmudist and authority on Jewish law.
His monumental work, *Beit
Habechirah,* is a digest summarizing the discussions of the Talmud
along with the commentaries of
the major subsequent rabbis in
a lucid style. Despite its stature,
the work was largely unknown for
many generations, and thus was
excluded from general summaries
of rabbinic law until recently.

A *rachil* is one who reveals secrets—even those that he was commanded to keep secret and conceal. But a trustworthy person not only conceals secrets, i.e. that which he was commanded to conceal, but even things heard by chance without being ordered to keep them secret. The trustworthy person keeps them secret and conceals them because he understands and recognizes that there is a need for it to be kept secret.

Rabbi Menachem Me'iri, *Chibur Hateshuvah* 1:2

Text 6

מקושש זה צלפחד, וכן הוא אומר ויהיו בני ישראל במדבר וימצאו איש וגו' (במדבר
טו,לב) ולהלן הוא אומר אבינו מת במדבר (שם כז,ג), מה להלן צלפחד, אף כאן
צלפחד, דברי רבי עקיבא. אמר לו רבי יהודה בן בתירא: עקיבא, בין כך ובין כך אתה
עתיד ליתן את הדין. אם כדבריך, התורה כיסתו ואתה מגלה אותו. ואם לאו אתה
מוציא לעז על אותו צדיק.

תלמוד בבלי, שבת צו,ב

"T he chopper [of wood, who violated Shabbat in the desert] was Tselafchad, as it says 'And the Children of Israel *were* *in the desert* and they found a man [chopping wood on the Shabbat]' (Numbers 15:32), and later it states 'Our father died *in the desert*' (ibid. 27:3). Just as the second verse refers to Tselafchad, so does the first verse refer to Tselafchad." These are the words of Rabbi Akiva.

Rabbi Yehudah ben Beteira responded, "Akiva, either way, you will have to give an account [for your words]. If you are correct, how can you reveal this fact when the Torah saw it fit to conceal? And if not, then you have maligned the name of a righteous person!"

Talmud, Shabbat 96b

Limits on Confidentiality
Secular Limits

Text 7a

While confidentiality is held to be central to the relationship between health care professional and patient there would be very few who would argue that this duty to maintain patient confidentiality should be considered absolute. The reasons for this are clear. The very principles that explain the importance of confidentiality also undermine it. Thus, while consequential reasoning and respect for autonomy generally require that we maintain medical confidences, in some cases the same consequential reasoning and respect for autonomy seem to require that we breach confidentiality. Consider the famous Tarasoff case (1976). In this case, a disturbed man revealed to his psychiatrist that he had homicidal thoughts towards his girlfriend. His confidentiality regarding this information was maintained, and the woman was not warned. The patient murdered her. On both consequentialist grounds and based on a general respect for autonomy, there are good reasons to argue that confidentiality of a patient with such murderous intentions should be breached in order to warn a third party at risk. While breaching confidentiality in this instance may result in an erosion of trust between patient and psychiatrist, perhaps even result in harm to others as a result, the alternative consequences of failing to prevent murder are severe. Similarly, although a breach of confidentiality undermines the patient's autonomy, removing his control over this information, if respect for autonomy is important in order to allow individuals control over their lives, then not attempting to prevent murder seems inconsistent with this respect for individual lives. Thus, we are left with a scenario where it is typically held that "confidentiality should be maintained without exception" but also agreed that "confidentiality should be broken when people were placed at risk."

Rebecca Bennett, "Confidentiality," in Richard Ashcroft et al. eds., *Principles of Health Care Ethics*, p. 326

Text 7b

The physician should not reveal confidential information without the express consent of the patient, subject to certain exceptions that are ethically justified because of overriding considerations.

When a patient threatens to inflict serious physical harm to another person or to him or herself and there is a reasonable probability that the patient may carry out the threat, the physician should take reasonable precautions for the protection of the intended victim, which may include notification of law enforcement authorities.

When the disclosure of confidential information is required by law or court order, physicians generally should notify the patient. Physicians should disclose the minimal information required by law, advocate for the protection of confidential information and, if appropriate, seek a change in the law.

Code of Medical Ethics, American Medical Association, Opinion 5.05 — Confidentiality

Question for Discussion

Based on Texts 7a and 7b, can you provide examples of situations that might justify a breach of confidentiality?

Text 8

Genetic knowledge has implications for individuals themselves, as well as other family members. In general, health professionals encourage people to pass on genetic risk information to their relatives. However, the disclosure of such information is not always straightforward and, consequently, some people may not be aware of their risk. If risk information is actively withheld, genetic counsellors may need to determine whether they have a duty to pass this on, particularly when preventive action can be taken.

Karn Forrest Keenan et al., "'It's Their Blood Not Mine': Who's Responsible for (Not) Telling Relatives About Genetic Risk?" *Health, Risk & Society* vol. 7:3 (September 2005): 209

Halachic Limits

Text 9a

ששמע גוים או מוסרים מחשבים עליו רעה או טומנים לו פח ולא גלה אזן חבירו
והודיעו . . . עובר על לא תעמוד על דם רעך.

רמב״ם, הלכות רוצח ושמירת נפש א,יד

If one hears of evildoers plotting to cause harm or intending to set a trap for his friend and does not inform him . . . he violates the prohibition of "You shall not stand by the shedding of your fellow's blood."

Rambam, *Mishneh Torah*, Laws of the Murderer and Guarding Life 1:14

Text 9b

למדנו מדברי הרמב״ם . . . שבכלל האיסור של לא תעמוד על דם רעך כלול לא רק
כשהמדובר על שפיכות דמים ממש, אלא הוא כולל על כל העומד מנגד ונמנע מלעשות
פעולה כדי להציל את חבירו מכל רעה שחורשים עליו או מכל פח שטומנים לו.

ציץ אליעזר טז,ד

We deduce from these words of Maimonides . . . that the prohibition of "You shall not stand by the shedding of your fellow's blood" does not only refer to an act of murder, but includes anyone who stands by and does not act to save a peer from any harm that is being planned for him, or any trap being set for him.

Rabbi Eliezer Waldenburg, *Tsits Eliezer* 16:4

Rabbi Eliezer Yehudah Waldenberg (1915–2006). Leading rabbi and judge on the Supreme Rabbinical Court in Jerusalem; considered an eminent authority on Jewish medical ethics and Jewish law. He published his halachic responsa, *Tsits Eliezer*, which is viewed as one of the great achievements of halachic scholarship of the 20th century. He served as rabbi for the Shaare Zedek Medical Center in Jerusalem.

כל הספרי מוסר הרעישו העולם על עון לשון הרע ואנכי מרעיש העולם להיפוך עון גדול
מזה וגם הוא מצוי יותר והוא מניעת עצמו מלדבר במקום הנצרך להציל את העשוק
מיד עושקו.

דרך משל במי שראה באחד שהוא אורב על חבירו בערמה על הדרך במדבר להרגו או
שראה חותר מחתרת בלילה בביתו או בחנותו היתכן שימנע מלהודיע לחבירו שיזהר
ממנו משום איסור לשון הרע הלא עונו גדול מנשוא שעובר על לא תעמוד על דם רעך
וכן בענין ממון הוא בכלל השבת אבידה.

ועתה מה לי חותר במחתרת או שרואה משרתיו גונבים ממונו בסתר או שותפו גונב
דעתו בעסק או שחבירו מטעהו במקח וממכר או שלוה מעות והוא גברא דלאו פרענא
הוא וכן בעניני שידוך והוא יודע שהוא איש רע ובליעל ורע להתחתן עמו כולן בכלל
השבת אבידת גופו וממונו.

פתחי תשובה, אורח חיים קנו

All the books of ethics make a tumult about
the prohibition of gossip. I make a tumult
about a greater wrong that is more prevalent, that of withholding information when it is necessary to communicate it in order to save a victim from
one who wishes to oppress him.

For example, if one sees someone ambushing another
on the road in the forest in order to kill him, or one
sees someone digging a tunnel at night into the house
or store of another, is it possible that because of the prohibition of tale-bearing he should not warn the victim
to be cautious? Doing this is a great sin, as it violates
the commandment "You shall not stand by the shedding of your fellow's blood." And regarding monetary
issues, there is the mitzvah of returning lost objects.

Now what difference is there between seeing the digger of the tunnel or seeing a friend's servants stealing his fortune, or seeing his partners take advantage of him in business, or seeing scoundrels cheat him, or seeing someone known not to repay a debt attempt to borrow money from him, or seeing an evil person being proposed to him in marriage? All of these cases are included in the mitzvah of returning lost objects and saving another from danger.

Rabbi Yisrael Isser Isserlin, *Pitchei Teshuva, Orach Chayim* 1:56

Text 9d

אם הוא רואה שאחד רוצה להשתדך עם אחד, וידוע לרואה הזה כי החתן יש לו
חסרונות עצומים . . . והמחותן אינו יודע מזה דבר ואילו היה יודע לא היה מתרצה לזה,
יש לגלותו לו . . . דהיינו אם החסרון הוא מצד חולי גופו, והמחותן אינו מכיר אותו מצד
שהוא דבר פנימי אשר לא נגלה לכל.

חפץ חיים, הלכות איסורי רכילות ט, ציורים ד–ו

If one sees that someone wants to marry a particular individual and the observer knows that the groom has major flaws . . . and that the other party is not aware of this, and that they would not want to go ahead with the marriage if they were aware of this fact, then this information should be disclosed by the observer. . . . This refers to a flaw due to illness which the other party is not aware of because it is internal and not apparent to all.

Rabbi Yisrael Meir Hakohen, *Chafets Chayim, Hilchot Rechilut* 9, Cases 4–6

Question for Discussion

What criteria must be present in order for one to be allowed to disclose a person's illness to a prospective spouse?

Text 10a

וַיֹּאמֶר ה' אֶל יְהוֹשֻׁעַ קֻם לָךְ לָמָּה זֶּה אַתָּה נֹפֵל עַל פָּנֶיךָ. חָטָא יִשְׂרָאֵל וְגַם עָבְרוּ אֶת בְּרִיתִי אֲשֶׁר צִוִּיתִי אוֹתָם וְגַם לָקְחוּ מִן הַחֵרֶם וְגַם גָּנְבוּ וְגַם כִּחֲשׁוּ וְגַם שָׂמוּ בִכְלֵיהֶם. וְלֹא יֻכְלוּ בְּנֵי יִשְׂרָאֵל לָקוּם לִפְנֵי אֹיְבֵיהֶם עֹרֶף יִפְנוּ לִפְנֵי אֹיְבֵיהֶם כִּי הָיוּ לְחֵרֶם לֹא אוֹסִיף לִהְיוֹת עִמָּכֶם אִם לֹא תַשְׁמִידוּ הַחֵרֶם מִקִּרְבְּכֶם. קֻם קַדֵּשׁ אֶת הָעָם וְאָמַרְתָּ הִתְקַדְּשׁוּ לְמָחָר כִּי כֹה אָמַר ה' אֱלֹקֵי יִשְׂרָאֵל חֵרֶם בְּקִרְבְּךָ יִשְׂרָאֵל לֹא תוּכַל לָקוּם לִפְנֵי אֹיְבֶיךָ עַד הֲסִירְכֶם הַחֵרֶם מִקִּרְבְּכֶם.

יהושע ז, י–יג

And the Lord said to Joshua, "Get up; why do you fall upon your face? Israel has sinned, and they have also violated My covenant which I commanded them; and they have also taken of the consecrated property, and have also stolen, and also dissembled, and they have also put it into their vessels.

"And the Children of Israel shall not be able to stand before their enemies; they will turn their backs before their enemies, because they have become accursed. I will not be with you anymore, if you do not destroy the consecrated property from among you.

"Arise, prepare the people, and say, 'Prepare yourselves for tomorrow; for so says the Lord G-d of Israel, "There is a transgressor in your midst, O Israel; you will not be able to stand before your enemies, until you remove the transgressor from among you."'"

Joshua 7:10–13

Text **10b**

אמר לפניו: רבונו של עולם, מי חטא. אמר לו: וכי דילטור אני לך, הטל גורלות.

תלמוד בבלי, סנהדרין יא,א

Joshua said to G-d, "Master of the Universe, who has sinned?"

G-d replied, "Am I a gossiper? Draw lots [to determine the culprit]."

Talmud, Sanhedrin 11a

Resolution of Case Study

Text 11

ישכנע הרופא את החולה שיסכים לגלות את המידע לקרוביו; ואם החולה עומד לשאת

אשה חייב החולה לגלות לה את מצבו, ואם לא מספר חייב הרופא להעביר לה את

המידע. אם הקרובים לא ישאו נשים אין להודיע להם.

ברכה לאברהם 313

The doctor should press the patient to reveal this information to his blood relatives. If the person with the disease is planning to marry, he is obligated to reveal his condition to the prospective spouse. If he does not tell, the doctor is obligated to relay this information. If none of the relatives are planning to marry, they should not be told about the illness.

Rabbi Yitschak Zilberstein, *Berachah LeAvraham*, p. 313

Rabbi Yitschak Zilberstein (1934–). Rabbi of Ramat Elchanan section of Bnei Brak and authority on Jewish law. Born in Poland, he was educated in Jerusalem and married the daughter of Rabbi Yosef Shalom Elyashiv. He is famous for his monthly class on Jewish medical ethics, which is attended by many religious and non-religious physicians. He has also published numerous essays on this subject.

Additional Considerations
My Money vs. Your Life

Text 12

ורשאין בני העיר להתנות על המדות ועל השערים, ועל שכר פועלים,
ולהסיע על קיצתן.

תלמוד בבלי, בבא בתרא ח,ב

The people of the city are authorized to make guidelines regarding measures, prices, and wages of laborers, as well as to fine those that transgress.

Talmud, Bava Batra 8b

Text 13a

מי שאבדה לו אבידה, ופגע באבידתו ובאבידת חבירו, אם יכול לחזור את שתיהן חייב
להחזירם; ואם לא, יחזיר את שלו, שאבידתו קודמת אפילו לאבידת אביו ורבו . . . ואף
על פי כן יש לו לאדם ליכנס לפנים משורת הדין ולא לדקדק ולומר שלי קודם,
אם לא בהפסד מוכח.

שולחן ערוך, חושן משפט רסז,א

If someone lost an object and found his object and his friend's lost object: If he can retrieve both of them, then he is obligated to do so. If he cannot, then he should retrieve his own, for his lost objects come even before those of his father and teacher . . . Still, a person should go beyond the letter of the law and not

be too particular in saying "My belongings come first"
unless the loss of his own object is very probable.

Text 13b

לאור האמור נמצאנו למדים לעניננו, שרופא המוצא את החולה שאין לו כושר ראיה
העונה לדרישות הציבור כתנאי למתן רשיון חייב למסור את הדברים לשלטונות מטעם
שהוא טובת הציבור ויסוד החיוב נובע מ״גמילות חסד״. ולכן אם קיים חשש שהחולה
ינקום ברכוש הרופא פטור הרופא מלמסור את הדברים לשלטונות, כי במצות שטעמם
״חסד״ קיים הכלל ״שלך קודם״, אבל מוטלת על הרופא חובה לשקול בפלס שכלו אם
החשש מוכח וברור ורק אז ממונו קודם. מה שאין כן כאשר החולה מוגבל בראייתו
והוא מסוכן מאד בנהיגתו מוטלת על הרופא חובה להתעלם מסכנת ממונו ולמסור את
הדברים לשלטונות, כי אז החולה עלול להרוג בני אדם ואנו מוזהרים על לא תעמוד
על דם רעך.

עמק הלכה אסיא 153

et us apply this principle to the present case.
When a physician finds that a patient suffers a
visual impairment that makes him ineligible to
hold a driver's license [and the patient has no intention
of giving up his license], the doctor should inform the
authorities, as this is in the public's best interest. This
obligation stems from the obligation to do kindness.

At the same time, if there is a possibility that the patient
will take revenge on the physician and cause him financial harm, the physician is exempt from informing the
authorities, for any mitzvah in the realm of chesed follows the rule "your own needs take precedence." The

physician must ascertain, however, that there is a genuine risk to his own well-being [before deciding not to report the patient to the authorities]; only in such a case do his own needs take precedence.

However, if the patient's sight is limited and his driving is very dangerous, then the physician must ignore his financial loss and inform the authorities, as in this case, the patient can kill people, and we are commanded, "Do not stand idly by the shedding of your brother's blood."

Rabbi Yitschak Zilberstein, *Emek Halachah Assia*, p. 153

Question for Discussion

What implications does this have for our case study regarding informing children that they may have Huntington's disease?

The Public Good

Text 14a

פדיון שבויים קודם לפרנסת עניים ולכסותן. ואין מצוה גדולה כפדיון שבויים. הילכך
לכל דבר מצוה שגבו מעות בשבילו, יכולים לשנותן לפדיון שבויים.
שולחן ערוך, יורה דעה רנב,א

The redemption of captives comes before feeding and clothing poor people. There is no mitzvah as great as the mitzvah of redeeming captives. Therefore, if there were any cause for which money was raised, it could be used for redeeming captives.

Rabbi Yosef Caro, Shulchan Aruch, *Yoreh De'ah* 252:1

Text 14b

אין פודין את השבויין יתר על כדי דמיהן, מפני תיקון העולם.
משנה, גיטין ד,ו

For the good of society, captives may not be redeemed for more than they are worth.

Mishnah, Gitin 4:6

	Lesson 1 Choosing Life	Lesson 2 Flesh of My Flesh	Lesson 3 Rolling The Dice
Values			
Surprising Facts			
Questions			
Action Items			
Favorite Readings			
Soundbites			

	Lesson 4 **New Beginnings**	**Lesson 5** **With You In Mind**	**Lesson 6** **Secret Code**
Values			
Surprising Facts			
Questions			
Action Items			
Favorite Readings			
Soundbites			

Key Points

1. Secular ethics views confidentiality as vital for practical therapeutic reasons as well as a necessary element of patient autonomy.

2. Jewish law exhorts every individual to refrain from passing around information regarding others. This is true even if the information is innocuous.

3. The major difference between secular ethics and Jewish law is that the duty imposed by Jewish law has a broader reach, extending to all information about any individual, whereas in secular ethics there is only a right to confidentiality once a relationship of trust has been established, as in the patient-physician relationship.

4. Both Jewish law and secular law impose an obligation to breach confidentiality when there is a likelihood of serious physical harm to a third party.

5. Jewish law extends this to include not only physical harm, but any other kind of harm such as financial harm.

6. In situations where Jewish law would normally require disclosure but doing so would lead to a financial loss, it would be permitted to withhold the information so long as maintaining confidentiality would not result in a threat to someone's life.

Additional Readings

Consent and Confidentiality in Genetics: Whose Information Is It Anyway?

A. Kent

Abstract

Against a background of increasing regulation regarding access to medical information and the presentation of patients' confidentiality, the case of genetic information raises interesting questions about whether the application of general rules is appropriate in all situations. Whilst all genetic information is not equally sensitive, some of it is highly predictive. It also allows deductions to be made about other family members. It may not be regarded as particularly sensitive when compared to other types of medical information and those to whom it applies may not be as anxious about preserving their confidentiality as compared with—for example, the prospect of seeing research into cause and cures for rare diseases put in hand. These distinctions also find resonance with the general public. Resolving conflicting tensions will require subtlety, not a blunt "one size fits all" model.

Against a background in which trust in the professionalism of clinicians and scientists has been shaken by a number of well publicised abuses, it is timely to discuss the issues of consent and confidentiality and the ways in which proper respect can be given to the wishes of those who seek medical treatment or who wish to participate in biomedical research.

The failure of existing regulatory mechanisms at Bristol, where professional shortcomings were known about but not acted on, and Alder Hey, where the trust of families in vulnerable situations was violated over a prolonged period for no good reason through the actions of an alleged "rogue pathologist", have resulted in a general tightening of the regulations about what may or may not be done and under what circumstances to patients and their samples. The inadequacies and competencies of the current situation are addressed in the forthcoming report of the Retained Organs Commission. This situation is likely to result in legislation, which will create offences under criminal law for those who fail to comply with the requirements of good practice in future.

The general tightening up of the regulations regarding consent and the protection of patient and family interests is a fact of life. In the light of the scandals referred to above it is hard to argue that it is not a good and a necessary development and I would be among the first to agree with the argument for a greater emphasis on seeking informed consent from patients and, in cases where individuals are unable to consent for themselves, from those who act in their interest.

In this as in other areas where the might of legislation is invoked to resolve a difficulty, however, hard cases can make bad law. Care must be taken in drawing the line between what is and what is not permissible, to ensure that an appropriate balance is struck between the interest and the rights of the individual and the legitimate interests and rights of the community to which that person belongs.

Not all medical information is equally sensitive. To treat it as if it were so is potentially to constrain some beneficial applications in ways which even those who might not wish to participate would not want to happen.

There is no absolute right to confidentiality, but there is a widely held rebuttable presumption that information obtained in the course of a medical intervention will be held in confidence by the person who obtains it unless there is a very good reason for disclosing it. This trust is the basis on which the system is able to operate and without it medical care and research would grind to a halt. But a "one size fits all" model does not work well and in the case of genetic information, rigid application of the rules can cause significant problems which are in no one's interest, be they patient or professional.

WHAT IS "GENETIC" INFORMATION?

By "genetic" information I mean information which may be obtained by a variety of routes that enables either a diagnosis or a prediction of either a current or a future health status that can eventually be directly related to identifiable alterations in a person's DNA. This information may be derived by direct observation of the DNA or chromosomes, through family history taking, from biochemical tests, or by clinical observations. The important element in its use in medicine or research is not the route by which it has been derived, but the reliability with which it can be used to devise and sustain valid conclusion.

Clearly, not all genetic information is equally powerful. To treat it as if it were is clumsy. Some is highly predictive of future health. Its acquisition and disclosure requires careful thought and the application of carefully designed and implemented protocols. Most is not and to treat it as if it were may create overkill. Unfortunately the limits on genetic information are not well understood. Too often it is treated, particularly by the media, as if it were like a train leaving the station and travelling along a track on which there were no stops, sidings or diversions, gathering speed inexorably until it crashes into the buffers at the terminus to the great detriment and damage of all around.

In the case of the gene for Huntington's disease there is some justice in this analogy, but even here, given our current knowledge, detection of the mutation only tells you that you will get the disease. It does not tell you when, exactly, you will start to show the symptoms, or what the precise pattern of progression will be in you— or how the interplay between you and those around you will affect their ability to provide the care and support you will need.

But Huntington's disease provides a poor model on which to base more general models for deriving consent or for protecting confidentiality. The Nuffield Council on Bioethics in its report on genetics and mental health[1] found that when the very rare genetic forms of mental disorder, such as Huntington's or familial Alzheimer's are eliminated, the highest increase in predictable risk of future mental health problems that could be attributed to observable genetic phenomena was sufficient to raise the risk above that of the population as a whole by only about two to three per cent. Compare this with the predictive power of environmental features with no obvious genetic component of future mental health status—such as divorce, loss of a home, the death of a close relative, and redundancy, then the relative importance of genetics in such cases becomes apparent.

Even where the gene in question is significant and highly penetrant, the opportunity to intervene to reduce, prevent or treat disease alters the way in which the information should be treated. For example, in the case of familial hypercholesterolaemia or familial bowel cancer knowledge of one's genetic status can be positively beneficial in that it allows intervention and can prevent unnecessary disease and disability. Development of an appropriate model for service delivery should take account of this, as those with experience of the condition and of providing services and support for those affected will quickly tell you.

WHAT INFORMATION IS IT ANYWAY?

Genetic information, by definition, does not apply uniquely to individuals. Knowledge of one person's genetic status allows us to draw inferences about those to whom he or she is related.

In most cases these will be of so little power or reliability as to be trivial, but in a number of instances, most notably those connected with significant single gene disorders, the inferences that can be drawn may be substantial. In such a situation, if I know something about myself does my brother or sister have a right to know

---

[1] Nuffield Council on Bioethics. Mental disorders and genetics: the ethical context. London: Nuffield Council on Bioethics, 1998.

it too, given that it also affects them? At what point is my wish to protect my privacy overridden by their wish or need to know in order to avoid potentially harmful consequences?

Work undertaken by the Genetic Interest Group[2] indicates that, among those living in families where there is a diagnosis of a substantial risk of genetic disease, there is a strongly held view that such information should not be seen as the private property of the individual. Rather it should be seen as family information held in common by all those to whom it applies. Of course, like all views that are simply stated, interpretation in practice is infinitely complex and subject to all the vagaries of human nature. The ideal world notion of important information being sensitively and carefully disclosed in a caring and supportive way does not always hold true. In some situations the giving or withholding of information and the manner in which it is done can be an exercise in power or a reflection of other aspects of the family context!

The familial nature of this type of genetic information also places on the professional the obligation to define where he or she stands in relation to the maintenance of individual confidentiality or the decision to override it in the pursuit of the greater good (or perhaps the lesser harm). Again, the view from families at risk is that, in the case of severe genetic disease where there is a potentially avoidable harm, professionals ought to be willing to override the wishes of the individuals and make the information available. This is not to suggest that people should be cavalier in their attitudes and disregard patients' wishes. To do so would very quickly result in legal challenges and close attention from professional and regulatory bodies such as the Royal College and the General Medical Council (GMC). Rather it is to postulate the need for the development of protocols and frameworks within which the decisions about the appropriate course of action in a given set of circumstances can be taken and recorded, in ways that are likely to protect the best interests of all concerned. While such a framework cannot guarantee that

legal action will be avoided, it will certainly minimise the chances of such litigation being successful.

RESEARCH

Research ethics committees rightly require that the confidentiality of those participating in approved programmes of research and development is not compromised. Whilst this is a feasible requirement in many types of research, when looking into causes and cures for rare genetic disorders it may not be possible. Indeed it may be counterproductive to try and achieve this. It may also be contrary to the expressed views of those with the condition in question.

Given the fact that it can take only two or three pieces of information to identify an individual to a very high degree of confidence, preserving the confidentiality of those with rare genetic disorders is, in many cases effectively impossible. In the case of many rare genetic disorders if you know the diagnosis, the health authority or trust and the name of the referring clinician then you can be pretty sure that you know the person. Indeed, for the research to be successful it may be essential that you are able to go back to the families and this indeed is likely to be what they would want, for it is only through the promotion of research that they will gain understanding of the situation in which they find themselves and eventually can have hope of making progress towards a cure.

Striking the right balance is difficult, particularly at the interface between research and clinical practice where initial observation of unexplained clinical signs and symptoms can move into more structured investigation almost imperceptibly, and where the nature of the referral almost begs the question about getting involved in research. The "Query xyz disorder or if not, what?" referral letter sets out both the clinical and the research agenda and it also asks the question which the families want urgently to be answered. Putting too rigid a bureaucracy around the means to answering it will frustrate these wishes. It will also act as a particular disincentive to those contemplating research with rare disorders and make the costs of doing such work rise significantly—an irony when it is often the fund raising efforts of those with the condition themselves

---

[2] Genetic Interest Group. Confidentiality guidelines. London: Genetic Interest Group, 1998.

which make it possible to contemplate doing the work in the first place.

Again, I am not arguing for carte blanche. Research must be regulated and it must be subject to proper ethical approval if potentially vulnerable individuals are not to be exploited unreasonably. But what works for a large scale multicentre clinical trial of a new drug for a common disease may be inappropriate for a study of a very rare genetic disorder requiring samples and case histories from clinicians throughout the UK and often further afield, each of whom may only know of one person or family with the condition in question. It is all a question of getting the balance right and of listening to the wishes of the individuals and the families who are at the heart of the problem.

SETTING THE CONTEXT

As has been stated earlier, not all genetic information is equally sensitive. It is also important to recognise that, whilst some of my genetic information may be highly sensitive, it may not be the aspect of my medical history that I am most concerned to keep private.

Thus my confidentiality may be severely breached by the unwarranted disclosure that I have cystic fibrosis (CF), but it is not—for example, significantly further damaged by the subsequent revelation that it is a consequence of the Delta F508 mutation. And whilst I may not mind your knowing that I have CF, I might be absolutely devastated were you to find out my HIV status, the fact that I had had several abortions and that my social father is not, in fact, my biological father. Improper disclosure of any of these could arguably do more damage than disclosing straightforward genetic information.

Rather then treating genetic information as if it were uniquely different and so warranting special treatment, we should be more concerned to ensure that existing mechanisms work well to protect individuals and preserve confidentiality in ways that are appropriate and necessary.

WHAT DOES THE PUBLIC THINK?

The discussion about access to medical information is often predicated on assumptions about the views of the general public. Yet when the question is asked of representatives of the public, the evidence is that the public is capable of making very sophisticated distinctions between different uses for medical information. The National Health Service (NHS) is currently engaged with a pilot project in West London known as "NHS LifeHouse". This is intended to link electronic patient records held in various locations in primary and secondary care to create a comprehensive electronic health record that will deliver point of care information that is relevant and up to date, whilst at the same time providing a resource for research and for health care planning.

Mindful of the fact that there are sensitivities associated with the use and abuse of computer records holding personal health data, this project takes as its baseline a commitment to transparency and public endorsement for its aims and objectives. This led to a number of consultations,[3] the results of which may provide some comfort for those who seek to regulate and control access to personal medical information in an appropriate way.

In respect of the clinical uses of personal medical information, the assumption seems to be that clinicians will and should talk to one another and that relevant information ought to be passed around between professionals who share an agreed code of conduct. When it comes to research, there is more difficulty, because many people do not see the NHS as an organisation which is research orientated. If the nature and purpose of the research is explained, however, then people are generally happy for this information to be shared, provided they are asked and that the information to be shared can be shown to be relevant. Similarly for service planning purposes, where personal identifiers are stripped away. Even the private sector can get a look in if the information is anonymised and the benefits are seen to flow to the NHS, rather than in the opposite direction, leading one to the conclusion that people are

---

[3] Sykes W, Hedges A. Preliminary focus groups: provisional notes. London: NHS LifeHouse, 2001.

aware of the complex uses that can be made of medical information, and are generally content that this should be the case when there is a clear explanation as to why, or that those who wish to regulate in order to protect confidentiality and ensure consent will have to be considerably more subtle than might have been anticipated by people seeking a quick fix to a current problem.

CONCLUSION

To conclude, I would like to return to my starting point and to the notion that hard cases can make bad law. I would like to leave you with a problem to think about and see how you would resolve it. It takes the form of a story.

Let us suppose that my brother and I are estranged. We share the same general practitioner (GP), who is aware of the fact that we are brothers, but who does not know about the hostility between us. Let us further suppose that I receive a diagnosis of a fatal, late onset dominantly inherited, genetic disorder. This means that my brother is at 50% risk and my GP knows this. Under the terms of the Data Protection Act, data controllers are obliged to tell data subjects if they hold significant information about them. My brother is unaware of the risk. I wish my confidentiality to be respected. You are my GP. You are also a DPA data controller. What do you do? Do you contact my brother and let him know you have information about him? Do you try and ascertain if he wants to know it? What if he not only doesn't want to know, but does not want to know that there is something he does not know? And what about my confidentiality? Oh and by the way, I also do not want my wife and children to know!

Answer, on a postcard, to . . . .!

DISCUSSION

Julian Peto was pleased to hear Alistair Kent's views and would like to see the survey of public attitudes on data and confidentiality. He believed the vast majority of the public would be happy to allow epidemiologists and other medical researchers to use their records once they understood the potential benefits of the research and how their data would be used. But first, the public

need to hear the arguments for the sharing of records. Alistair Kent agreed, adding that as long as patients understood the benefits of research they would be happy to give the go ahead to the use of their records. Such consent might be given generally, not for each specific case.

Onora O'Neill asked how a family at risk of a genetic disease could give an objective view. She also asked what was meant by family. Was it the social concept of family, or the genetic concept? In reply, Alistair Kent said that research carried out by the Centre for Family Research had revealed idiosyncratic ideas of what families are, based not just on genetics. He also advised caution before resorting to complex legislation on consent. This could result in inflexible rules that would not allow for changes to be made.

Journal of Medical Ethics 29, no. 1 (February 2003): 16-18. Reprinted with permission by publisher

House Votes To Expand National DNA Arrest Database

Declan McCullagh

Millions of Americans arrested for but not convicted of crimes will likely have their DNA forcibly extracted and added to a national database, according to a bill approved by the U.S. House of Representatives on Tuesday.

By a 357 to 32 vote, the House approved legislation that will pay state governments to require DNA samples, which could mean drawing blood with a needle, from adults "arrested for" certain serious crimes. Not one Democrat voted against the database measure, which would hand out about $75 million to states that agree to make such testing mandatory.

"We should allow law enforcement to use all the technology available to them . . . to reduce expensive and unjust false convictions, bring closure to victims by solving cold cases, better identify criminals, and keep those who commit violent crime from walking the streets," said Rep. Harry Teague, the New Mexico Democrat who sponsored the bill.

But civil libertarians say DNA samples should be required only from people who have been convicted of crimes, and argue that if there is probable cause to believe that someone is involved in a crime, a judge can sign a warrant allowing a blood sample or cheek swab to be forcibly extracted.

"It's wrong to treat someone as guilty before they're convicted," says Jim Harper, director of information policy studies at the Cato Institute. "It inverts the concept of innocent until proven guilty."

House Speaker Nancy Pelosi and the Democratic leadership scheduled Tuesday's debate on the bill—called the Katie Sepich Enhanced DNA Collection Act of 2010—using a procedure known as the "suspension calendar" intended to be reserved for non-controversial legislation.

"Suspension of the rules is supposed to be for praising the winner of the NCAA championship or renaming Post Offices," Harper says. "Things like collecting Americans' DNA are supposed to be fully debated in Congress."

In a surprise move, as the U.S. Congress was expanding the FBI's DNA database, the U.K.'s new coalition government was pledging sharp curbs on its own databases.

Created in the mid-1990s, the UK National DNA Database originally was supposed to store data on convicted criminals, but grew to include records on more than 5 million Britons, including many who were only arrested on suspicion of a crime.

U.K. Deputy Prime Minister Nick Clegg promised once-in-a-century privacy reforms in a speech on Wednesday: "We won't hold your Internet and e-mail records when there is just no reason to do so. CCTV will be properly regulated, as will the DNA database, with restrictions on the storage of innocent people's DNA. Britain must not be a country where our children grow up so used to their liberty being infringed that they accept it without question."

Background

The United States has followed a similar pattern: first, DNA was collected from convicted criminals, and then the practice was expanded to sweep in Americans arrested on suspicion of a crime.

A 2000 federal law called the DNA Analysis Backlog Elimination Act required that DNA samples be taken from anyone convicted of or on probation for certain serious crimes. This was challenged in court on Fourth and Fifth Amendment grounds, but a federal appeals court upheld the DNA collection requirement as constitutional.

A second bill that President Bush signed in January 2006 said any federal police agency could "collect DNA samples from individuals who are arrested." Anyone who fails to cooperate is, under federal law, guilty of an additional crime.

In addition, federal law and subsequent regulations from the Department of Justice authorize any means "reasonably necessary to detain, restrain, and collect a DNA sample from an individual who refuses to cooperate in the collection of the sample." The cheek swab or blood tests can be outsourced to "private entities."

A May 2009 ruling from a federal judge in California was the first decision to say that police can forcibly take DNA samples from Americans who have been arrested but not convicted of a crime. U.S. Magistrate Judge Gregory Hollows said the requirement of DNA-sampling felony arrestees did not violate the Fourth Amendment's prohibition of "unreasonable searches and seizures"—but noted that he took no position on whether or not DNA sampling for misdemeanor offenses was reasonable and constitutional.

But that law applied only to federal agencies, and the bill approved this week would provide a strong incentive for state and local governments to follow suit.

If states do follow suit, it's difficult to overstate how many more DNA samples would flood into the FBI's Convicted Offender DNA Index System (CODIS) database. Federal agencies arrested about 133,000 people in 2004, according to data compiled by the Urban Institute under a Justice Department grant.

But local and state governments arrested nearly 14 million Americans that year, not counting traffic offenses, according to FBI data.

Rep. Teague's proposal would extend DNA sampling and testing to anyone arrested on suspicion of burglary or attempted burglary; aggravated assault; murder or attempted murder; manslaughter; sex acts that can be punished by imprisonment for more than one year; and sex offenses against minors. The attorney general would be required to report to Congress which states have and have not signed up for the DNA database.

Rep. Dave Reichert (R-Wash.), a former sheriff who spoke on the House floor in favor of the bill, said the measure is supported by the National Sheriffs' Association, the National District Attorney's Association,

and the Rape, Abuse, and Incest National Network (RAINN).

The legislation would allow states to receive 15 percent "bonuses" from the Edward Byrne Memorial Justice Assistance Grant Program. The program gave out $165 million in local funding and $318 million in state funding for fiscal year 2009, not counting stimulus grants.

"We're strongly opposed to expanding collection," says Marc Rotenberg, executive director of the Electronic Privacy Information Center in Washington, D.C. He suggested the U.S. should follow the lead of the European Court of Human Rights, which ruled two years ago that holding DNA samples from people arrested but not convicted of a crime violates their privacy rights.

Cnet news, May 19, 2010.
Reprinted with permission by cnet.com

Protecting Privacy and the Public—Limits on Police Use of Bioidentifiers in Europe

George J. Annas, J.D., M.P.H.

Since 9/11, police and military around the world have sought to increase their arsenals of bioidentifiers, and privacy advocates have sought to cabin their use. In what may turn out to be the most important court decision involving the privacy limits on police use of bioidentifiers by any court in the world to date, the European Court of Human Rights ruled late last year that the United Kingdom's laws governing the collection and retention of DNA profiles and samples by law enforcement officials violate the human rights of members of the Council of Europe.[4] The Council of Europe, founded by 10 countries in 1949, currently has 47 member countries. The Council adopted the European Convention

---

[4] S. and Marper v. The United Kingdom, [2008] ECHR 30562/04.

for the Protection of Human Rights and Fundamental Freedoms in 1950, and it is the core document of the most comprehensive regional system of human rights protection in the world. Remarkably, the opinion was unanimous—signed by all 17 judges who were sitting as a Grand Chamber of the Human Rights Court—holding that the United Kingdom's retention policy "constitutes a disproportionate interference with the . . . right to respect for private life and cannot be regarded as necessary in a democratic society."[5]

The United Kingdom has been the world leader in collecting and using DNA profiles for criminal investigations since its first DNA dragnet, recounted vividly in Joseph Wambaugh's 1989 book, *The Blooding*. The book recounts how application of Alec Jeffreys's then-new DNA profiling technique was used to conduct a DNA dragnet that involved the collection of blood samples from more than 5000 men who lived in the vicinity of the location where two teenage girls had been brutally raped and murdered in 1983 and 1986.[6] Use of DNA profiling by the police was initially justified for identifying rapists and child molesters but has gradually expanded to involve more and more criminal suspects, although its usefulness in improving crime detection remains contested.[7] The expansion of bioidentification databases has also been justified by the threat of terrorism.[8] Because of the pioneering work in this area in the United Kingdom, the rules it adopts and the procedures it follows have considerable influence, especially in the United States, where our trend is to collect and retain DNA samples from all persons arrested for felonies.[9]

The constitutionality of the police's taking and using biometric data for identification and investigation, including not just DNA profiles but also fingerprints

themselves, has never been examined by the U.S. Supreme Court. One recurring question is whether DNA information is in some way unique, such that it calls for special legislation and regulation, or whether our privacy laws that protect private information (including medical information) are sufficient. In addition, whether Europe takes privacy more seriously than America is open to debate.[10] Finally, whether the European opinion will influence judicial decisions in the United States depends on both the respect U.S. judges accord to non-U.S. judicial opinions and differences in the language of the European Convention and the U.S. Constitution.

S. and Marper in the United Kingdom

S. was arrested and charged with attempted robbery when he was 11 years of age; he was later acquitted. Michael Marper, an adult, was arrested and charged with harassment of his partner.

Marper and his partner were reconciled before a pre-trial review, and the case was formally discontinued. Both arrests occurred in 2001. In each case, the police took both fingerprints and DNA samples.

S. and Marper asked that their fingerprints and DNA samples be destroyed, and in both cases the police refused. An administrative court refused to reverse this decision, and it was upheld in a Court of Appeal decision on a two-to-one vote.

One of the judges in the majority, Lord Justice Waller, argued that although the actual DNA sample had major differences from the DNA profiles and fingerprints, retention of the samples themselves could be justified for five reasons that outweighed any risk to privacy[11]:

"Retention of samples permits (a) the checking of the integrity and future utility of the DNA database system; (b) a reanalysis for the upgrading of DNA profiles

---

[5] Ibid.

[6] Wambaugh J. The blooding. New York: William Morrow, 1989.

[7] McCartney C. The DNA Expansion Programme and criminal investigation. Br J Criminol 2006;46:175-92.

[8] Williams R, Johnson P. Circuits of surveillance. Surveill Soc 2004;2:1-14.

[9] Simoncelli T, Steinhardt B. California's Proposition 69: a dangerous precedent for criminal DNA databases. J Law Med Ethics 2006;34:199-213.

[10] National Research Council. Bits of power: issues in global access to scientific data. Washington, DC: National Academy Press, 1997.

[11] R (on the application of S) v. Chief Constable of South Yorkshire; R (on the application of Marper) v. Chief Constable of South Yorkshire, [2002] EWCA Civ 1275.

where new technology can improve the discriminating power of the DNA matching process; (c) reanalysis and thus an ability to extract other DNA markers and thus offer benefits in terms of speed, sensitivity and cost of searches of the database; (d) further analysis in investigations of alleged miscarriages of justice; and (e) further analysis so as to be able to identify any analytical or process errors."

An appeal to the House of Lords was dismissed, with Lord Steyn giving the lead judgment. He argued, among other things, that the reason U.K. law permitted the retention of DNA profiles and samples was to prevent cases in which persons who had been acquitted of rape or murder nonetheless later commit these crimes and escape prosecution because their samples had not been retained. He also relied on evidence that suggested that almost 6000 DNA profiles that had been linked with crime-scene stain profiles involving 53 murders and 94 rapes would have been destroyed under the rules requiring destruction after acquittal.

Lord Steyn concluded that any interference with private life was proportionate to what was necessary for investigation of the crime: that profiles and samples were kept only for the limited purpose of detection, investigation, and prosecution of crime; were not made public; and were not identifiable by a nonexpert. He also did not believe that retention of a sample in any way stigmatized the person whose sample was retained by treating them as a suspect in future crimes or that there was any difference between retaining a DNA profile and retaining a DNA sample.[12]

S. and Marper in the European Court of Human Rights

S. and Marper thereafter brought a complaint to the European Court of Human Rights, arguing that the actions of the United Kingdom in retaining their fingerprints, DNA profile, and DNA samples for purposes of criminal investigation violated their rights under Article 8 (right to respect for private and family life) of the European Convention which provides that:

"1. Everyone has the right to respect for his private and family life, his home and his correspondence.

2. There shall be no interference by a public authority with the exercise of this right except such as is in accordance with the law and is necessary in a democratic society in the interests of national security, public safety or the economic well-being of the country, for the prevention of disorder or crime, for the protection of health or morals, or for the protection of the rights and freedoms of others."

The court found that at least 20 of the 47 member states in the Council of Europe permit the compulsory taking of DNA information and its storage in national databases. Of these 20 members, the United Kingdom is the only one "expressly to permit the systematic and indefinite retention of DNA profiles and cellular samples of persons who have been acquitted or in respect of whom criminal proceedings have been discontinued," and also is the only one "expressly to allow the systematic and indefinite retention of both profiles and samples of convicted persons."[13]

S. and Marper argued that retention of their DNA samples, DNA profiles, and fingerprints interfered with their right to respect for private life because this personal information is linked to personal identity and is the type of information they were entitled to keep within their control.

DNA samples were of particular concern because they "contained full genetic information about a person including genetic information about his or her relatives." The government agreed that all three were "personal data" but disagreed that any fell within the provisions of Article 8 of the European Convention because, unlike the actual taking of the information, the retention of it "did not interfere with the physical and psychological integrity of the person, nor did it breach their right to personal development or to establish and develop relationships with other human beings."[14]

---

[12] S. and Marper v. The United Kingdom, [2008] ECHR 30562/04

[13] Ibid.

[14] Ibid.

The Human Rights Court Decision

The court began its assessment by noting that the concept of "private life" is a broad one, covering not only the physical and psychological integrity of a person but also gender identification, name and sexual orientation, health information, ethnic identity, and other elements "relating to a person's right to their image." Most important, "the mere storing of data relating to the private life of an individual amounts to an interference within the meaning of Article 8."[15] The court reviewed the retention of DNA samples, DNA profiles, and fingerprints separately.

Regarding DNA samples, the primary concern of S. and Marper was that the samples could be used in the future in new and currently unknown ways. The court agreed that such a concern, although speculative and not yet realized, "is legitimate and relevant to a determination of the issue of whether there has been an interference." The court continued:

"[samples] contain much sensitive information about an individual, including information about his or her health. Moreover, samples contain a unique genetic code of great relevance to both the individual and his relatives. . . . Given the nature and amount of personal information contained in cellular samples, their retention per se must be regarded as interfering with the right to respect for the private lives of the individuals concerned."[16]

Next is the DNA profile, which the United Kingdom argued was "nothing more than a sequence of numbers or a bar-code containing information of a purely objective and irrefutable character." The court had little sympathy for this argument, noting that although the information itself may be considered objective, the way it is used undercuts this description. In particular, the court noted that the profiles have been used for "familial searching with a view to identifying a possible genetic relationship between individuals" and that this use alone "is sufficient to conclude that their reten-

tion interferes with the right to the private life of the individual concerned." In addition, the court noted that police also use DNA profiles to assess the probable ethnic origin of a perpetrator, "which makes retention all the more sensitive and susceptible of affecting the right to private life."

Fingerprints obviously do not contain the type of personal, familial, ethnic, and health information contained in DNA. In previous cases, the court had concluded that retention of fingerprints and their closest analogue, photographs, by the police after an arrest did not present a privacy problem because they did not contain any subjective information that "called for refutation." For example, the court had previously found that retention of photographs taken at a demonstration did not interfere with private life, at least if authorities had not tried to identify the persons photographed by comparing the photograph with others in a data bank. On the other hand, the court found that retention of the recording of a person's voice did amount to interference with the right to respect for private life if it was used to try to identify the person "in conjunction with other personal data." Applying these cases to fingerprints, the court found that although fingerprints are neutral, objective, and unintelligible to the untutored eye, fingerprints nonetheless "contain unique information about the individual concerned[,] allowing his or her identification with precision in a wide range of circumstances." Because of this, they are capable of affecting private life, and therefore their blanket and indefinite retention "without the consent of the individual concerned cannot be regarded as neutral or insignificant."[17]

Justification for Retention in a Democracy

The only remaining issue was whether the United Kingdom had a sufficient justification for retaining the DNA samples, DNA profiles, and fingerprints under Article 8 of the European Convention. S. and Marper argued that the justification of prevention or detection of crime was too vague and open to abuse and that indefinite retention could not be regarded as necessary in a democratic society for the purpose of preventing crime and was, in any event, disproportionate and

---

[15] S.and Marper v. The United Kingdom, [2008] ECHR 30562/04.

[16] Ibid.

[17] Ibid.

particularly detrimental to children and members of certain ethnic groups overrepresented in the database.

The United Kingdom defended its indefinite retention as being of "inestimable value in the fight against crime and terrorism and the detection of the guilty" and the elimination of the innocent from suspicion. The United Kingdom also cited examples of successful prosecutions involving the retention of samples from people who had not been convicted, and it argued that the retention could not be regarded as excessive because the DNA samples and the DNA profiles were kept only for specific limited statutory purposes and were stored securely. In the government's view, there was no stigmatization and "no practical consequences for the applicants unless the records matched a crime-scene profile."[18]

The court found that the justification of preventing crime was so general that it could "give rise to extensive interpretation," saying:

"It is as essential, in this context, as in telephone tapping, secret surveillance and covert intelligence-gathering, to have clear, detailed rules governing the scope and application of measures, as well as minimum safeguards concerning, inter alia, duration, storage, usage, access of third parties, procedures for preserving the integrity and confidentiality of data and procedures for its destruction, thus providing sufficient guarantees against the risk of abuse and arbitrariness."[19]

The court agreed that prevention and detection of crime, particularly organized crime and terrorism, are both legitimate and increasingly reliant on modern scientific techniques, including DNA analysis. Nonetheless, the court was concerned that in the United Kingdom no distinctions are made on the basis of the gravity of the offense charged or the age of the suspect, and there are no time limits on retention, few opportunities to have the material destroyed, and no opportunity for independent review if a request for destruction is denied.

The court found especially troubling the risk of stigmatization from indefinite storage, which it believed

undercut the presumption of innocence to which people who had not been convicted of any crime are entitled. Instead, these innocents were treated exactly the same as convicted criminals. This is even worse in the case of minors and members of ethnic minorities, who are overrepresented in the database. The court also found the retention of DNA samples to be "particularly intrusive given the wealth of genetic and health information contained therein."[20]

The court's ultimate conclusion, nonetheless, made no distinctions among DNA samples, DNA profiles, and fingerprints because of the "blanket and indiscriminate nature of the powers of retention" and the failure of the United Kingdom to strike a "fair balance between the competing public and private interests." The court accordingly held that blanket and indefinite retention of all three identifiers constituted a disproportionate interference with the applicants' right to respect for private life and cannot be regarded as necessary in a democratic society. Therefore, the practice was in violation of Article 8 of the European Convention.[21]

Implications of the Decision

The numbers are impressive. With more than 5 million DNA profiles and samples (representing 9% of the population, nearly all men), the United Kingdom's criminal DNA database is one of the largest in the world.[22] Of the 5 million, almost 1 million are from persons who were never convicted of any crime, and about half a million are from juveniles. The response to the European Court's decision in the United Kingdom has been largely positive. The journal *Nature,* for example, editorialized that although "technology can be a powerful force for human rights," it could also lead us down the road to a "surveillance society."[23]

The editors were particularly concerned that "without strong safeguards [legitimate databases] . . . could slowly and steadily be linked into an all-pervasive monitoring

---

[18] Ibid.

[19] Ibid.

[20] Ibid.

[21] Ibid.

[22] DNA and human rights: throw it out. Economist 2008;12:73-4.

[23] Watching Big Brother. Nature 2008;456:675-6.

system that would make George Orwell's concept of 1984 look technologically tame all in the name of security, efficiency and convenience."[24] Alec Jeffreys himself also agreed with the decision, telling the *Guardian* newspaper that DNA samples should not be kept and that the DNA profiles of innocent people should not be in the data bank.[25]10 The U.K. government itself has issued a responsive set of proposals (out for public comment until August 7) to reform its practices.[26] The major proposal is to end the practice of retaining DNA samples at all and to destroy them soon after the DNA profile is created.[27] As for the DNA profiles, as well as fingerprints, these would be retained for 6 years for those not convicted and for 12 years for those not convicted but charged with serious violent, sexual, or terrorism-related offenses.[28] There would be separate but similar rules for minors. The proposal to destroy all DNA samples is stunning, goes well beyond the ruling, and is to be applauded. The 6- and 12-year retention times, on the other hand, seem excessive, and they may be reduced further depending on public reaction.

The Marper opinion should also serve as an opportunity to reevaluate biometric identification policies in the United States. Fingerprinting, for example, has long been limited to arrestees and some federal employees, leaving other Americans alone, although since 9/11 there have been many additional instances of fingerprinting, including fingerprinting of visitors to the Statue of Liberty. New U.S. regulations also permit the storing of DNA data from arrestees from the states that collect their DNA and from all noncitizens detained by authorities for any purpose even if no charge is made or conviction obtained.[29]

It has been observed that all three identifiers in the United States "reflect arrest patterns, policing patterns, policing practices, and biases in judicial outcomes and as such are likely to reflect race, class, and geographic inequities."[30] Nonetheless, once entered in a data bank, they take on the appearance of objective, even scientific, data. Perhaps this is why their use in law enforcement has been widely supported in the United States, even though, there is no independent, comprehensive, scientific, peer-reviewed study of the overall effectiveness of DNA data banks in solving crimes.[31] Instead we have simple assertions, such as that of Senator Jon Kyl (R-AZ), one of the authors of a 2005 federal DNA act, that "We know from past experience that collecting DNA at arrest or deportation will prevent rapes and murders that would otherwise be committed."[32]

Only the 47 member states of the Council of Europe are bound by the ruling, but the ruling could nonetheless cause other countries and individual states to reexamine their policies. Most relevant in this regard are the conclusions of the Human Rights Court that simple assertions of the effectiveness of a DNA profile or sample in solving or preventing crime, or even terrorism, are not sufficient justification for the privacy invasion inherent in the bioidentifier data bank. Second, the collection and indefinite retention of fingerprints requires justification itself—and thus it should no longer be sufficient (if it ever was) to justify retention of DNA profiles because they are the same or substantially similar to fingerprints, as I have been guilty of doing

[24] Ibid.

[25] Sturcke J. DNA pioneer Alec Jeffreys: drop innocent from database. Guardian. April 15, 2009:1.

[26] Keeping the right people on the DNA database: science and public protection. London: Home Office, May 2009. (Accessed June 18, 2009, at http://www.homeoffice.gov.uk/documents/cons-2009-dna-database/dna-consultation?view=Binary.)

[27] Ibid.

[28] Ibid.

[29] Hsu SS. New rule expands DNA collection to all people arrested. Washington Post. December 12, 2008:A2.

[30] Cole SA. Fingerprint identification and the criminal justice system: historical lessons for the DNA debate. In: Lazer D, ed. DNA and the criminal justice system: the technology of justice. Cambridge, MA: MIT Press, 2004:63-89; Duster T. Selective arrests, an ever-expanding DNA forensic database, and the specter of an early-twenty first-century equivalent of phrenology. In: Lazer D, ed. DNA and the criminal justice system: the technology of justice. Cambridge, MA: MIT Press, 2004:315-34

[31] McCartney C. The DNA Expansion Programme and criminal investigation. Br J Criminol 2006;46:175-92; . Rothstein MA, Talbott MK. The expanding use of DNA in law enforcement: what role for privacy? J Law Med Ethics 2006; 34:153-64.

[32] Hsu SS. New rule expands DNA collection to all people arrested. Washington Post. December 12, 2008:A2.

myself.[33] Third, juveniles are a special case, and it will be extremely difficult to justify retention of any of their biomarkers, although there may be convictions of specific violent crimes that can provide that justification. Fourth, no matter how one comes out on the collection, storage, and use of fingerprints, photographs, and DNA profiles, there seems to be insufficient justification to ever retain DNA samples. Requiring their routine destruction after a DNA profile is created seems to be a case of "genetic exceptionalism," but it really is not. It is simply the recognition that the DNA molecule itself can be considered a medical record, and like an electronic medical record, can be read by a machine to disclose sensitive private information about people and their family members, unrelated to anything relevant to the criminal justice system.[34]

Biometric identifiers have complex privacy implications that demand much more rigorous analysis than they have received. Former Homeland Security Secretary Michael Chertoff, for example, may have been trying to deflect close analysis of the privacy aspects of fingerprints when he said during a Canadian press conference, "a fingerprint is hardly personal data because you leave it on glasses and silverware and articles all over the world, they're like footprints. They're not particularly private."[35] Of course, the same could be said about DNA samples: you shed them inadvertently, including leaving them on "glasses and silverware." In this respect, fingerprints should be treated, as the European court did, more like DNA samples than footprints. Jennifer Stoddart, the Privacy Commissioner of Canada, responded to Chertoff that, under Canadian law (as well as under the privacy policy of the U.S. Department of Homeland Security),[36] fingerprints are personal information, and she worried that the increasing reliance by the United States on the collection of biometric data in the name of national security and identifying suspected terrorists might lead Canada to lessen its standards of safeguarding personal information.[37]

All these issues should be subject to wide-ranging debate in the United States. It has, for example, been suggested that one means of doing away with the racial and ethnic inequalities inherent in the current method of obtaining biometric information from arrestees is to have a universal criminal database that collects biometric information from everyone.[38] This suggestion, if implemented, could be viewed as converting a free country into a "nation of suspects."[39] It would not automatically make us a *1984* society in which all our conversations would be monitored and deviation from the government's line would be grounds for punishment, but it could radically alter the way we view ourselves and our relationship to our government. Nonetheless, whether such a universal system of DNA profiling would be acceptable to the Human Rights Court was not specifically decided.

The European Court of Human Rights is, I think, correct to emphasize the differences between democracies and police states as reflected in the types of personal information police are permitted to collect and retain about citizens. Each individual point of data may seem insignificant, but when data sets are merged, privacy is effectively destroyed. No one has made the privacy point better than Aleksandr Solzhenitsyn in his novel *Cancer Ward*, in which he writes that, in a totalitarian state, people are obliged to answer questions

---

[33] Annas GJ. Privacy rules for DNA databanks: protecting coded 'future diaries.' JAMA 1993;270:2346-50.

[34] Ibid.

[35] Swire P. Chertoff says fingerprints aren't 'personal data.' Washington, DC: Think Progress, April 16, 2008. (Accessed April 18, 2009, at http://thinkprogress.org/2008/04/16/chertoff-fingerprints/.)

[36] The Privacy Office. Privacy impact assessment: official guidance. Washington, DC: Department of Homeland Security, 2007.

[37] Letter to the Minister of Public Safety and Emergency Preparedness Canada. Ottawa: Office of the Privacy Commissioner of Canada, April 11, 2008. (Accessed April 18, 2009, at http://www.privcom.gc.ca/media/nr-c/2008/let_080411_e.asp.)

[38] Kaye DH, Smith ME. DNA databases for law enforcement: the coverage question and the case for a population-wide database. In: Lazer D, ed. DNA and the criminal justice system: the technology of justice. Cambridge, MA: MIT Press, 2004:247-83.

[39] Annas GJ. Privacy rules for DNA databanks: protecting coded 'future diaries.' JAMA 1993;270:2346-50. Glantz LH. A nation of suspects: drug testing and the Fourth Amendment. Am J Public Health 1989;79:1427-31.

on a variety of forms, and each answer "becomes a little thread" permanently connecting him to the government:

"There are thus hundreds of little threads radiating from every man. . . . They are not visible, they are not material, but every man is constantly aware of their existence. . . . Each man, permanently aware of his own invisible threads, naturally develops a respect for the people who manipulate the threads . . . and for these people's authority."[40]

Bioidentifiers implicate privacy even more than answers on forms such as tax returns, because they identify us directly and can be seen as an integral part of us. When the police have and use DNA in investigations of criminal activity, the European Court of Human Rights seems correct to conclude that privacy is being invaded, and if the sources of that DNA are innocent of any crime, this use cannot be easily justified in a democratic society.

The New England Journal of Medicine 361, no. 2 (July 9 2009): 196–201.
Reprinted with permission by publisher

---

[40] Solzhenitsyn A. Cancer ward. New York: Farrar, Strauss & Giroux, 1969.

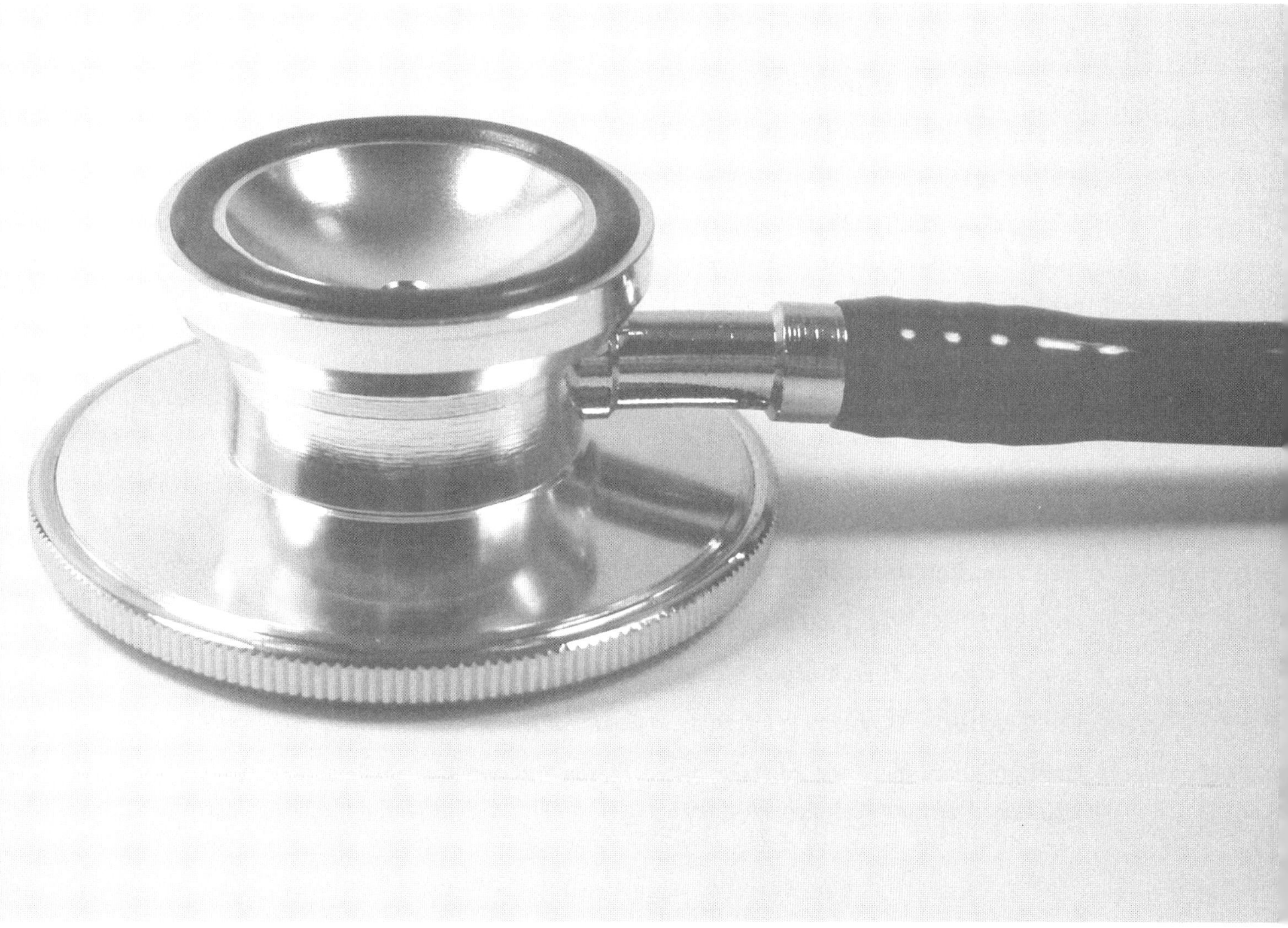

Selected Bibliography

Abraham, Abraham S. *Nishmat Avraham*. Mesorah Publications, 2000.

Abraham, Abraham S. *The Comprehensive Guide to Medical Halachah*. Feldheim Publishers, 1990.

Bleich, J. David. *Time of Death in Jewish Law*. Berman Books, 1991.

Bleich, J. David. *Bioethical Dilemmas—A Jewish Perspective*, Vol. II. Targum Press, 2006.

Bleich, J. David. *Bioethical Dilemmas—A Jewish Perspective*. Ktav Publishing House, 1998.

Bleich, J. David. *Bioethical Issues in Rabbinic Tradition*. The Academy for Jewish Studies Without Walls, 1975.

Bleich, J. David. *Judaism and Healing: Halakhic Perspectives*. Ktav Publishing House, 2003.

Feldman, David M., and Fred Rosner, eds. *Compendium on Medical Ethics: Jewish Moral, Ethical and Religious Principles in Medical Practice*. Federation of Jewish Philanthropies of New York, 1984.

Feldman, David M. *Birth Control in Jewish Law: Marital Relations, Contraception, and Abortion As Set Forth in the Classic Texts of Jewish Law*. New York University Press, 3rd ed., 1995.

Feldman, Emanuel, and Joel B. Wolowelsky, eds. *Jewish Law and the New Reproductive Technologies*. Ktav Publishing House, 1997.

Finkelstein, Baruch, and Michal Finkelstein. *The Third Key: The Jewish Couple's Guide to Fertility*. Feldheim Publishers, 2005.

Flancbaum, Louis J. *"And You Shall Live By Them": Contemporary Jewish Approaches to Medical Ethics*. Mirkov Publications, 2001.

Freedman, Benjamin. *Duty and Healing: Foundations of a Jewish Bioethic*. Routledge, 1999.

Freudenthal, Gad, ed. *AIDS in Jewish Thought and Law*. Ktav Publishing House, 1998.

Grazi, Richard V. *Be Fruitful and Multiply*. Feldheim Publishers, 1994.

Grazi, Richard V. *Overcoming Infertility: A Guide for Jewish Couples*. Toby Press, 2005.

Guggenheim, Refoel, Leonardo Leupin, Yves Nordmann, and Raphael Patcas. *The Value of Human Life: Contemporary Perspectives in Jewish Medical Ethics*. Feldheim Publishers, 2010.

Halperin, Mordechai, David Fink, and Shimon Glick, eds. *Jewish Medical Ethics 1989–2004.* Schlesinger Institute, 2004.

Herring, Basil F. *Jewish Ethics and Halacha for Our Time: Sources and Commentary.* Ktav Publishing House, Vol. 1, 1984, Vol. 2, 1989.

Hurwitz, Peter J., Jacques Picard, Avraham Steinberg, eds. *Jewish Ethics and the Care of the End-of-Life Patients.* Ktav Publishing House, 2006.

Isaacs, Ronald H. *Judaism, Medicine and Healing.* Jason Aronson Publishers, 1998.

Jakobovits, Immanuel. *Jewish Medical Ethics: A Comparative and Historical Study of the Jewish Religious Attitude to Medicine and Its Practice.* Bloch Publishing Company, 1997.

Koenigsberg, Mordechai, ed. *Halachah and Medicine Today.* Feldheim Publishers, 1997.

Levin, Faitel. *Halacha, Medical Science, and Technology: Perspectives on Contemporary Halacha Issues.* Moznaim, 1987.

Meier, Levi, ed. *Jewish Values in Bioethics.* Human Sciences Press, 1986.

Meier, Levi, ed. *Jewish Values in Health and Medicine.* University Press of America, 1991.

Rosner, Fred, and J. David Bleich, eds. *Jewish Bioethics.* Ktav Publishing House, 2000.

Rosner, Fred, and Moshe D. Tendler. *Practical Medical Halachah.* Ktav Publishing House, 3rd rev. ed., 1997.

Rosner, Fred, and Robert Schulman. *Medicine and Jewish Law,* Vol. III. Yashar Books, 2005.

Rosner, Fred. *Biomedical Ethics and Jewish Law.* Ktav Publishing House, 2001.

Rosner, Fred. *Contemporary Biomedical Ethical Issues and Jewish Law.* Ktav Publishing House, 2006.

Rosner, Fred, ed. *Medicine and Jewish Law,* Jason Aronson Publishers, 1990.

Rosner, Fred, ed. *Medicine and Jewish Law,* Vol. II. Jason Aronson Publishers, 1993.

Rosner, Fred. *Encyclopedia of Medicine in the Bible and Talmud.* Jason Aronson Publishers, 2000.

Rosner, Fred. *Medical Encyclopedia of Moses Maimonides.* Jason Aronson Publishers, 1998.

Rosner, Fred. *Medicine in the Bible and the Talmud: Selections from Classical Jewish Sources.* Ktav Publishing House, 1995.

Rosner, Fred. *Modern Medicine & Jewish Law.* Yeshiva University Press, 1972.

Rosner, Fred. *Modern Medicine and Jewish Ethics.* Ktav Publishing House, 2nd rev. ed., 1991.

Rosner, Fred. *Pioneers in Jewish Medical Ethics.* Jason Aronson Publishers, 1997.

Rosner, Fred. *Practical Medical Halachah.* Jason Aronson Publishers, 3rd rev. ed., 1997.

Rosner, Fred. *The Medical Legacy of Moses Maimonides.* Ktav Publishing House, 1997.

Schneerson, Menachem Mendel. *Healthy in Body, Mind & Spirit: Based on the Teachings of the Lubavitcher Rebbe, Rabbi Menachem M. Schneerson.* Compiled by Sholom Ber Wineberg. Sichos in English, 2005.

Shulman, Nisson E. *Jewish Answers to Medical Questions: Questions and Answers from the Medical Ethics Department of Chief Rabbi of Great Britain.* Jason Aronson Publishers, 1998.

Sinclair, Daniel B. *Tradition and the Biological Revolution: The Application of Jewish Law and the Treatment of the Critically Ill.* Edinburgh University Press, 1989.

Slae, Menachem. *Smoking and Damage to Health in Halacha.* Acharai Publications, 1990.

Sokol, Binyomin. *Halakha and Medicine: A Physician's Manual, Hilchot Shabbat.* Regensberg Institute, 1986.

Steinberg, Avraham. *Encyclopedia of Jewish Medical Ethics.* Feldheim Publishers, 2003.

Steinberg, Avraham, ed. *European Colloquium on Medical Ethics: Jewish Perspectives.* Magnes Press, 1989.

Tatz, Akiva. *Dangerous Disease and Dangerous Therapy in Jewish Medical Ethics: Principles and Practice.* Targum Press, 2010.

Tendler, Moshe D. *Responsa of Rav Moshe Feinstein: Care of the Critically Ill.* Ktav Publishing House, 1996.

Teutsch, David A. *Bioethics: Reinvigorating the Practice of Contemporary Jewish Ethics.* Wayne State University Press, 2005.

Wiener, Yaakov. *Ye Shall Surely Heal: Medical Ethics from a Halachic Perspective.* Jerusalem Center for Research, 1995.

Author's Acknowledgments

Eight years ago, I was approached by **Stuart Green**, a pediatric neurologist, to study Jewish Medical Law with him. He was joined by another eminent pediatric neurosurgeon, **Anthony Hockley**. A short while later, the **West Midlands Jewish Medical Ethics Forum** was born. This attracted an eclectic group of health care professionals ranging from students to senior consultants, covering the whole gamut of medical practice.

Much of the material in this course is derived from lectures I originally delivered to the forum and I am grateful to all its members for the debate and discussion that has sharpened the focus of many of the lessons. Unfortunately both Anthony and Stuart passed away suddenly at a relatively young age. I am sure that their *neshamot* are deriving pleasure from the Torah learning that has resulted from their initiative.

As the fame of the forum spread, members of the community who were not part of the medical fraternity asked for an opportunity to learn about these topics. I would like to thank all the regular attendees of the weekly **SMILES Lecture Series** whose comments and feedback helped me adapt these lectures into a format that was suitable for lay people.

In the summer of 2007, I was talking to **Rabbi Mendy Wineberg** of Kansas City who suggested that I make this material available to **JLI**. It is he who first introduced me to **Rabbi Efraim Mintz,** Executive Director of **JLI**. Rabbi Mintz enthusiastically championed the idea of making this material available to an international audience.

I would like to pay particular tribute to **Dr. Chana Silberstein,** Director of Curriculum for **JLI** who has been involved at every stage of this course from developing the concept to the editing of the finished article.

The **JLI** Editiorial board of **Rabbi Shalom Adler, Rabbi Levi Kaplan, Rabbi Yosef Loschak, and Rabbi Dr. Shlomo Pereira** provided valuable input in the initial drafting stages of the course.

Rabbi Mordechai Wollenberg, Rabbi Aaron Modcha Lipsey, and my brother **Rabbi Eli Pink** also provided incisive comments on the initial draft of the lessons.

The course was piloted by **Rabbi Levi Kaplan, Rabbi Levi Mendelow,** and **Rabbi Avrohom Steinmetz.** The feedback they and their students provided helped align the final product with the **JLI** genre.

Rabbi Feitel Levin reviewed the first three lessons of the course. His detailed critique and insightful comments were extremely helpful. **Rabbi Yosef Feigelstock** reviewed Lesson Four and **Rabbi Shlomo Yaffe** reviewed Lessons Five and Six.

I am grateful for all the help received from the staff of **JLI** Central, including **Rabbi Zalman Abraham, Rabbi Avrohom Bergstein, Rabbi Mordechai Dinerman, Mrs. Miri Birk, Mrs. Chana Lightstone,** and **Mrs. Rivka Sternberg.** They have all contributed to the professionally designed book that you have in front of you.

The Rohr Jewish Learning Institute benefits from the constant support of the vice chairman of Merkos L'inyonei Chinuch, **Rabbi Moshe Kotlarsky** and the unwavering encouragement of its principal benefactors, **Mr. & Mrs. George and Pamela Rohr.**

And finally I thank my wife and children who have graciously accepted the increased workload I have borne, over and above the demands on any shliach's time, as a result of my work for this course.

May the merit of the hours of Torah study undertaken by tens of thousands of **JLI** participants as a result of this course be the true reward for all those who have been involved in its production.

Rabbi Yehuda Pink MSc

Solihull, West Midlands, UK
Chai Elul 5770

Acknowledgments

The subject of medical ethics is relevant and compelling to a broad audience. Doctors, nurses, and other health professionals grapple with these issues on a daily basis. Legal experts are often called upon to help clarify definitions and boundaries, as new technologies challenge our preconceived notions about the meaning of birth and death, parenthood and personhood. And in an age that allows many more options for intervention, yet is plagued with diminishing resources, all of us will sooner or later be faced with decisions in the medical arena that force us to confront our deepest values.

Jewish medical ethics provides a unique contribution to this ever-changing interdisciplinary area. A seamless integration of the old and the new, the field meshes the timeless values of our Torah and the pragmatic wisdom of contemporary rabbinic authorities who keep current with the evolving medical realities so they can provide practical guidance for real people forced to make real decisions.

Every **JLI** course is a vast collaborative effort. We are grateful first and foremost to **Rabbi Yehuda Pink,** our course author, who is renowned throughout the UK for his lucid and enlightening presentation of Jewish medical ethics. We are privileged to have been able to draw upon his extensive knowledge of both the medical and halachic literature, bringing a tremendous breadth of information to this course. Rabbi Pink's meticulously prepared material is the foundation of **JLI**'s adaptation of **Medicine and Morals** for the international market.

Because of the sensitive nature of the matters addressed in this course, each lesson has been reviewed for accuracy by a rabbi specializing in practical applications of the subject matter. We are deeply indebted to **Rabbi Feitel Levin** for his thoughtful review of the first three lessons, **Rabbi Yosef Feigelstock** for his review of Lesson Four, and **Rabbi Shlomo Yaffe** for his thoughful comments to Lessons Five and Six.

The **JLI** Editorial Board has guided the development and revision of our course and ensured that the course material is sensitive to the needs of our students. Many thanks to **Rabbi Levi Kaplan,**

Rabbi Yosef Loschak, Rabbi Dr. Shlomo Pereira, Rabbi Levi Mendelow, Rabbi Avraham Steinmetz, and **Rabbi Shalom Adler** for the review and piloting of the course material.

This semester marks the unveiling of a number of special initiatives. We are proud to partner with the **Kohelet Foundation,** an organization devoted to dramatically improving the effectiveness, affordability, and enrollment of American Jewish day schools. We are grateful to the president of the Kohelet Foundation, **Mr. David Magerman**, the visionary promoting the concept of supporting Jewish day schools through engaging parents in Jewish learning. We are also much indebted to the director of the Kohelet Foundation, **Mrs. Holly Cohen**, who has worked closely with **JLI** in the pilot cities to ensure an exemplary program.

This semester also marks the launch of the **Rohr JLI/Touro Division of Continuing Professional Development**. We are grateful to **Dr. Alan Kadish**, president of Touro College, for his encouragement of this important initiative, and to **Dr. Anthony Polemeni**, vice president of Touro College's Division of Graduate Studies, for his indefatigable advocacy of this promising collaboration from its inception. **Rabbi Joseph Zuker** has played a critical role as liaison between Touro and **JLI**, aiding in bringing this program to fruition. **Professor Dan Stein** has offered invaluable assistance in developing the program's online platform. We are greatly indebted to **Rabbi Dr. Michael Shmidman**, dean of the Graduate School of Jewish Studies, for academic oversight and review of our materials, and to **Dr. Steven Huberman**, dean of the Graduate School of Social Work, for thoughtful guidance on the development of a program of continuing professional education.

This is the fourth time we have offered a course that has been accredited to provide continuing legal education credits, and the second time that we have offered a course that has been accredited to provide continuing medical education credits. Many thanks to **Dr. Michael Akerman** for his dedicated assistance in bringing this course to the wider medical community and his patient guidance through the CME accreditation process. **Rabbi Mendy Halberstam** authored our scholarly and thorough legal notes, a vital tool for **JLI** chapters offering CLE. **Mrs. Rivka Sternberg** oversaw the application process, coordinating the efforts across the U.S. and Canada. **Ms. Musie Karp** served as the CLE/CME liaison at **JLI Central**, assisting our affiliates in meeting local continuing education guidelines. It is thanks to their coordinated efforts that we have succeeded in ensuring that this multidisciplinary course could be brought to the attention of professionals in the field.

We are greatly indebted to **Rabbi Mordechai Dinerman**, our associate editor, for his extensive contributions to the course. Rabbi Dinerman approaches his work with careful precision and thoughtful analysis. His valuable editorial suggestions were invaluable in assisting us in adapting the material for our **JLI** audience. Rabbi Dinerman also prepared and proofed our Hebrew sources and references, and assisted in the selection of our additional readings. His breadth of knowledge and formidable research skills are an incredible asset to our operation.

We are also grateful to **Mrs. Leah-Perl Shollar** who has spearheaded our entry into the world of online learning. She has adapted the current course to the online environment, and reconfigured the content to ensure a more satisfying learning experience for the distant learner. Mrs. Shollar's exceptional talents at pedagogic design are greatly valued by **JLI** and we eagerly anticipate the expansion of this new area of instruction.

The multimedia and instructional support team create extraordinary enhancements to ensure the effective delivery of our course material. **Rabbi Avraham Bergstein** demonstrates through his delightful work that "a picture is worth a thousand words." He is a master of using the visual to enhance conceptual understanding. Rabbi Bergstein created the Powerpoint slides that accompany each lesson and also crafted the lesson maps that serve as a powerful guide to lesson preparation.

Each trimester, **JLI** creates short trigger videos for each lesson to spark discussion and thought. **Mrs. Chana Lightstone** scripts and coordinates the development of the videos, which are thoughtfully produced under the talented and artistic hands of **Rabbi Levi Teldon** and **Mr. Moshe Raskin**.

JLI is blessed with an exceptional production team. **Rabbi Mendel Sirota**, production manager, sets perfection as **JLI**'s baseline standard. He orchestrates the myriad tasks that are necessary to our overall operation, including posting and personalizing marketing materials, overseeing the delivery of our books, and ensuring that our affiliates receive all support materials in a timely manner. **Mrs. Chana Lightstone**, our research associate, is creative and resourceful in addressing a wide variety of informational and logistical challenges. **Mrs. Rachael Wilkenfeld**, our proofreader, meticulously prepares our manuscripts for print. **Nachman Levine**, our layout designer and research editor, brings to our work not only an artistic eye but also a scholarly one. Thank you, **Spotlight Design,** for proving that you *can* judge a book by its covers. Finally, we would like to acknowledge the efforts of **Shimon Leib Jacobs,** who oversees our printing and shipping.

We extend our thanks to **Rabbi Zalman Abraham**, director of marketing, who is responsible for the strategic and creative thrust of our campaign, as well as the members of our **JLI** marketing board, **Rabbi Simcha Backman, Rabbi Ronnie Fine, Rabbi Ovadia Goldman, Rabbi Mendel Halberstam**, and **Rabbi Yehudah Shemtov. Mrs. Miri Birk** has very devotedly pursued a number of public relations initiatives on behalf of the course. Our thanks as well to **Rabbi Shraga Sherman**, who reviews our marketing materials.

The hardworking support staff at **JLI Central** is critical to our success and growth:

JLI's administrative staff, **Mrs. Musie Kesselman, Mrs. Mindy Wallach, Mrs. Fraydee Kessler,** and **Mrs. Chana Shaffer-Minkowitz**, attend to the many details that hone our professional edge to perfection. **Mrs. Shaina Basha Mintz, Mrs. Nechama Shmotkin**, and **Ms. Musie Karp** oversee our accounts. **Rabbi Mendel Bell**, webmaster *par excellence*, ensures the integrity of our online environment. **Rabbi Levi Kaplan** directs our International division and adapts our material for our Hebrew-speaking and Spanish-speaking markets. **Rabbi Mendel Popack,** director of **JLI Academy,** is the organizing force behind our annual **JLI** conference and is devoted to providing our affiliates with the development tools they need. We also warmly welcome **Rabbi Dubi Rabinowitz**, chief operating officer, who invites us to constantly rethink our roles and to reconfigure ourselves for exceptional efficiency and outstanding results.

Special thanks to **Project Chai** for providing resource materials for the research of Lesson Four. We are deeply appreciative as well to **Rabbi Dr. Edward Reichman**, Associate Professor of Emergency Medicine and Associate Professor of Philosophy and History of Medicine at the Albert Einstein College of Medicine of Yeshiva University. Dr. Reichman graciously responded to queries from our editorial team and clarified a number of important points.

We are immensely grateful for the encouragement of our chairman and vice chairman of Merkos Le'Inyonei Chinuch—Lubavitch World Headquarters, **Rabbi Moshe Kotlarksy**. We are also blessed to have the unwavering support of **JLI**'s principal benefactor, **Mr. George Rohr**, who has fully invested in our work and has been vital to the monumental expansion of the organization.

JLI's dedicated executive board—**Rabbi Chaim Block, Rabbi Hesh Epstein, Rabbi Yosef Gansburg, Rabbi Shmuel Kaplan, Rabbi Avremel Sternberg**, and **Rabbi Yisrael Rice**—devote countless hours to the development of **JLI**. Their dedicated commitment and sage direction has helped **JLI** continue to grow and flourish.

We owe a particular debt of thanks to **Rabbi Yisrael Rice**, chairman of our flagship division whose patient and thoughtful guidance has been an exceptional source of support throughout a period of rapid development.

The constant progress in **JLI** is a testament to the visionary leadership of our director, **Rabbi Efraim Mintz**, who is never content to rest on his laurels and who boldly encourages continued innovation and change.

Finally, **JLI** represents an incredible partnership of more than 300 shluchim giving of their time and talent to further Jewish adult education. We thank them for generously sharing their thoughts, feedback, questions, and teaching experiences. They are our most valuable critics, and our most cherished contributors.

Inspired by the call of the **Lubavitcher Rebbe** of righteous memory, it is the mandate of the **Rohr JLI** to allow all Jews throughout the world to experience and take part in the Torah learning that is their heritage. May this course succeed in fulfilling that sacred charge.

On behalf of the **Rohr Jewish Learning Institute**,

Chana Silberstein PhD

Ithaca, New York

Chai Elul, 5770

JLI International Desk

Rabbi Avrohom Sternberg
Chairman
New London, CT

Rabbi Levi Kaplan
Coordinator

JLI Supplementary Courses

Rabbi Levi Kaplan
Director
Brooklyn, NY

Authors

Rabbi Zalman Abraham
Brooklyn, NY

Rabbi Levi Jacobson
Toronto, ON

Mrs. Malka Touger
Jerusalem, Israel

Mrs. Shimonah Tzukernik
Brooklyn, NY

Rabbi Benyomin Walters
Chicago, IL

JLI Teacher Training

Rabbi Berel Bell
Director
Montreal, QC

myShiur:
Advanced Learning Initiative

Rabbi Shmuel Kaplan
Chairman
Potomac, MD

Rabbi Levi Kaplan
Director

Authors

Rabbi Moshe Lieberman
Newton, MA

Rabbi Zalman Abraham
Brooklyn, NY

Rabbi Levi Kaplan
Brooklyn, NY

Rabbi Leizer Teitelbaum
Brooklyn, NY

National Jewish Retreat

Rabbi Hesh Epstein
Chairman
Columbia, SC

Bruce Backman
Rabbi Mendy Weg
Liaisons

Rabbi Boruch Cohen
Coordinator

Mrs. Shaina B. Mintz
Administrator

Sinai Scholars Society
in partnership with
Chabad on Campus

Rabbi Menachem Schmidt
Chairman
Philadelphia, PA

Rabbi Moshe Chaim Dubrowski
Chabad on Campus

Rabbi Yitzchok Dubov
Director

Torah Café Online Learning

Rabbi Levi Kaplan
Director

Rabbi Simcha Backman
Consultant

Rabbi Mendel Bell
Webmaster

Getzy Raskin
Filming and Editing

Rabbi Mendy Elishevitz
Website Design

Moshe Raskin
Video Editing

Mrs. Miri Birk
Adminisrator

Torah Studies

Rabbi Yossi Gansburg
Chairman
Toronto, ON

Rabbi Meir Hecht
Director

Rabbi Yechezkel Deitsch
Mrs. Nechama Shmotkin
Administrators

JLI Academy

Rabbi Hesh Epstein
Chairman

Rabbi Mendel Popack
Director

Steering Committee

Rabbi Yoel Caroline
Rabbi Mordechai Grossbaum
Rabbi Levi Mendelow

Beis Medrosh L'Shluchim
in partnership with
Shluchim Exchange

Rabbi Sholom Zirkind
Administrator

Rabbi Yitzchok Steiner
Coordinator

Rabbi Mendel Margolin
Producer

Steering Committee

Rabbi Simcha Backman
Rabbi Mendy Kotlarsky
Rabbi Efraim Mintz

JLI Central
Founding Department Heads

Rabbi Zalman Charytan
Acworth, GA

Rabbi Mendel Druk
Cancun, Mexico

Rabbi Menachem Gansburg
Toronto, ON

Rabbi Yoni Katz
Brooklyn, NY

Rabbi Chaim Zalman Levy
New Rochelle, NY

Rabbi Elchonon Tenenbaum
Napa Valley, CA

Rohr JLI Affiliates

Share the Rohr JLI experience with friends and relatives worldwide

ALABAMA

BIRMINGHAM
Rabbi Yossi Friedman
205.970.0100

ARIZONA

CHANDLER
Rabbi Mendel Deitsch
480.855.4333

FLAGSTAFF
Rabbi Dovie Shapiro
928.255.5756

GLENDALE
Rabbi Sholom Lew
602.375.2422

PHOENIX
Rabbi Zalman Levertov
Rabbi Yossi Friedman
602.944.2753

SCOTTSDALE
Rabbi Yossi Levertov
Rabbi Yossi Bryski
480.998.1410

ARKANSAS

LITTLE ROCK
Rabbi Pinchus Ciment
501.217.0053

CALIFORNIA

AGOURA HILLS
Rabbi Moshe Bryski

BAKERSFIELD
Rabbi Shmuel Schlanger
661.835.8381

BEL AIR
Rabbi Chaim Mentz
310.475.5311

BRENTWOOD
Rabbi Boruch Hecht
Rabbi Mordechai Zaetz
310.826.4453

BURBANK
Rabbi Shmuly Kornfeld
818.954.0070

CALABASAS
Rabbi Eliyahu Friedman
818.585.1888

CARLSBAD
Rabbi Yeruchem Eilfort
Rabbi Michoel Shapiro
760.943.8891

CHATSWORTH
Rabbi Yossi Spritzer
818.718.0777

CONTRA COSTA
Rabbi Yaakov Kagan
Rabbi Dovber Berkowitz
925.937.4101

ENCINO
Rabbi Joshua Gordon
Rabbi Eli Rivkin
818.758.1818

FOLSOM
Rabbi Yossi Grossbaum
916.608.9811

GLENDALE
Rabbi Simcha Backman
818.240.2750

HUNTINGTON BEACH
Rabbi Aron Berkowitz
714.846.2285

IRVINE
Rabbi Alter Tenenbaum
Rabbi Elly Andrusier
949.786.5000

LAGUNA BEACH
Rabbi Elimelech Gurevitch
949.499.0770

LOMITA
Rabbi Eli Hecht
Rabbi Sholom Pinson
310.326.8234

LONG BEACH
Rabbi Abba Perelmuter
562.621.9828

MARINA DEL REY
Rabbi Danny Yiftach
Rabbi Mendy Avtzon
310.859.0770

MISSION VIEJO
Rabbi Zalman Aron Kantor
949.770.1270

MONTEREY
Rabbi Dovid Holtzberg
831.643.2770

MT. OLYMPUS
Rabbi Sholom Ber Rodal
323.650.1444

NEWHALL
Rabbi Elchonon Marosov
661.254.3434

NEWPORT BEACH
Rabbi Reuven Mintz
949.721.9800

NORTH HOLLYWOOD
Rabbi Nachman Abend
818.989.9539

NORTHRIDGE
Rabbi Eli Rivkin
818.368.3937

PACIFIC PALISADES
Rabbi Zushe Cunin
310.454.7783

PASADENA
Rabbi Chaim Hanoka
626.564.8820

RANCHO CUCAMONGA
Rabbi Sholom B. Harlig
909.949.4553

RANCHO PALOS VERDES
Rabbi Yitzchok Magalnic
310.544.5544

REDONDO BEACH
Rabbi Dovid Lisbon
310.214.4999

SACRAMENTO
Rabbi Mendy Cohen
916.455.1400

S. BARBARA
Rabbi Yosef Loschak
805.683.1544

S. CLEMENTE
Rabbi Menachem M. Slavin
949.489.0723

S. CRUZ
Rabbi Yochanan Friedman
831.454.0101

S. DIEGO
Rabbi Motte Fradkin
858.547.0076

S. FRANCISCO
Rabbi Peretz Mochkin
415.571.8770

S. MONICA
Rabbi Boruch Rabinowitz
310.394.5699

S. RAFAEL
Rabbi Yisrael Rice
415.492.1666

S. ROSA
Rabbi Mendel Wolvovsky
707.577.0277

SIMI VALLEY
Rabbi Nosson Gurary
805.577.0573

STOCKTON
Rabbi Avremel Brod
209.952.2081

STUDIO CITY
Rabbi Yossi Baitelman
818.508.6633

TEMECULA
Rabbi Yitzchok Hurwitz
951.303.9576

THOUSAND OAKS
Rabbi Chaim Bryski
805.493.7776

TUSTIN
Rabbi Yehoshua Eliezrie
714.508.2150

Ventura
Rabbi Yakov Latowicz
Mrs. Sarah Latowicz
805.658.7441

West Hills
Rabbi Avrahom Yitzchak Rabin
818.337.4544

Yorba Linda
Rabbi Dovid Eliezrie
714.693.0770

COLORADO
Aspen
Rabbi Mendel Mintz
970.544.3770

Boulder
Rabbi Pesach Scheiner
303.494.1638

Denver
Rabbi Yossi Serebryanski
303.744.9699

Highlands Ranch
Rabbi Avraham Mintz
303.694.9119

Longmont
Rabbi Yaakov Dovid Borenstein
303.678.7595

Vail
Rabbi Dovid Mintz
970.476.7887

Westminster
Rabbi Benjy Brackman
303.429.5177

CONNECTICUT
Branford
Rabbi Yossi Yaffe
203.488.2263

Glastonbury
Rabbi Yosef Wolvovsky
860.659.2422

Greenwich
Rabbi Yossi Deren
Rabbi Menachem Feldman
203.629.9059

Litchfield
Rabbi Yoseph Eisenbach
860.567.3609

New London
Rabbi Avrohom Sternberg
860.437.8000

Orange
Rabbi Sheya Hecht
Rabbi Adam Haston
203.795.5261

Simsbury
Rabbi Mendel Samuels
860.658.4903

Stamford
Rabbi Yisrael Deren
Rabbi Levi Mendelow
203.3.CHABAD

Westport
Rabbi Yehuda L. Kantor
Mrs. Dina Kantor
203.226.8584

West Hartford
Rabbi Yosef Gopin
Rabbi Shaya Gopin
860.659.2422

DELAWARE
Wilmington
Rabbi Chuni Vogel
302.529.9900

FLORIDA
Aventura
Rabbi Laivi Forta
305.933.0770

Bal Harbour
Rabbi Dov Schochet
305.868.1411

Boca Raton
Rabbi Moishe Denberg
Rabbi Zalman Bukiet
561.417.7797

Bonita Springs
Rabbi Mendy Greenberg
239.949.6900

East Boca Raton
Rabbi Ruvi New
561.417.7797

Boynton Beach
Rabbi Yosef Yitzchok Raichik
561.732.4633

Bradenton
Rabbi Menachem Bukiet
941.388.9656

Brandon
Rabbi Mendel Rubashkin
813.657.9393

Coconut Creek
Rabbi Yossi Gansburg
954.422.1987

Coral Gables
Rabbi Avrohom Stolik
305.490.7572

Deerfield Beach
Rabbi Yossi Goldblatt
954.422.1735

Delray Beach
Rabbi Sholom Ber Korf
561.496.6228

Fort Lauderdale
Rabbi Yitzchok Naparstek
954.568.1190

Fort Myers
Rabbi Yitzchok Minkowicz
Mrs. Nechama Minkowicz
239.433.7708

Hollywood
Rabbi Leizer Barash
954.965.9933

Rabbi Zalman Korf
Rabbi Yakov Garfinkel
954.374.8370

Kendall
Rabbi Yossi Harlig
305.234.5654

Key Biscayne
Rabbi Yoel Caroline
305.365.6744

Key West
Rabbi Yaakov Zucker
305.295.0013

Miami Beach
Rabbi Aron Rabin
Rabbi Mendy Halberstam
305.535.0094

Naples
Rabbi Fishel Zaklos
239.262.4474

North Miami Beach
Rabbi Moishe Kievman
305.770.1919

Orlando
Rabbi Yosef Konikov
407.354.3660

Parkland
Rabbi Mendy Gutnik
954.796.7330

Pinellas County
Rabbi Shalom Adler
727.789.0408

S. Petersburg
Rabbi Alter Korf
727.344.4900

Sarasota
Rabbi Chaim Shaul Steinmetz
941.925.0770

Satellite Beach
Rabbi Zvi Konikov
321.777.2770

South Palm Beach
Rabbi Leibel Stolik
561.889.3499

South Tampa
Rabbi Mendy Dubrowski
813.287.1795

Sunny Isles Beach
Rabbi Alexander Kaller
Classes in Russian
305.803.5315

Tallahassee
Rabbi Schneur Zalmen Oirechman
850.523.9294

Venice
Rabbi Sholom Ber Schmerling
941.493.2770

Walnut Creek
Rabbi Zalman Korf
954.374.8370

Weston
Rabbi Yisroel Spalter
954.349.6565

West Palm Beach
Rabbi Yoel Gancz
561.659.7770

GEORGIA
Alpharetta
Rabbi Hirshy Minkowicz
770.410.9000

RANDOLPH
Rabbi Avraham Bechor
973.895.3070

ROCKAWAY
Rabbi Asher Herson
Rabbi Mordechai Baumgarten
973.625.1525

SPARTA
Rabbi Shmuel Lewis
973.726.3333

TEANECK
Rabbi Ephraim Simon
201.907.0686

TENAFLY
Rabbi Mordechai Shain
Rabbi Yitzchak Gershovitz
201.871.1152

TOMS RIVER
Rabbi Moshe Gourarie
732.349.4199

WAYNE
Rabbi Michel Gurkov
973.694.6274

WEST ORANGE
Rabbi Efraim Mintz
Rabbi Mendy Kasowitz
973.731.0770

WOODCLIFF LAKE
Rabbi Dov Drizin
201.476.0157

NEW MEXICO
S. FE
Rabbi Berel Levertov
505.983.2000

NEW YORK
ALBANY
Rabbi Yossi Rubin
518.482.5781

BEDFORD
Rabbi Arik Wolf
914.666.6065

BINGHAMTON
Mrs. Rivkah Slonim
607.797.0015

BRIGHTON BEACH
Rabbi Zushe Winner
Rabbi Avrohom Winner
718.946.9833

CEDARHURST
Rabbi Shneur Zalman Wolowik
516.295.2478

DIX HILLS
Rabbi Yaakov Saacks
631.351.8672

DOBBS FERRY
Rabbi Benjy Silverman
914.693.6100

EAST HAMPTON
Rabbi Leibel Baumgarten
631.329.5800

GREAT NECK
Rabbi Yoseph Geisinsky
516.487.4554

ITHACA
Rabbi Eli Silberstein
607.257.7379

KINGSTON
Rabbi Yitzchok Hecht
845.334.9044

LARCHMONT
Rabbi Mendel Silberstein
914.834.4321

LONG ISLAND CITY
Rabbi Zev Wineberg
347.262.5540

NEW YORK
Rabbi Yisrael Kugel
212.799.0809

NYC GRAMERCY PARK
Rabbi Naftali Rotenstreich
212.924.3200

NYC KEHILATH JESHURUN
Rabbi Elie Weinstock
212.774.5636

OCEANSIDE
Rabbi Levi Gurkov
616.764.7385

OSSINING
Rabbi Dovid Labkowski
914.923.2522

PORT WASHINGTON
Rabbi Shalom Paltiel
516.767.8672

RIVERDALE
Rabbi Levi Shemtov
718.549.1100

ROCHESTER
Rabbi Nechemia Vogel
585.271.0330

ROSLYN
Rabbi Yaakov Reiter
516.484.8185

SEA GATE
Rabbi Chaim Brikman
Mrs. Rivka Brikman
718.266.1736

STATEN ISLAND
Rabbi Moshe Katzman
Rabbi Shmuel Bendet
718.370.8953

STONY BROOK
Rabbi Shalom Ber Cohen
631.585.0521

WEST HEMPSTEAD
Rabbi Yossi Lieberman
Rabbi Mordechai Dinerman
516.596.8691

NORTH CAROLINA
ASHEVILLE
Rabbi Shaya Susskind
828.505.0746

CHARLOTTE
Rabbi Yossi Groner
Rabbi Shlomo Cohen
704.366.3984

GREENSBORO
Rabbi Yosef Plotkin
336 617 8120

RALEIGH
Rabbi Aaron Herman
919.637.6950

Rabbi Pinchas Herman
Rabbi Sholom Ber Estrin
919.847.8986

OHIO
BEACHWOOD
Rabbi Yossi Marosov
216.381.4736

BLUE ASH
Rabbi Yisroel Mangel
513.793.5200

COLUMBUS
Rabbi Areyah Kaltmann
Rabbi Levi Andrusier
614.294.3296

DAYTON
Rabbi Nochum Mangel
Rabbi Dr. Shmuel Klatzkin
937.643.0770

TOLEDO
Rabbi Yossi Shemtov
419.843.9393

OKLAHOMA
OKLAHOMA CITY
Rabbi Ovadia Goldman
405.524.4800

TULSA
Rabbi Yehuda Weg
918.492.4499

OREGON
ASHLAND
Rabbi Avi Zwiebel
541.482.2778

PORTLAND
Rabbi Moshe Wilhelm
Rabbi Mordechai Wilhelm
503.977.9947

PENNSYLVANIA
AMBLER
Rabbi Shaya Deitsch
215.591.9310

BALA CYNWYD
Rabbi Shraga Sherman
610.660.9192

CLARKS SUMMIT
Rabbi Benny Rapoport
570.587.3300

DEVON
Rabbi Yossi Kaplan
610.971.9977

NEWTOWN
Rabbi Aryeh Weinstein
215.497.9925

PHILADELPHIA: CENTER CITY
Rabbi Yochonon Goldman
215.238.2100

PITTSBURGH
Rabbi Yisroel Altein
412.422.7300 ext. 269

PITTSBURGH: SOUTH HILLS
Rabbi Mendy Rosenblum
412.278.3693

READING
Rabbi Yosef Lipsker
610.921.2805

RYDAL
Rabbi Zushe Gurevitz
215.572.1511

RHODE ISLAND
WARWICK
Rabbi Yossi Laufer
401.884.7888

SOUTH CAROLINA
COLUMBIA
Rabbi Hesh Epstein
803.782.1831

TENNESSEE
BELLEVUE
Rabbi Yitzchok Tiechtel
615.646.5750

CHATTANOOGA
Rabbi Shaul Perlstein
423.490.1106

MEMPHIS
Rabbi Levi Klein
901.766.1800

KNOXVILLE
Rabbi Yossi Wilhelm
865.588.8584

TEXAS
FORT WORTH
Rabbi Dov Mandel
817.263.7701

HOUSTON
Rabbi Moishe Traxler
713.774.0300

HOUSTON: RICE UNIVERSITY AREA
Rabbi Eliezer Lazaroff
Rabbi Yitzchok Schmukler
713.522.2004

PLANO
Rabbi Mendel Block
Rabbi Yehudah Horowitz
972.596.8270

S. ANTONIO
Rabbi Chaim Block
Rabbi Yossi Marrus
210.492.1085

UTAH
SALT LAKE CITY
Rabbi Benny Zippel
801.467.7777

VERMONT
BURLINGTON
Rabbi Yitzchok Raskin
802.658.5770

VIRGINIA
ALEXANDRIA/ARLINGTON
Rabbi Mordechai Newman
703.370.2774

FAIRFAX
Rabbi Leibel Fajnland
703.426.1980

NORFOLK
Rabbi Aaron Margolin
Rabbi Levi Brashevitzky
757.616.0770

RICHMOND
Rabbi Dr. Shlomo Pereira
804.740.2000

TYSONS CORNER
Rabbi Levi Deitsch
Rabbi Chezzy Deitsch
703.356.3451

WASHINGTON
OLYMPIA
Rabbi Cheski Edelman
360.584-4306

SEATTLE
Rabbi Elazar Bogomilsky
206.527.1411

SPOKANE COUNTY
Rabbi Yisroel Hahn
509.443.0770

WISCONSIN
MEQUON
Rabbi Menachem Rapoport
262.242.2235

MILWAUKEE
Rabbi Mendel Shmotkin
414.961.6100

PUERTO RICO
CAROLINA
Rabbi Mendel Zarchi
787.253.0894

ARGENTINA
BUENOS AIRES
Rabbi Hirshel Hendel
5411 4807 7073

Rabbi Mendy Grunblatt
5411 4772 1024

AUSTRALIA
BRISBANE
Rabbi Chanoch Sufrin
617.3843.6770

MELBOURNE
Rabbi Schneier Lange
613.9522.8222

Rabbi Shimshon Yurkowicz
613.9822.3600

SYDNEY
Rabbi Levi Wolff
612.9389.5622

BONDI
Rabbi Pinchas Feldman
612.9387.3822

DOUBLE BAY
Rabbi Yanky Berger
612.9327.1644

DOVER HEIGHTS
Rabbi Benzion Milecki
612.9337.6775

NORTH SHORE
Rabbi Nochum Schapiro
Mrs. Fruma Schapiro
Rabbi Shmuly Kopel
612.9488.9548

VICTORIA
SOUTH YARRA
Rabbi Yehuda Hoch
03.9613.0738

AUSTRIA
VIENNA
Rabbi Shaya Boas
431.369.1818 ext. 123

BELGIUM
ANTWERP
Rabbi Mendy Gurary
32.3.239.6212

BRAZIL
RIO DE JANEIRO
Rabbi Yehoshua Goldman
Rabbi Avraham Steinmetz
21.3543.3770

S. PAULO
Rabbi Avraham Steinmetz
55.11.3081.3081

CANADA
ALBERTA
CALGARY
Rabbi Mordechai Groner
403.238.4880

NOTES

NOTES

NOTES

NOTES

NOTES

NOTES

NOTES

THE JEWISH LEARNING MULTIPLEX
Brought to you by the Rohr Jewish Learning Institute

In fulfillment of the mandate of the Lubavitcher Rebbe, of blessed memory,
whose leadership guides every step of our work,
the mission of the Rohr Jewish Learning Institute is to transform
Jewish life and the greater community through the study of Torah,
connecting each Jew to our shared heritage of Jewish learning.

While our flagship program remains the cornerstone of our organization,
JLI is proud to feature additional divisions catering to specific populations,
in order to meet a wide array of educational needs.

Torah Studies provides a rich and nuanced
encounter with the weekly Torah reading.

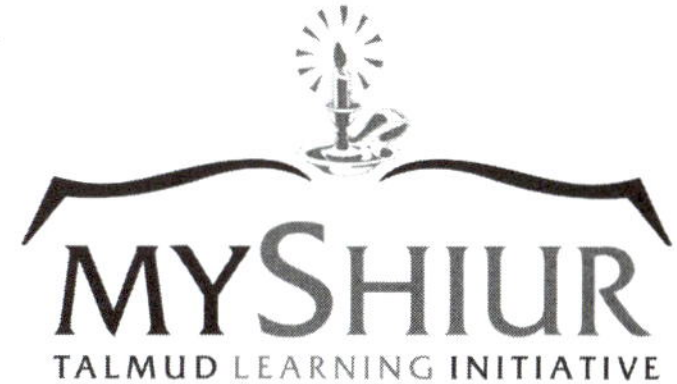

MyShiur courses are designed to assist
students in developing the skills needed
to study Talmud independently.

This rigorous fellowship program invites select college
students to explore the fundamentals of Judaism.

Jewish teens forge their identity as they engage in
Torah study, social interaction, and serious fun.

The rigor and excellence of JLI courses,
adapted to the campus environment.

TorahCafe.com provides an exclusive selection
of top-rated Jewish educational videos.

This yearly event rejuvenates mind, body, and spirit with
a powerful synthesis of Jewish learning and community.

The Rosh Chodesh Society gathers Jewish women
together once a month for intensive textual study.

Select affiliates are invited to partner with peers and noted
professionals, as leaders of innovation and excellence.

Mission participants delve into our nation's rich past while
exploring the Holy Land's relevance and meaning today.

(310) 377-1511.

Chad.

Monday night.